BUSINESS ENGLISH ESSENTIALS

SIXTH EDITION

Greta LaFollette Henderson
Former Instructor
Kinman Business University
Spokane, Washington

Price R. Voiles
Editor in Chief
Typing, Communications, and Records Management
Gregg Division, McGraw-Hill Book Company

GREGG DIVISION
McGraw-Hill Book Company

New York   Atlanta   Dallas   St. Louis
San Francisco   Auckland   Bogotá   Düsseldorf
Johannesburg   London   Madrid   Mexico   Montreal
New Delhi   Panama   Paris
São Paulo   Singapore   Sydney
Tokyo   Toronto

Sponsoring Editor: Joseph Tinervia

Editor: Michael Esposito

Production Supervisor: Frank Bellantoni

Design Supervisor: Frank Medina

Cover Designer: Mark Watts

Library of Congress Cataloging in Publication Data

Henderson, Greta La Follette Whiteside, date.
  Business English essentials.

  Includes index.
    1. English language—Business English. 2. Commer-
cial correspondence. I. Voiles, Price R., joint
author. II. Title.
PE1115.H54 1980   808'.066'651   79-9219
ISBN 0-07-027984-5

BUSINESS ENGLISH ESSENTIALS, Sixth Edition

    7890 DODO 8876543

To the Student

How many jobs in business, industry, and government that require specialized knowledge and skill can you name? You undoubtedly could list a large number of such occupations—many of which have titles that clearly indicate the special knowledge or skill that those engaged in them must have. For example, a lawyer obviously must know a great deal about the subject of law, a typist must be highly skillful in typewriting, and an accountant must have a thorough understanding of accounting principles and procedures. Now, how many jobs that do *not* require a solid knowledge of language and skill in communicating with others can you name? The chances are extremely good that you could identify none—for the simple reason that, to one extent or another, *every* job requires both a knowledge and a command of language usage. Unquestionably, then, your objectives in taking this course are to refine and perhaps to expand your understanding of standard English and to develop proficiency in using it when you write or speak for a business purpose. *Business English Essentials* is therefore designed to assist you in meeting both of these objectives in a logical, effective manner.

REVIEW OF LANGUAGE STRUCTURE

The English courses you completed most recently probably were devoted to the study of novels and other types of literature, the preparation of book reports and themes, and other activities essential to one's cultural development. If so, you may have forgotten at least part of what you once knew about the structural framework of English and feel that you need to refresh your memory. Therefore, you will find that Part One of *Business English Essentials* provides the study and practice materials you need to brush up on the parts of speech, phrases, clauses, and sentences.

ENGLISH FOR BUSINESS COMMUNICATION

After reviewing the general framework of English, you naturally will want to concentrate on those principles of grammar and usage that will have immediate, practical value to you as a business writer and speaker. Thus you will find that the units and worksheets comprising Part Two place special emphasis on the fundamentals that significantly influence the effectiveness of written and oral messages prepared for a business purpose and a business audience.

STYLE IN BUSINESS WRITING

Writing letters, memos, reports, and similar types of messages obviously involves the use of punctuation, capitalization, numbers, and abbreviations. In Part Three, then, you will study and practice applying the principles of style that business writers follow in order to ensure that their readers will be able to correctly, quickly, and easily interpret messages in the manner they were intended.

BUSINESS LETTERS, MEMOS, AND REPORTS

Having acquired the language-usage knowledge and skill needed to do so, you are now fully prepared to concentrate on the principles and techniques of writing various types of business letters, memos, and reports. In Part Four you will notice that the study topics and the writing assignments pertain not only to the most common types of communications you will be likely to need to write on the job but also to the kinds of messages you will need to write in order to get a job.

OTHER BUSINESS COMMUNICATION SKILLS

As part of your preparation for entering the business world, you obviously will want to assess your reading, listening, and speaking skills and to take whatever steps may be necessary and appropriate to improve them. In a comprehensive but intensive course of this type, it is difficult to do more than alert you to the vital importance of having a high degree of skill in each of these areas of communication. Therefore, Part Five of this program will have fulfilled its objective if the comments and suggestions it contains help you assess your proficiency in these other business communication skills and prompt you to take whatever steps may be appropriate.

SOME SPECIAL COMMENTS

As you will notice, *Business English Essentials* presents all the study materials in the first half of the book and the practice, or worksheet, exercises in the second half, which starts on page 133. Among the worksheets, you will find a number that are designed to assist you in further developing your spelling and other basic vocabulary skills. In completing these exercises, you will find an authoritative, up-to-date dictionary an indispensable aid—as does everyone whose work involves the use of language. Although the spelling and other aspects of word usage in this book are based upon *Webster's New Collegiate Dictionary* (Eighth Edition), which is published and copyrighted by G. & C. Merriam Company, Springfield, Massachusetts, you may prefer to use some other reference. If so, your teacher can help you choose the dictionary and other reference materials best suited to your needs.

In this course, as in other courses you have taken, your teacher probably will ask you to complete quizzes and objective tests from time to time. Each of these activities will be helpful to *you* in measuring *your* progress toward achieving *your* goals. We wish you outstanding success in meeting your objectives in this course and in your chosen career.

GRETA L. HENDERSON
PRICE R. VOILES

Contents

v

Worksheet Contents/Scoreboard

Index

PART ONE

Review of Language Structure

The overall structure, or framework, of business English is the same as that of the English you undoubtedly have studied in previous courses. Both types of English involve sentences, clauses, phrases, and words; however, business English places special emphasis on those principles that have practical application in writing and speaking for business purposes. Therefore, the main objectives of this part of this course are to help you recall information that you may have forgotten and to refresh your skills in applying that information.

UNIT 1: The Sentence

The sentence is the principal means by which we write and speak our thoughts and by which we read and listen to those of others. At the same time, it is the language-usage unit from which the fundamental principles of grammar, usage, and style are derived. Consequently, a thorough understanding of the sentence is vitally important.

☐ DEFINITION

Sentence.   A *sentence* is a group of words that expresses a complete thought and makes sense when it stands by itself. When written, such a group of words begins with a capital letter and ends with a period, a question mark, or an exclamation point. Note how each of the following groups of words fits the definition and meets the style (capitalization and punctuation) requirements of a sentence.

The president of the company announced the opening of a new branch office.

What type of equipment would you recommend for our word processing center?

You gave an excellent report!

1

☐ ESSENTIAL PARTS

Every sentence contains two main parts, a *subject* and a *predicate.*

Subject.   The *subject* tells who is speaking, who is spoken to, or who or what is spoken about. Although the subject may consist entirely of a "naming" word, it often includes one or more descriptive words.

> *I* received a copy of the agenda this morning. (*I,* which tells who is speaking, is the complete subject of this sentence.)
>
> *You* should apply for that job. (*You,* which tells who is spoken to, is the complete subject of the sentence.)
>
> *Our new equipment* has saved us time and money. (*Equipment,* which tells what is spoken about, is the subject—or, as it is sometimes called, the "simple subject." This naming word plus the descriptive words *our* and *new* make up the complete subject.)
>
> *Mrs. Ames* was living in Iowa. (*Mrs. Ames* tells who is spoken about and is the complete subject.)

Predicate.   The *predicate* tells something about the action, condition, or state of being of the subject. It includes at least one word that *expresses* action, condition, or state of being and generally includes one or more other words that complete or clarify the meaning of the "action" or other word.

> Several people at the scene of the accident *fled.* (*Fled,* which tells what action the people took, is the complete predicate of the sentence.)
>
> Your comments *seemed appropriate.* (As this sentence illustrates, the complete predicate may include a word that describes or modifies the subject of the sentence.)
>
> Every member of your staff *was very helpful.* (*Was,* which expresses state of being, is the simple predicate. It and the other italicized words make up the complete predicate.)
>
> Ms. Beverly Corbett *will send you a copy of the report.* (*Will send* is the simple predicate. It and the other italicized words make up the complete predicate.)

☐ RELATION TO CLAUSES, PHRASES, AND PARTS OF SPEECH

Independent Clause.   An *independent clause* contains a subject and a predicate and expresses a complete thought. When written, therefore, an independent clause can stand alone as a sentence if it is properly punctuated.

> INDEPENDENT CLAUSE: your instructions are always easy to understand
>
> SENTENCE: Your instructions are always easy to understand.

In many instances, an independent clause functions as the *main clause* of a sentence. Note the italicized independent clauses in these sentences, for example.

> *One of your co-workers told me* that you will be promoted within the near future.
>
> *Mr. Benitez is in charge of the firm's word processing department,* and *Miss Sullivan manages its data processing operations.*

Dependent Clause.   A *dependent clause* contains a subject and a predicate, but it does not express a complete thought and cannot stand alone as a sentence. Such a clause usually begins with *although, because, that, when, if,* or a similar word that makes the meaning of the clause dependent upon some part of an independent clause in a complete sentence.

> although the machine is new   because our costs have risen
> when you are ready to leave   that you will be promoted within the near future

As illustrated below, a dependent clause makes sense only when it is used with an independent clause.

Although the machine is new, we have had a few problems with it.

Mrs. Richardson wants you to call her *when you are ready to leave.*

Phrase. A *phrase* contains neither a subject nor a predicate and expresses an incomplete thought. Phrases, such as those listed below, are used as parts of sentences and clauses.

have set	to a customer	to do better	prepared accurately
are planning	for ourselves	writing memos	sitting outside

To do better is the goal that we *have set for ourselves.*

Parts of Speech. The *parts of speech* are the eight classes into which words are divided on the basis of how they are used in sentences, clauses, and phrases. The parts of speech, which are illustrated and identified in the following sentence, will be discussed in Units 2–7.

Oh (*interjection*), Miss Lee (*noun*) called (*verb*) and (*conjunction*) asked (*verb*) me (*pronoun*) about (*preposition*) the (*adjective*) extremely (*adverb*) long (*adjective*) delay (*noun*).

☐ STRUCTURE

The number and kinds of clauses that a sentence contains determine whether it is *simple, compound, complex,* or *compound-complex* in structure.

Simple Sentence. A *simple sentence* contains one independent clause only.

Your recommendations make a great deal of sense to us.

Every customer has the right to expect prompt and courteous service.

As illustrated below, a simple sentence may have a *compound subject,* a *compound predicate,* or both a compound subject and a compound predicate. That is, the complete subject may contain two or more naming words (nouns or pronouns) and two or more words that express action, condition, or state of being (verbs) in the complete predicate.

Ms. Johannsen and her assistant are working on the annual report. (This simple sentence has a compound subject—*Ms. Johannsen* and *assistant.*)

You, Mr. Kelley, or Mrs. Favata prepared the requisition and sent it to Dr. Wiley. (This simple sentence has a compound subject—*you, Mr. Kelley,* and *Mrs. Favata*—and a compound predicate—*prepared* and *sent.*)

Compound Sentence. A *compound sentence* consists of two or more independent, or main, clauses.

The proposed budget has been submitted to the general manager, but it has not been approved yet. (The two independent clauses are joined by the conjunction *but.*)

This year the meeting will be in San Francisco; next year it will be in Chicago. (The two independent clauses are separated by the semicolon.)

Complex Sentence. A *complex sentence* contains one independent, or main, clause and one or more dependent clauses. In the following examples, the dependent clauses appear in italics.

I believe *that you have all the necessary qualifications.*

When I asked Mr. Sullivan, he was unable to tell me *what the total cost would be.*

3

Compound-Complex Sentence. A *compound-complex sentence* contains two or more independent, or main, clauses and one or more dependent clauses. Note that the dependent clauses in the following sentences appear in italics.

We wanted to visit you *while we were in Omaha,* but your secretary said *that you were away on a business trip.*

Two versions of the story are being circulated, and no one seems to know *which of them is accurate.*

☐ FUNCTION

On the basis of what it does, a sentence may be classified as *declarative, imperative, interrogative,* or *exclamatory.* As you study these four classes of sentences, note the comments concerning the correct choice of punctuation.

Declarative Sentence. A *declarative sentence* makes a statement of fact, belief, opinion, or possibility. As illustrated below, always use a period at the end of a declarative sentence.

The title *Ms.* does not indicate the marital status of a woman, nor does *Mr.* indicate the marital status of a man. (Fact.)

The number *13* is unlucky. (Belief—of some people at least!)

The Evergreen Inn is the best restaurant in this area. (Opinion.)

You may receive a bonus at the end of the year. (Possibility.)

Imperative Sentence. An *imperative sentence* expresses a command or a request. The subject *you* is often understood, not stated, in this type of sentence. Note the use of a period after an imperative sentence.

Be sure to sign all four copies of the contract. (The subject *you* is understood.)

Please ask her to call me before noon tomorrow. (The subject *you* is understood.)

Will you please send us your payment immediately. (Even though this request is phrased as a question, it can correctly end with a period. The sentence makes a request that requires an "action" response, not a "Yes" or "No" answer.)

Interrogative Sentence. An *interrogative sentence* asks a question that requires a written or spoken answer, not an "action" response. An interrogative sentence always ends with a question mark.

Why would you like to work for our company?

Do you speak or write any foreign languages?

Exclamatory Sentence. An *exclamatory sentence* expresses strong feeling or emotion. The use of an exclamation point at the end of the sentence tells the reader that the writer intends the statement to have such special force. Most business writers use exclamatory sentences very sparingly.

The job is yours!
We won!
It's a tremendous bargain!

ASSIGNMENT

4

○ Worksheets 1, 2, 3, and 4

UNIT 2: Nouns

☐ DEFINITION

Noun. A *noun* is the name of a person, place, thing, or quality. Thus, as illustrated below, a noun may be a single word or a group of two or more words that function together as one name.

manager	Phyllis	state	North Dakota	machine	airport	shake-up
attorney	Martin	city	New Orleans	business	honesty	sincerity

Some compound nouns, which are those that consist of more than one word, are written as one word; others are written as two or more separate words; and others are written as two or more hyphenated words. Since there is no consistent pattern for writing such nouns, the best procedure is to consult the dictionary whenever you are in doubt. When using the dictionary, be sure to note the part-of-speech label (*n* for noun, *adj* for adjective, and so on), as the way in which a compound should be written often depends upon how it is used as a part of speech.

payoff (adjective, noun)	side step (noun)	time stamp (noun)
pay off (verb)	sidestep (verb)	time-stamp (verb)

☐ CLASSES

Nouns are often divided into various classes, such as those described and illustrated below. As you will readily see, a particular noun may be classified in more than one way; for example, *magazine* may be classified as a common noun as well as a concrete noun.

Common Nouns. A *common noun* is a general name that can be used to refer to any one of a number of persons, places, things, or qualities.

executive	accountant	island	machine	document	college	faith	envelope
secretary	customer	ocean	factory	magazine	student	truth	industry

Proper Nouns. A *proper noun* is a particular name used to refer to a specific person, place, or thing. Unlike common nouns, proper nouns are always capitalized.

Mario	Mrs. Edwards	San Francisco	Europe	Atlantic Ocean	Hunter College
Susan	Juan Torres	Winnipeg	Florida	Fulton Avenue	Lincoln Center

Concrete Nouns. A *concrete noun* is the name of something that can be seen, heard, touched, tasted, or smelled.

paper	desk	whistle	smoke	gasoline	flower	fog	Central Park
stone	chair	scream	water	mechanic	garage	ice	Ford Theater

Abstract Nouns. An *abstract noun* is the name of something that cannot be seen, heard, touched, tasted, or smelled.

experience	opportunity	education	honesty	wisdom	time	anger	hope
knowledge	friendship	happiness	integrity	security	luck	truth	idea

Collective Nouns. A *collective noun* is the name of something that is composed of two or more persons or things.

army	committee	staff	faculty	congregation	majority	family	jury
crew	orchestra	tribe	council	commission	minority	flock	herd

Gerunds (Verbal Nouns). A *gerund* is a verb form ending in *ing* that is used as a noun in a phrase, a clause, or a sentence. Note that *ing* must be added to a word such as *plan, call, increase,* or *write* before it can be used as a gerund. Such words as *thing, bring, string,* and *ring* are not gerunds, even though they end in *ing*.

> A great deal of *planning* will be required. (*Planning* is the object of the preposition *of* in the prepositional phrase *of planning.*)
>
> We thought that the *ringing* would never stop. (*Ringing* is the subject in the dependent clause *that the ringing would never stop.*)
>
> *Writing* is a major part of many jobs. (*Writing* is the subject of the sentence.)

☐ PROPERTIES

Nouns have the properties, or characteristics, of *person, number, gender,* and *case.*

Person. *Person* is used as a grammatical term to indicate whether a word refers to someone making a statement, to someone being spoken to, or to someone or something being spoken about. All nouns name persons and things about which statements are made; thus all nouns are *third person.*

> *Mr. O'Malley* became *manager* of the *office* in *Houston* about a *year* ago.
>
> *Technology* has had a tremendous *impact* on *communication* in *business* and in all other *areas* of *society.*

Number. Most nouns have two different forms to indicate the *number* of persons, places, or things they name. The *singular* form indicates one or, in the case of collective nouns, one group. The *plural* form, which usually consists of the singular form plus *s* or *es,* indicates two or more or, in the case of collective nouns, two or more groups.

SINGULAR:	premium	procedure	faculty	survey	tax	child
PLURAL:	premiums	procedures	faculties	surveys	taxes	children

Gender. All nouns reflect *gender,* or sex. Those that refer to males are of *masculine* gender; to females, of *feminine* gender; to either or both males and females, of *common* gender; to neither males nor females, of *neuter* gender.

MASCULINE:	man	husband	son	father	prince	boy	king
FEMININE:	woman	wife	daughter	mother	princess	girl	queen
COMMON:	person	spouse	child	parent	governor	student	citizen
NEUTER:	catalog	house	budget	garage	library	career	domain

Although a number of nouns have a masculine form and a feminine form (*host, hostess; steward, stewardess; salesman, saleswoman;* and so on), the preferred practice is to use a term of common gender. Thus *host* is commonly used for members of both sexes; *flight attendant* is used instead of *steward* or *stewardess;* and *salesperson, sales representative,* or some other term of common gender is used instead of *salesman* or *saleswoman.*

Case. *Case* is simply a grammatical term that refers to the relationship between two or more words appearing in a sentence, clause, or phrase. As it applies to nouns, the most important thing to remember is that many nouns change form to show ownership or possession—*possessive case*—by adding an apostrophe or an apostrophe and *s.*

SINGULAR POSSESSIVE:	owner's	company's	attorney's	boss's	committee's
PLURAL POSSESSIVE:	owners'	companies'	attorneys'	bosses'	committees'

Nouns that refer to objects generally show possession through an *of* phrase. However, those that refer to time and money are commonly used as possessives, as illustrated in the last two sentences below.

> The foundation *of the building* collapsed. (**NOT:** *the building's foundation.*)
>
> The cost *of the repairs* was quite reasonable. (**NOT:** *the repairs' cost.*)
>
> Both of you deserve a *week's* vacation. (**NOT:** *vacation of a week.*)
>
> Please get a *dollar's* worth of nails. (**NOT:** *worth of a dollar.*)

□ USES

The following are some of the ways in which nouns are frequently used in ordinary business writing and speech.

Subject of Sentence or Clause.   As a *subject,* a noun tells who or what is being talked about.

> *Miss Norton* thinks that her *recommendations* will be accepted. (*Miss Norton* is the subject of the sentence; *recommendations* is the subject of the dependent clause.)

Direct Object of Verb.   The *direct object* names the receiver or the result of the action expressed by the verb.

> Some stockholders sold their *shares* when they heard the *news.* (*Shares* is the direct object of the verb *sold; news* is the direct object of the verb *heard.*)

Indirect Object of Verb.   The *indirect object* tells to whom something is given or for whom something is done.

> Some dealers gave their *customers* rebates. (*Customers* is the indirect object and *rebates* is the direct object of the verb *gave.*)

Object of Preposition.   A *preposition* is a word that connects a noun or pronoun, known as the *object of the preposition,* to a preceding word in the sentence. The preposition, the object of the preposition, and the modifiers (if any) of the object form a *prepositional phrase.*

> I left a message for *Mr. Polisky* on your *desk.* (*Mr. Polisky* is the object of the preposition *for; for* connects *Mr. Polisky* to *message;* the prepositional phrase *for Mr. Polisky* modifies the noun *message. Desk* is the object of the preposition *on; on* connects *desk* to the verb *left;* the prepositional phrase *on your desk* modifies the verb *left.*)

Appositive.   An *appositive* is one or more words that clarify a preceding noun or pronoun.

> We *accountants* must complete these reports before the end of this week. (The noun *accountants* clarifies the pronoun *we.*)
>
> Both of them, *Kurt and Brenda,* exceeded their sales budgets last month. (*Kurt and Brenda* clarifies the pronoun *them.*)
>
> Her new administrative assistant, *Ralph Saunders,* previously worked for Mr. Glenn. (The noun *Ralph Saunders* clarifies the noun *administrative assistant.*)

Predicate Nominative.   A *predicate nominative* is a word that follows a verb and renames the subject of the sentence or clause in which it appears.

> Dr. Lundquist is the *executor* of the estate. (*Executor* follows the verb *is* and renames the subject of the sentence, *Dr. Lundquist.*)

□ SPECIAL COMMENTS CONCERNING NOUNS

1. A word used as a noun in one sentence may be used as a different part of speech in another sentence.

> Mr. and Mrs. Perez are building a new *home*. (Noun)
>
> Please give me your *home* telephone number. (Adjective)
>
> Lorraine went *home* at 3 o'clock this afternoon. (Adverb)

> The Hagners have lived in *Minneapolis* for several years. (Noun)
>
> What is the name of your *Minneapolis* representative? (Adjective)

2. Numbers may be either nouns or adjectives, depending upon how they are used.

> If your suggestion is accepted, you will receive *$100*. (Noun)
>
> We have only *five* copies of the pamphlet on hand. (Adjective)

3. Possessive nouns are often used as adjectives modifying nouns.

> Many people are unaware of *Henry's* contributions to the success of the company. (The possessive noun *Henry's* functions as an adjective modifying the noun *contributions*.)

4. The words *a, an,* and *the* (known as "articles") often precede and pinpoint nouns.

> A *reporter* asked the *senator* for an *explanation*.

ASSIGNMENT

○ Worksheets 5, 6, and 7

UNIT 3: Pronouns

□ DEFINITION

Pronoun. A *pronoun* is a word that takes the place of a noun. Therefore, the use of pronouns eliminates the monotonous repetition of nouns, such as that occurring in the following sentence:

> Miss Pollock signed the memo that Miss Pollock's assistant typed for Miss Pollock before Miss Pollock left for a meeting with the members of Miss Pollock's staff.

Notice how the use of the pronouns *her* and *she* eliminates the repetition of the noun *Miss Pollock* and makes the sentence flow smoothly.

> Miss Pollock signed the memo that *her* assistant typed for *her* before *she* left for a meeting with the members of *her* staff.

To avoid confusion, the *antecedent*—the word or words to which a pronoun refers—must be clear. Notice the uncertainty that this sentence produces:

> Mr. Wheeler informed Mr. Dawson that he probably would be unable to attend the convention because he had not been able to obtain confirmation of his hotel reservations. (*Who* probably would be unable to attend the convention? *Who* had not been able to obtain confirmation of *whose* hotel reservations?)

The only way to clear up the confusion is to revise the sentence in such a way that the antecedent of each pronoun is clear. Here are some acceptable revisions of the example sentence:

Because Mr. Wheeler had not been able to obtain confirmation of *his* hotel reservations, *he* informed Mr. Dawson that *he* probably would be unable to attend the convention. (The pronouns clearly refer to *Mr. Wheeler.*)

Mr. Wheeler informed Mr. Dawson that *he* probably would be unable to attend the convention because *he* had not been able to obtain confirmation of Mr. Dawson's hotel reservations. (The first *he* refers to *Mr. Dawson;* the second *he* refers to *Mr. Wheeler.*)

Mr. Wheeler, *who* had not been able to obtain confirmation of *his* hotel reservations, informed Mr. Dawson that *he* probably would be unable to attend the convention. (The pronouns clearly refer to *Mr. Wheeler.*)

☐ CLASSES

Personal Pronouns. The *personal pronouns* refer to specific persons or things. As illustrated in the following sentences, certain personal pronouns refer to the person speaking; others refer to the person spoken to; and others refer to the person or thing spoken about. (See the chart on page 13.)

I should have asked *my* supervisor to explain the procedure to *me.* (*I, my,* and *me* refer to the person speaking.)

You probably will want to renew *your* subscription right away. (*You* and *your* refer to the person spoken to.)

Larry Stern was offered the job, but *he* did not accept *it.* (*He* refers to *Larry Stern,* the person spoken about. *It* refers to *job,* the thing spoken about.)

Compound Personal Pronouns. The *compound personal pronouns* end in *self* (singular) or *selves* (plural). These are the only compound personal pronouns recognized in standard English usage:

myself   ourselves   yourself   yourselves   himself   herself   itself   themselves

We have no choice but to do the work *ourselves.* (The pronoun *we,* which does not require a stated antecedent, is the antecedent of *ourselves.*)

You may prefer to inspect this shipment *yourself.* (The pronoun *you,* which does not require a stated antecedent, is the antecedent of *yourself.*)

Kevin blamed *himself* for the errors in the report. (The pronouns *himself, herself, itself,* and *themselves* require stated antecedents. *Kevin* is the antecedent of *himself* in this sentence.)

Indefinite Pronouns. *Indefinite pronouns,* such as those listed below, do not refer to specific persons or things.

all   one   both   some   none   anybody   anyone   everything   several   somebody
any   few   each   many   most   nothing   no one   something   neither   someone

Everyone feels that *something* needs to be done about that particular problem.

Many were aware of the proposed merger, but *no one* could be certain that it would become a reality.

As illustrated below, a number of words used as indefinite pronouns may also be used as modifiers.

Most customers placed their orders early. (*Most* modifies the noun *customers.*)

Is *either* one of the signatures legible? (*Either* modifies the indefinite pronoun *one.*)

Demonstrative Pronouns. The *demonstrative pronouns,* which point out or point to, are *this, that, these,* and *those.*

This is yours and *that* is mine; however, *these* are theirs and *those* are ours.

9

When used as modifiers, *this* and *that* modify singular nouns and pronouns; *these* and *those* modify plural nouns and pronouns.

This container is full, but *that* one is empty. (*This* modifies the noun *container,* and *that* modifies the indefinite pronoun *one.*)

We have lowered the prices of *these* radios and of *those* calculators. (*These* modifies the plural noun *radios,* and *those* modifies the plural noun *calculators.*)

Interrogative Pronouns. An *interrogative pronoun* introduces a question. These are often used as interrogative pronouns:

who   what   which   whom   whose

What can we do to increase productivity without sacrificing quality?

Whom do you plan to invite to participate in the panel discussion?

Relative Pronouns. *Relative pronouns* join dependent clauses to independent clauses in complex and compound-complex sentences. As illustrated in the following sentences, the relative pronoun may function as a subject or an object as well as a connecting word.

Mr. Fernandez may know the name of the company *that* manufactures these desks. (*That* connects the dependent clause *that manufactures these desks* to the independent clause; it also functions as the subject of the dependent clause. The dependent clause modifies the noun *company*—it tells which company.)

Mrs. Merola said *that* she would be in Milwaukee next Wednesday. (*That* simply connects the dependent clause *that she would be in Milwaukee next Wednesday* to the independent clause.)

We should send this letter to everyone *who* participates in the survey. (*Who* connects the dependent clause *who participates in the survey* to the independent clause; it also functions as the subject of the dependent clause.)

Do you know anyone *whom* we could hire on a part-time basis? (*Whom* connects the dependent clause *whom we could hire on a part-time basis* to the independent clause. *Whom* also functions as the direct object of *could hire.*)

The following are commonly used relative pronouns. Usage notes are shown in parentheses.

who (refers to persons)   which (refers to animals or things)
whom (refers to persons)   that (refers to persons, animals, or things)

Relative and interrogative pronouns are similar. The use of the pronoun in a sentence determines its classification.

Do you know anyone *who* has the necessary qualifications? (*Who* is a relative pronoun because it introduces a clause that modifies the pronoun *anyone.*)

Who owns the garage on Elm Street? (*Who* is an interrogative pronoun. It does not introduce a clause that modifies some other word in the sentence.)

☐ PROPERTIES

Since pronouns are substitutes for nouns, they have the same properties, or characteristics, as nouns: *person, number, gender,* and *case.* Thus one of the most important principles of standard English usage is this: *A pronoun must agree with its antecedent in person, number, and gender.* As you will see in the following discussion, an understanding of *case* is important too—even though the case of a pronoun depends upon how it is used, not upon what its antecedent is.

Person.   As illustrated below and as shown in the Personal Pronoun Chart on page 13, certain personal pronouns refer to the person speaking (first person); others refer to the person spoken to (second person); and others refer to the person or thing spoken about (third person).

I should renew *my* subscription to that magazine this week. (*I* and *my* refer to the person speaking. They are first person pronouns.)

You should submit *your* recommendations to Ms. Rodgers. (*You* and *your* refer to the person spoken to. They are second person pronouns.)

Paul said that *he* approved the requisition and sent *it* on to *his* supervisor. (*He* and *his* refer to *Paul,* the person spoken about. *It* refers to *requisition,* the thing spoken about. *He, his,* and *it* are third person pronouns.)

Compound personal pronouns also indicate whether they refer to the person speaking, the person spoken to, or the person or thing spoken about.

I mailed the package *myself.* (The antecedent of *myself* is *I,* the person speaking.)

You should order a copy for *yourself.* (The antecedent of *yourself* is *you,* the person spoken to.)

The managers did the work *themselves.* (The antecedent of *themselves* is *managers,* the persons spoken about.)

Indefinite pronouns refer to persons and things spoken about; thus they are third person. As antecedents, they require third person pronouns.

Each of the men did *his* share of the work. (The antecedent of *his* is the indefinite pronoun *each.* Note that the masculine pronoun *his* is used in this sentence because the indefinite pronoun *each* refers to the masculine noun *men.*)

Most of the stores have awnings in front of *them.* (The indefinite pronoun *most* is the antecedent of *them.*)

Number.   With the exception of the second person pronoun *you,* the form of a personal or compound personal pronoun indicates whether the pronoun is *singular* or *plural* in number. As indicated in the Personal Pronoun Chart on page 13 and as illustrated below, *you* may refer to one person or two or more persons.

John and *I* were at the reception, but *we* did not stay very long. (*I* is first person singular; *we* is first person plural.)

You may want to check the figures *yourself.* (*Yourself* makes it clear that *you* refers to one person.)

You should be proud of *yourselves.* (*Yourselves* makes it clear that *you* refers to two or more persons.)

When I spoke to Inez, *she* was working on the project by *herself.* (*She* and *herself* are singular third person pronouns; the antecedent of each of these pronouns is the singular noun *Inez.*)

Larry and Bob said *they* would make the necessary arrangements *themselves.* (The antecedent of *they* and *themselves,* which are plural third person personal pronouns, is *Larry* and *Bob.*)

Other pronouns, such as the following, indicate number by their meaning.

SINGULAR: each   either   everyone   nobody   no one   nothing   one   something
PLURAL: both   few   many   several   these   those

Each must do *his* or *her* share of the work. (All the pronouns are singular.)

Several are planning to take *their* vacations in August. (Both pronouns are plural.)

Some pronouns may be either singular or plural, depending upon how they are used. These are examples of such pronouns:

some   who   that   which   whose   most   all   whom

Some of the water has evaporated. (*Some,* which refers to *water,* is singular here.)

Some of the members were absent. (*Some* refers to *members* and is plural here.)

Please sign the memo *that* is on your desk. (*That* refers to *memo* and is singular.)

Please address the envelopes *that* are on your desk. (*That* refers to *envelopes* and is plural.)

Gender. Some singular pronouns are clearly *masculine, feminine,* or *neuter* in gender. Most pronouns, however, are of *common* gender.

MASCULINE: he   him   his   himself   FEMININE: she   her   hers   herself

NEUTER: it   its   itself   everything   nothing   anything   something

COMMON: I   we   you   they   all   both   anyone   everyone   someone   who   that

Mario will place the order *himself.* (The antecedent of the masculine pronoun *himself* is *Mario.*)

Eleanor dictated the letters to *her* secretary. (The antecedent of the feminine pronoun *her* is *Eleanor.*)

The city will have to solve *its* fiscal problems *itself.* (The antecedent of the neuter pronouns *its* and *itself* is *city.*)

We hope *they* will call *us* as soon as *they* arrive at the airport. (These pronouns may refer to men or women or to both men and women; therefore, they are of common gender.)

Each of the customers expects to receive *his or her* monthly statements on time. (*Each* may refer to both male and female customers; therefore, *his or her* is used to refer to *each.*)

Case. The form of a pronoun may change to indicate its *case;* this is especially true of personal pronouns. (See the Personal Pronoun Chart on page 13.) The three cases are listed, explained, and illustrated below.

1. The *nominative case* is used when a pronoun is the subject or the predicate nominative, as illustrated below.

I hope that *you* will attend the meeting. (The pronoun *I* is the subject of the verb *hope;* the pronoun *you* is the subject of the verb *will attend.*)

Who are *they?* (The pronoun *they* is a predicate nominative; it renames the subject *who.*)

2. The *objective case* is used when a pronoun is the object of a verb or a preposition, or the subject or object of an infinitive (*to go, to do, to call, to see,* and so on).

John wants *us* to go with *him.* (*Us* is the object of the verb *wants* and the subject of the infinitive *to go. Him* is the object of the preposition *with.*)

We may decide to visit *them* next week. (*Them* is the object of the infinitive *to visit.*)

3. The *possessive case* is used when a pronoun shows ownership, authorship, or a similar relationship to some other word and modifies that word.

I must answer *her* letter. (*Her* modifies the noun *letter.* It tells whose letter.)

Such possessive pronouns as *yours, theirs,* and *ours* show ownership, authorship, or a similar relationship and take the place of a word stated previously in the sentence or a word clearly understood, not stated.

These copies are *yours.* (*Yours* shows ownership and takes the place of the noun *copies.* In effect, *yours* takes the place of *your copies* in this sentence: *These copies are your copies.*)

PERSONAL PRONOUN CHART

PERSON	NOMINATIVE CASE		OBJECTIVE CASE		POSSESSIVE CASE	
	SINGULAR	PLURAL	SINGULAR	PLURAL	SINGULAR	PLURAL
First (the speaker)	I	we	me	us	my, mine	our, ours
Second (spoken to)	you	you	you	you	your, yours	your, yours
Third (spoken about)	he she it	they	him her it	them	his her, hers its	their, theirs

ASSIGNMENT

○ Worksheets 8, 9, and 10

UNIT 4: Verbs

☐ DEFINITION

Verb.   A *verb* is a word that expresses action, condition, or state of being. The following are a few examples of commonly used verbs:

choose	write	hope	change	be	buy	seem	develop	complete	assist
enclose	think	plan	accept	do	pay	feel	receive	believe	prefer

A verb is an essential part of the predicate of every sentence and every clause. Without at least one verb, a group of words can be neither a sentence nor a clause.

Both of them *change* jobs quite often.

Most people *think* that they *pay* too much for such services.

☐ CLASSES

Verbs are generally divided into two classes—*transitive* and *intransitive*.

Transitive Verbs.   A *transitive verb* shows physical or mental action and has a direct object when the subject is the doer of the action.

This company *manufactures* office products. (*Company,* the subject, is the doer of the action. The direct object is *office products.*)

The architect *submitted* new plans. (*Architect,* the subject, is the doer of the action. The direct object is *plans.*)

Any sentence or clause in which the subject is the receiver or the result of the action contains a transitive verb.

Office products *are manufactured* by this company. (*Office products,* the subject, names the result of the action expressed by *are manufactured.*)

New plans *were submitted* by the architect. (*Plans,* the subject, is the receiver of the action expressed by *were submitted.*)

13

Intransitive Verbs. An *intransitive verb* shows physical or mental action but does not have a direct object.

Their sales *increased* significantly. (*Significantly* modifies *increased*.)

Each driver *proceeded* cautiously. (*Cautiously* modifies *proceeded*.)

Some intransitive verbs show state of being (living or existence), not action. These verbs are often referred to as *linking verbs*. As illustrated below, a linking verb links its subject to a *predicate nominative* (a word that renames the subject) or a *predicate adjective* (a word that modifies the subject).

These procedures *seem* efficient. (*Efficient,* the predicate adjective, modifies the subject, *procedures.*)

Dr. Gomez *is* a well-known surgeon. (*Surgeon,* the predicate nominative, renames the subject, *Dr. Gomez.*)

☐ VERB PHRASES

Definition. A *verb phrase* is two or more words consisting of a *main* verb and one or more *helping* verbs. The main verb is always the last word in the phrase; the verb or verbs appearing before the main verb are helping verbs.

You *could have answered* Mildred's question. (*Answered* is the main verb; *could* and *have* are helping verbs.)

Sometimes it is difficult to tell whether a word is part of a verb phrase or a predicate adjective. If the word cannot be used as a verb, consider it a predicate adjective. However, if it can be used as a verb, consider it the main verb in the verb phrase. Note these examples:

Our plane *was delayed* for two hours. (*Delayed* can be used as a verb; therefore, it is the main verb in the verb phrase.)

The driver *may have been* seriously *injured*. (*Injured* can be used as a verb; it is part of the verb phrase.)

Ms. Ryder, one of the witnesses, *was* cooperative throughout the investigation. (*Cooperative* cannot be used as a verb. It modifies the subject, *Ms. Ryder,* and is a predicate adjective.)

Commonly used helping verbs (sometimes called *auxiliary verbs*) are as follows:

be	are	been	will	might	have	have had	would
am	was	being	may	could	has	had been	does
is	were	shall	can	should	do	has been	did

☐ TENSES

The *tense* of a verb or verb phrase reflects the time of an action or a state of being.

Present Tense. The *present tense* indicates now—the present time.

We *are* fortunate in many respects.

Mr. Barbera *has* the files in his office.

The present tense is also used to indicate things that are true at all times, as in the following examples:

The sun *rises* in the east and *sets* in the west.

We always *give* your orders immediate attention.

14

Past Tense.   The *past tense* indicates that the action took place some time in the past or that the state of being existed some time in the past.

> Ed *was* there at 9 o'clock.   Almost everyone *agreed* with us.

Future Tense.   The *future tense* indicates that the action or state of being will occur or exist at some future time. The future tense is always expressed by *will* or *shall* plus a main verb.

> We *shall notify* you within the next ten days.   Your flight *will leave* soon.

Present Perfect Tense.   The *present perfect tense* indicates that the action or state of being is complete (perfect) at the present time. This tense is always formed by using *has* or *have* with a main verb.

> Our building *has drawn* many compliments.   Two firms *have built* new warehouses.

Past Perfect Tense.   The *past perfect tense* indicates that the action or the state of being was complete (perfect) at some particular past time. It is always formed by using *had* with a main verb.

> You *had left* before I arrived.   We *had known* of his plans before he told us.

Future Perfect Tense.   The *future perfect tense* indicates that the action or state of being will be complete (perfect) at some particular time in the future. This tense is always formed by using *shall have* or *will have* with a main verb.

> By the time he arrives, we *shall have been* here more than an hour.

> Jerry *will have received* an appointment to the academy before next summer.

☐ VOICE

The term *voice* describes the relationship between a subject and a verb that expresses action. The two voices of verbs are *active* and *passive*.

Active Voice.   When the subject is the doer of the action expressed by the verb, the verb is in *active voice*.

> These laws *protect* the rights of consumers.   The store *gave* me a refund.

Passive Voice.   When the subject names the receiver or the result of the action expressed by the verb, the verb is in *passive voice*. The passive voice always includes a form of the verb *be* (*be, am, is, are, was, were, been,* or *being*) as a helping verb and a past participle as a main verb.

> The rights of consumers *are protected* by these laws.

> I *was given* a refund by the store. **OR:** A refund *was given* to me by the store.

☐ USAGE PRINCIPLES

1. A subject and its verb must agree in number. A singular subject requires a singular verb; a plural subject requires a plural verb. **NOTE:** The pronoun *you* is always considered to be plural and requires a plural verb.

> There *are* many *jobs* available. (**NOT:** There *is* many *jobs* available.)
>
> *Neither* of these products *is* defective. (**NOT:** *Neither* of these products *are* defective.)
>
> *One* of my co-workers *was* ill yesterday. (**NOT:** *One* of my co-workers *were* ill yesterday.)
>
> *You were* out of the office when I called. (**NOT:** *You was* out of the office when I called.)
>
> *Some* of them *are being checked* by Ruth. (**NOT:** *Some* of them *is being checked* by Ruth.)

2. A verb must agree with its subject in person. Study the following examples to see how this principle is applied.

You are the best-qualified candidate. (**NOT:** *You is* the best-qualified candidate.)

I am planning to be there next week. (**NOT:** *I is planning* to be there next week.)

She is in Chicago today, and *he is* in Atlanta or Tampa.

3. The correct form of a verb must be used to reflect a particular tense. One of the most glaring errors is the use of the wrong tense form.

I *saw* them last week. (**NOT:** I *seen* them last week.)

Who *did* it? (**NOT:** Who *done* it?)

We *have* already *eaten* lunch. (**NOT:** We *have* already *ate* lunch.)

Have you *written* to Mrs. Favata recently? (**NOT:** *Have* you *wrote* to Mrs. Favata recently?)

ASSIGNMENT

○ Worksheets 11, 12, 13, and 14

UNIT **5**: Adjectives

The use of adjectives helps to make both written and oral communications more interesting and more meaningful to readers and listeners. While they appear in all types of business communications, adjectives are especially important in those that have a sales or sales-promotion purpose.

☐ DEFINITION

Adjective. An *adjective* modifies a noun or a pronoun. Adjectives answer such questions as these: Which? What kind of? How many? Whose?

Several multinational corporations have *their* offices in *this* building.

Everyone who is *present* will receive *a valuable, practical* gift.

☐ CLASSES

Descriptive Adjectives. A *descriptive adjective* describes a quality or a characteristic of someone or something. It tells "what kind of."

Careful consideration will be given to your proposals.

What *government* regulations are applicable in this situation?

Demonstrative Adjectives. A *demonstrative adjective* tells "which." The demonstrative pronouns—*this, that, these,* and *those*—may be used as demonstrative adjectives. Note that *this* and *that* modify singular nouns or pronouns and *these* and *those* modify plural nouns or pronouns.

This house is in excellent condition, but *that* one needs extensive repairs.

These letters are ready to be signed, but *those* contracts are not.

Limiting Adjectives. A *limiting adjective* tells "how many" or "in what order."

We have openings for *three* maintenance workers and *several* sales correspondents.

You are *next* on the list of those to be promoted.

Proper Adjectives. A *proper adjective* is a proper noun or a word derived from a proper noun that modifies a noun or a pronoun.

What is the telephone number of your *Philadelphia* office?

Does your company have many *European* customers for its products?

Compound Adjectives. A *compound adjective* consists of two or more words that act together as a one-thought modifier.

This housing development consists entirely of *two-story* homes.

Please list all *out-of-stock* items, and issue an *up-to-date* report.

The *high school* principal agreed with those who wanted to adjust *real estate* taxes.

Articles. *A, an,* and *the* are adjectives known as *articles.*

The company plans to open *an* office in Detroit and *a* warehouse in Dayton.

The article *an* is used when the word following it begins with a vowel (*a, e, i, o,* or *u*) or a vowel sound. *A* is used when the word following it begins with a consonant (any letter other than *a, e, i, o,* or *u*) or a consonant sound.

We shall make *an* effort to comply.   Your friend has *an* unusual first name.
What is *a* reasonable offer?   Your idea is *a* very good one.

Note that the letter *u* is sometimes pronounced "uh" (a vowel sound) and sometimes "you" (a consonant sound). Be guided by the sound, as illustrated below.

an unconstitutional act   *a* uniform   *an* understanding   *a* unique problem

☐ DEGREE FORMS

Many adjectives have three different forms that are used in comparisons of persons and things: the *positive degree* form, the *comparative degree* form, and the *superlative degree* form.

POSITIVE DEGREE:	heavy	good	long	appropriate
COMPARATIVE DEGREE:	heavier	better	longer	more (*or* less) appropriate
SUPERLATIVE DEGREE:	heaviest	best	longest	most (*or* least) appropriate

Positive Degree. The *positive degree* expresses the quality of someone or something by itself.

Miss Garcia made a *good* suggestion.

Do you think red would be an *appropriate* color?

Comparative Degree. The *comparative degree* expresses the quality of one person or thing compared with that of one other person or thing.

Miss Garcia made a *better* suggestion than I did.

Do you think red would be a *more appropriate* color than green? (**OR:** *less appropriate*)

If adding *er* to the basic adjective (positive degree) would make the comparative degree form difficult to pronounce or awkward-sounding, use *more* (or *less*) with the basic adjective. Do not use both the *er* ending and *more* (or *less*).

Is there a *simpler* procedure? (**NOT:** Is there a *more simpler* procedure?)

17

Superlative Degree. The *superlative degree* expresses the quality of one person or thing compared with that of two or more other persons or things.

Miss Garcia made the *best* suggestion of all those that were made at the meeting.

Do you think red would be the *most appropriate* color?

If adding *est* to the basic adjective (positive degree) would make the superlative degree form difficult to pronounce or awkward-sounding, use *most* (or *least*) with the basic adjective. Do not use both the *est* ending and *most* (or *least*).

The *prettiest* rose will win an award. (**NOT:** The *most prettiest* rose will win an award.)

☐ ABSOLUTE ADJECTIVES

Definition. An *absolute adjective* is one that (at least technically) cannot be used in a comparison because of its meaning. Such adjectives as the following do not have comparative and superlative degree forms:

fiscal	unique	monetary	single	only	financial	annual

Some absolute adjectives, such as those listed below, are sometimes used with *more nearly* or *less nearly* and with *most nearly* or *least nearly.*

perfect	unique	average	square	round	correct	accurate

For the special effect that their doing so produces, some business writers and speakers deliberately use such expressions as "the most perfect," "the most unique," and so forth, especially in sales-promotion materials. In this course, be sure to consider the sentences and other worksheet materials as excerpts from ordinary business writing and speech—and avoid violations of the most widely accepted principles of English usage.

ASSIGNMENT

○ Worksheets 15, 16, 17, and 18

UNIT 6: Adverbs

Like adjectives, adverbs play an important part in written and oral communications. Both adjectives and adverbs are modifiers—and their uses and characteristics are comparable, at least in a general sense.

☐ DEFINITION

Adverb. An *adverb* is a word that modifies a verb, an adjective, or another adverb. Adverbs answer such questions as these: How? When? To what extent or degree? How often? Where?

Interest in solar energy has grown *rapidly.* (Has grown *how?*)

I paid the balance of my account *yesterday.* (Paid *when?*)

These cartons are *almost* ready to ship. (Ready *to what extent or degree?*)

Everyone makes mistakes *occasionally*. (Makes mistakes *how often?*)
The sign indicates that all pets must be left *outdoors*. (Must be left *where?*)

Many adverbs end in *ly,* but some do not. Note that a large number of adverbs are formed by adding *ly* to such adjectives as *quiet, final, rapid,* and *usual.*

quietly	rapidly	mostly	surely	sincerely	too	there	seldom
finally	usually	nearly	wholly	recently	very	quite	already

In the following sentences, note that words often used as other parts of speech can also be used as adverbs.

Pat went *home*. (Adverb)
Her *home* is in Washington. (Noun)

He was ill *Friday*. (Adverb)
Tomorrow is *Friday*. (Noun)

They were sitting *outdoors*. (Adverb)
We like the great *outdoors*. (Noun)

Nancy left *early*. (Adverb)
She chose *early* retirement. (Adjective)

More of them are needed. (Pronoun)
More orders have arrived. (Adjective)
Which is *more* appropriate? (Adverb)

Most of those are ready. (Pronoun)
Most people agree with you. (Adjective)
She is *most* competent. (Adverb)

☐ CLASSES

Adverbs are sometimes divided into classes on the basis of what they do. These classes include the following: *manner*—those that tell "how"; *place*—those that tell "where"; *time*—those that tell "when"; *frequency*—those that tell "how often"; *reason*—those that tell "why"; and so on.

☐ DEGREE FORMS

Many adverbs, like many adjectives, may be used in comparisons. The principles that apply to the positive, comparative, and superlative degree forms of adjectives (*see* pages 17–18) also apply to the degree forms of adverbs.

POSITIVE: Dr. Merola arrives at the office *early*.

COMPARATIVE: Dr. Merola arrives at the office *earlier* than I do.

SUPERLATIVE: Of all my co-workers, Dr. Merola arrives at the office *earliest*.

POSITIVE: Miss Hill does her work *carefully*.

COMPARATIVE: Miss Hill does her work *more carefully* than either of us. (OR: *less carefully*.)

SUPERLATIVE: Of all of us, Miss Hill does her work *most carefully*. (OR: *least carefully*.)

As a general rule, adverbs formed by adding *ly* to other words (*cordial, immediate, practical,* and so on) require the use of *more* (or *less*) in the comparative degree and *most* (or *least*) in the superlative degree.

Like absolute adjectives, such absolute adverbs as the following cannot be compared because of their meaning:

there	here	now	outside	then	very	almost	quite	too

ASSIGNMENT

○ Worksheets 19, 20, and 21

UNIT 7: Prepositions, Conjunctions, and Interjections

This unit reviews the two classifications of connecting words—*prepositions* and *conjunctions*. It also covers *interjections*—a class of words used sparingly in ordinary business writing.

☐ PREPOSITIONS

Definition. A *preposition* is a connecting word that shows the relationship between a following noun or pronoun and some other word in a sentence or a clause. The words listed below are commonly used as prepositions.

about	against	before	between	for	into	off	past	under	upon
across	around	below	by	from	like	on	through	until	with
after	at	beside	down	in	of	over	to	up	within

Use. Prepositions are used in *prepositional phrases,* each of which is a group of words that functions as one part of speech in a sentence or clause. A prepositional phrase consists of a preposition, the noun or pronoun object of the preposition, and the modifiers (if any) of the noun or pronoun object.

Ms. Soriano has gone *to Cleveland.* (*To Cleveland* functions as an adverb modifying the verb phrase *has gone.* It tells where Ms. Soriano has gone.)

The letter *from her* arrived last Friday. (*From her* functions as an adjective modifying the noun *letter.* It tells which letter.)

In the morning would be the best time to call them. (*In the morning* functions as a noun; it is the subject of the sentence. Note that *to* is followed by the verb *call;* therefore, it is part of the infinitive phrase *to call them* and not part of a prepositional phrase.)

We thanked each interviewee *for cooperating.* (Note that the object of *for* is the gerund *cooperating. For cooperating* functions as an adverb modifying *thanked;* it tells why.)

A word used as a preposition in one sentence may be used as part of a compound word that functions as a different part of speech in another sentence. If the word is followed by a noun or pronoun object, it is a preposition; otherwise, it is part of a compound word.

The majority of the union members decided to walk *out.* (*Out* is part of the compound verb *walk out* in the infinitive phrase *to walk out.*)

Employees of other companies staged a walk*out* in sympathy with the striking workers. (*Out* is part of the compound noun *walkout.*)

I didn't see anyone walk *out* the door. (*Out* is followed by the noun object *door;* therefore, it is part of the prepositional phrase *out the door,* which functions as an adverb modifying the verb *walk.* It tells where.)

☐ CONJUNCTIONS

Definition. A *conjunction* is a word that connects words, phrases, or clauses. The various classes into which conjunctions are grouped are discussed on the next page.

20

Coordinate Conjunctions. A *coordinate conjunction* is one that joins words, phrases, or clauses that are grammatically equal, as illustrated by the following sentences. The coordinate conjunctions are *and, but, or,* and *nor.*

> John Stefano *and* Karen McBride are members of the board of directors, *but* they *and* another board member were not at the last meeting. (The first *and* joins two nouns; the second *and* joins a pronoun and a noun. *But* connects the two independent clauses in this compound sentence.)

> Vincent has not seen the final report, *nor* have I. (*Nor* joins the two independent clauses in this compound sentence.)

> Please call *or* write Ms. Rodriguez within the next few days. (*Or* joins two verbs—*call* and *write.*)

> I am sure that Ms. Stevens will be happy to hear from you *and* that she will accept your invitation. (*And* joins two dependent clauses.)

Correlative Conjunctions. *Correlative conjunctions* are pairs of coordinate conjunctions used to join grammatically equal elements of a sentence. Commonly used correlative conjunctions are as follows:

both . . . and	either . . . or	as . . . as	whether . . . or
not only . . . but also	neither . . . nor	so . . . as	

> This statement of account is *not only* inaccurate *but also* incomplete. (*Not only* and *but also* join the two predicate adjectives *inaccurate* and *incomplete.*)

> *Both* he *and* she have enrolled in the company's in-service training program. (*Both* and *and* join the two pronouns *he* and *she,* which make up the compound subject of the sentence.)

> *Either* you *or* Nancy Gillette will need to draft the contract. (*Either* and *or* join the two parts of the compound subject—the pronoun *you* and the noun *Nancy Gillette.*)

> We stock *neither* vinyl *nor* cork tiles in our 86th Street store. (*Neither* and *nor* connect the two adjectives *vinyl* and *cork,* which modify the noun *tiles.*)

Conjunctive Adverbs. *Conjunctive adverbs* are a special kind of coordinate conjunctions. They are used only to connect independent clauses. Examples of commonly used conjunctive adverbs are as follows:

accordingly consequently furthermore however moreover nevertheless therefore

> More than a hundred signed up for the excursion; *however,* fewer than half of them actually went on the trip.

Note that words used as conjunctive adverbs may also be used as ordinary adverbs. In the preceding sentence, *however* was used to join two independent clauses; therefore, it functioned as a conjunctive adverb. In the sentence below, the same word is used as an ordinary adverb.

> We must install a new press, *however* expensive it may be. (*However* modifies the adjective *expensive.*)

Subordinate Conjunctions. A *subordinate conjunction* is a word used to join a dependent (subordinate) clause to an independent (main) clause in a complex or compound-complex sentence. The following words are frequently—but not always—used as subordinate conjunctions:

after	as soon as	before	until	when	which	who	whose
although	because	that	what	where	while	whom	why

Please send us a replacement copy *as soon as* you can. (*As soon as* connects the dependent clause *as soon as you can* to the main clause in this complex sentence. *As soon as you can,* which functions as an adverb modifying the verb *send,* tells when.)

Do you know *why* they want to terminate the agreement? (*Why* introduces and connects the dependent clause *why they want to terminate the agreement* to the independent clause. The dependent clause functions as the noun object of the verb phrase *do know.*)

The forms *that* we need are out of stock, and I don't know *when* they will be available. (*That* connects the dependent clause *that we need,* which functions as an adjective modifying *forms,* to the first independent clause in this compound-complex sentence. *When* introduces the dependent clause *when they will be available,* which functions as the noun object of the verb phrase *do know,* to the second independent clause.)

☐ INTERJECTIONS

Definition.   An *interjection* expresses strong feeling or emotion. An interjection has no grammatical relationship to the rest of the sentence; it is always followed by an exclamation point or a comma.

Excellent! They showed their good judgment and their good taste by choosing you.

Oh, I forgot to tell Jack where we would meet him.

Use.   Interjections, like exclamatory sentences, must be used sparingly if they are to be effective. They are more frequently used in speech than in writing.

ASSIGNMENT
○ Worksheets 22, 23, 24, and 25

UNIT 8: Phrases and Clauses

Various types of phrases and clauses were briefly introduced and illustrated in the preceding units. Thus this unit is designed to reinforce your understanding of the construction and use of the different kinds of word groups.

☐ PHRASES

A *phrase,* as defined previously, is a group of words that does not contain a subject or a predicate. Such a word group always functions as a single part of speech—for example, a noun, an adjective, an adverb, or a verb.

Verb Phrases.   A *verb phrase* consists of a main verb plus one or more helping verbs. The main verb is always the last verb in the phrase, and it is sometimes separated from the helping verb or verbs, as illustrated below. The predicate of a sentence or a clause always contains a verb or a verb phrase.

Mr. Sivinski *will be arriving* at O'Hare at 4:15 p.m. (*Arriving* is the main verb; *will* and *be* are helping verbs.)

Are you and Miss Davega definitely *scheduled* to work at the exhibit? (*Scheduled* is the main verb; *are* is a helping verb.)

Infinitive Phrases.   An *infinitive phrase* consists of an infinitive (*to* plus a verb) plus one or more modifiers, a subject, an object (direct or indirect), or a combination of these. Infinitive phrases always function as nouns, adjectives, or adverbs.

> *To become an executive* is the goal of many people in the business world. (This infinitive phrase functions as a noun; it is the subject of the sentence.)

> Please list the name and address of each person *to be notified in case of an emergency.* (This infinitive phrase includes two modifying prepositional phrases. It functions as an adjective modifying the noun *person.*)

> Mr. Reeves called this morning *to cancel his appointment.* (This infinitive phrase, which tells why, functions as an adverb modifying the verb *called.*)

Prepositional Phrases.   A *prepositional phrase* consists of a preposition and a noun or pronoun object plus the modifiers, if any, of the object. These phrases function as nouns, adjectives, or adverbs.

> *From New York to Los Angeles* is a long trip to make by bus. (This phrase, which functions as a noun, is used as the subject of the sentence.)

> They would like to find an apartment *with a full-size kitchen.* (This prepositional phrase functions as an adjective modifying *apartment.*)

> We waited *for an hour,* but you didn't show up. (*For an hour* functions as an adverb. It modifies the verb *waited.*)

Gerund Phrases.   As you will remember, a *gerund* is verb form ending in *ing* that is used as a noun. Thus, like any other noun, a gerund may be modified by an adjective; in addition, a gerund may, like any other verb, be modified by one or more adverbs, have a direct object, and have an indirect object. Therefore, a *gerund phrase* consists of the gerund, its modifiers (if any), and its object or objects (if any). A gerund phrase always functions as a noun.

> We were surprised by *George's resigning.* (The possessive noun *George's* functions as an adjective modifying the gerund *resigning.* The gerund phrase functions as the noun object of the preposition *by.*)

> *Your sending me a duplicate copy* will be very much appreciated. (The possessive pronoun *your* functions as an adjective modifying the gerund *sending. Copy* is the direct object and *me* is the indirect object of the gerund. The complete phrase is the subject of the sentence.)

> *Ordering early* is the best procedure. (The gerund *ordering* is modified by the adverb *early.* This gerund phrase is the subject of the sentence.)

> Thank you for *notifying them.* (The pronoun *them* is the direct object of the gerund *notifying.* The complete phrase is the object of the preposition *for.*)

□ DEPENDENT CLAUSES

As you will remember, a *dependent clause* is a group of words that contains a subject and a predicate but that does not make sense when it stands by itself. Dependent clauses appear in complex and compound-complex sentences, where they function as nouns, adjectives, or adverbs.

Noun Clauses.   A *noun clause* is a dependent clause that functions as a noun in a sentence.

> *Who will be appointed to the commission* is anyone's guess. (This dependent clause is the subject of the sentence.)

Mrs. Thomas told me *that she had worked in your Biloxi office for two years.* (This dependent clause functions as the direct object of the verb *told.*)

Please give a new price list to *whoever requests one.* (This dependent clause functions as the object of the preposition *to.*)

Adjective Clauses. An *adjective clause* is a dependent clause that modifies a noun or a pronoun.

Enclosed is a copy of the letter *that I received from him last week.* (This dependent clause modifies the noun *letter.* It tells which.)

Anyone *who would like to take this civil service examination* may apply at any post office. (This dependent clause modifies the pronoun *anyone.*)

Adverbial Clauses. *Adverbial clauses* answer such questions as these: How? When? Where? Why?

The changes were made *while you were on vacation.* (This adverbial clause tells when; it modifies the verb phrase *were made.*)

We are returning the refrigerator *because it has a dent in the door.* (This dependent clause tells why; it modifies the verb phrase *are returning.*)

☐ INDEPENDENT CLAUSES

An independent clause makes complete sense by itself. Therefore, it may be used by itself as a sentence, or it may be used as a main clause in a compound, complex, or compound-complex sentence. It does not function as a part of speech.

Your envelopes will be printed in dark blue ink. (Sentence.)

Ms. Lee did not sign the memo because it contained too many errors. (Main clause in a complex sentence.)

Ruby told me that you were on a business trip; however, *she did not say* where you were or when you would return. (Main clauses in a compound-complex sentence.)

I read the instructions twice, but *I did not understand them.* (Main clauses in a compound sentence.)

ASSIGNMENT

○ Worksheets 26, 27, 28, and 29

PART TWO

English for Business Communication

When we write or speak for a purely social purpose, many — if not most — of us pay little attention to the manner in which we use English. For example, we may express ourselves in incomplete sentences, use a number of the latest slang expressions, say "me" when we know we should be saying "I," and so on — and still communicate very effectively. In a business situation, though, all of us need to adhere to the principles of standard English usage — those presented in Units 9 through 24 — in order to get the results we want from speaking or writing.

UNIT 9: Nouns—Plural Forms

The dictionary is an invaluable reference that provides the answers to a wide variety of questions pertaining to words and word usage: spelling, syllabication, pronunciation, origin, definition, and so on. With respect to the plurals of nouns, however, the dictionary you are using probably will not show the vast majority of those that are formed simply by adding *s* or *es* to the singular nouns. Instead, you are likely to find that it lists those plurals that are formed in an irregular manner, the plurals of those nouns that have more than one acceptable plural form, and perhaps some plurals— even though they are formed regularly—that are commonly misspelled. Thus the rules presented and illustrated in this unit will save you many trips to the dictionary— as well as alert you to situations in which you should consult the dictionary.

☐ GENERAL PRINCIPLES

As you study these general principles for forming the plurals of nouns, note that they do not indicate the exceptions to the rules. Also note that the examples do not include the alternate plural forms for those nouns that have two or more equally acceptable plurals. Unless otherwise indicated, the principles apply to common nouns.

Most Nouns.   The plural of most nouns is formed by adding *s* to the singular.

SINGULAR:	material	envelope	contract	customer	committee	brochure
PLURAL:	materials	envelopes	contracts	customers	committees	brochures

Nouns Ending in *s, x, ch, sh,* or *z*.   If the singular noun ends in *s, x, ch, sh,* or *z,* the plural is formed by adding *es.*

SINGULAR:	business	address	tax	branch	witness	switch	buzz
PLURAL:	businesses	addresses	taxes	branches	witnesses	switches	buzzes

Nouns Ending in *y*.   If the singular noun ends in *y* and the *y* is preceded by a vowel (*a, e, i, o,* or *u*), the plural is usually formed by adding *s*.

SINGULAR:	holiday	survey	attorney	essay	alloy	alley	boy
PLURAL:	holidays	surveys	attorneys	essays	alloys	alleys	boys

However, if the *y* is preceded by a consonant (any letter other than *a, e, i, o,* or *u*), the plural is formed by changing the *y* to *i* and adding *es*.

SINGULAR:	opportunity	industry	monopoly	apology	vacancy	enemy
PLURAL:	opportunities	industries	monopolies	apologies	vacancies	enemies

Nouns Ending in *o*.   The plural of many nouns ending in *o*, including those pertaining to music or one of the other arts, is formed by adding *s*.

SINGULAR:	alto	duo	contralto	oratorio	piano	solo	soprano
PLURAL:	altos	duos	contraltos	oratorios	pianos	solos	sopranos

SINGULAR:	radio	trio	dynamo	embryo	folio	memo	portfolio
PLURAL:	radios	trios	dynamos	embryos	folios	memos	portfolios

In other instances, the plural is formed by adding *es*.

SINGULAR:	echo	ego	hero	potato	tomato	veto
PLURAL:	echoes	egoes	heroes	potatoes	tomatoes	vetoes

Some nouns ending in *o* have two acceptable plural forms. The form listed first should generally be considered the preferred form.

SINGULAR:	cargo	commando	memento	motto	mosquito	zero
PLURAL:	cargoes	commandos	mementos	mottoes	mosquitoes	zeros
	cargos	commandoes	mementoes	mottos	mosquitos	zeroes

Unless you are certain of the correct spelling of the plural of a noun ending in *o*, then, the best policy is to consult your dictionary.

Nouns Ending in *f* or *fe.*   The plural of many nouns ending in *f* or *fe* is formed by changing the *f* or *fe* to *v* and adding *es*.

SINGULAR:	calf	half	knife	scarf	shelf	wife	thief
PLURAL:	calves	halves	knives	scarves	shelves	wives	thieves

In other instances, the plural is formed by simply adding *s*.

SINGULAR:	belief	brief	chief	cliff	plaintiff	safe	staff
PLURAL:	beliefs	briefs	chiefs	cliffs	plaintiffs	safes	staffs

Compound Nouns.   If a compound noun is written as two or more hyphenated words or as two or more separate words, change the principal word to its plural form.

SINGULAR:	sister-in-law	chief of police	price list	account receivable
PLURAL:	sisters-in-law	chiefs of police	price lists	accounts receivable

If the compound noun is written as one word, the plural is usually formed by changing the last part of the compound to its plural.

SINGULAR:	airport	bookcase	bookkeeper	bookshelf	checkbook	letterhead
PLURAL:	airports	bookcases	bookkeepers	bookshelves	checkbooks	letterheads

Letters and Figures.   The plural of a capital letter or of a number written in figures is often formed by simply adding *s*. The exceptions are the capital letters *A, I,* and *U,* for which the plurals must be formed by adding *'s* in order to avoid confusing the plurals of the letters with the words *As, Is,* and *Us.*

Bs	Cs	Ds	Hs	Js	Ks	1s	2s	3s	10s	11s	12s

For the sake of clarity, the plural of a small letter is formed by adding *'s.*

a's	b's	c's	two *m's* in *recommend*	three *l's* in *parallel*

Proper Nouns.   Except when referring to the Rocky Mountains as "the Rockies" or to the Allegheny Mountains as "the Alleghenies," do not change the spelling of a singular proper noun when forming the plural. Simply add *s* or *es.*

SINGULAR:	Mary	Jones	Spellman	Fitch	Gibson	Marx
PLURAL:	Marys	Joneses	Spellmans	Fitches	Gibsons	Marxes

Personal Titles.   Memorize the correct plural form of these personal titles:

SINGULAR:	Mr.	Mrs.	Miss	Ms.	Dr.
PLURAL:	Messrs.	Mmes. *or* Mesdames	Misses	Mses. *or* Mss.	Drs.

Foreign Nouns.   Some nouns of foreign origin have both an English plural and a foreign plural; others have only a foreign plural. If the noun has an English plural, it is formed in the regular way (by adding *s* or *es*). In general, the foreign plural is formed by changing the singular ending as shown below.

	us to *i*	*um* to *a*	*is* to *es*	*a* to *ae*	*on* to *a*	*ex* to *ices*	*ix* to *ices*
SINGULAR:	alumnus	medium	analysis	alumna	criterion	index	appendix
ENGLISH PLURAL:	——	mediums	——	——	criterions	indexes	appendixes
FOREIGN PLURAL:	alumni	media	analyses	alumnae	criteria	indices	appendices

Nouns With One Form for Singular and Plural.   Some nouns have one form for both the singular and the plural. Such nouns as those listed below may be used with either a singular verb or a plural verb, depending upon the meaning intended.

corps	deer	salmon	series	sheep	trout	rendezvous

Note that the singular form of *corps* is pronounced to rhyme with *core,* not *corpse;* the plural is pronounced to rhyme with *cores.* Also note that the singular of *rendezvous* rhymes with *due;* the plural rhymes with *dues.*

Nouns Always Singular.   Some nouns are always or almost always singular and require singular verbs when they are used as subjects. A few nouns of this type have the appearance of plurals.

equipment	news	education	advice	music	information	merchandise
weather	milk	assistance	integrity	civics	attention	cooperation

This *equipment needs* to be repaired. (**NOT:** *These equipment need* to be repaired.)

The *news* of your promotion *comes* as no surprise. (**NOT:** The *news* of your promotion *come* as no surprise.)

Nouns Always Plural.   Some nouns are always or almost always plural in meaning and in usage.

premises	pliers	scissors	trousers	thanks	remains
credentials	goods	auspices	riches	proceeds	belongings

The *scissors are* dull. (**NOT:** The *scissors is* dull.)

The *premises were being patrolled* by private guards until yesterday. (**NOT:** The *premises was being patrolled* by private guards until yesterday.)

Nouns With Irregular Plurals.   A few nouns have plurals formed in highly irregular ways. Note these examples:

SINGULAR:	child	ox	man	woman	goose	mouse
PLURAL:	children	oxen	men	women	geese	mice

☐ THE USE OF PLURALS OF FOREIGN NOUNS

In some instances, the foreign plural is used in preference to the English plural. In others, the English plural is used with one meaning, and the foreign plural is used with a different meaning. In some situations, the English plural and the foreign plural are equally acceptable. When in doubt as to which form to use, consult your dictionary.

Agenda.   *Agenda,* the foreign plural of *agendum,* is generally used in business to refer to a list or an outline of things to be done at a meeting or conference; it is used with a singular verb. *Agendas,* the English plural of *agenda,* is used with a plural verb to refer to two or more lists or outlines of things to be done at meetings and conferences. *Agendums,* the English plural of *agendum,* is rarely—if ever—used in business.

Alumnae.   *Alumnae,* the foreign plural of *alumna,* is used to refer to female graduates of a school.

Alumni.   *Alumni,* the foreign plural of *alumnus,* is used to refer to male graduates of a school. It is also used when reference is being made to a group consisting of both male and female graduates of a school.

Criteria.   *Criteria,* the foreign plural of *criterion,* is used in preference to the English plural, *criterions. Criterion* is used with a singular verb when reference is made to one standard, model, example, test, rule, or measure. *Criteria* is used with a plural verb.

Data.   *Data,* the foreign plural of *datum,* is commonly used in business as both a singular noun and a plural noun; it may refer either to a single fact or principle or to a collection of facts or principles. *Data* is therefore generally used with a singular verb. *Datums,* the English plural, is generally restricted to references to facts or principles pertaining to topography or mathematics.

Indexes.   *Indexes,* the English plural of *index,* is commonly used in business to refer to alphabetic and numeric listings. *Indices,* the foreign plural, is most often used to refer to signs or indications of economic conditions.

Media.   *Media,* the foreign plural of *medium,* is generally used to refer to newspapers, magazines, radio, television, and similar means of communication. *Mediums,* the English plural, is generally used for all other meanings.

Memoranda. *Memoranda*, the foreign plural of *memorandum,* and *memorandums,* the English plural, are both commonly used in business to refer to letter-type communications written by employees to other employees of the same company.

ASSIGNMENT

○ Worksheets 30 and 31

UNIT 10: Nouns—Possessive Forms

Ownership, authorship, or a similar relationship between one person or thing and another may be indicated by an "of" phrase or some other type of prepositional phrase. In other instances, however, the shorter—and preferred—way to indicate such a relationship is to use a possessive noun. This unit provides guidance in forming and using both types of possessive constructions.

☐ SINGULAR POSSESSIVES

The following principles govern the formation of the possessives of singular nouns.

Nouns Not Ending in *s* or the Sound of *s*. To form the possessive of a singular noun that does not end in *s* or the sound of *s*, simply add *'s*.

the *company's* records	one *person's* opinion	in *Ellen's* office	a *child's* wish
my *assistant's* name	at *Bob's* suggestion	an *employee's* rights	a *mayor's* aide

Nouns Ending in *s* or the Sound of *s*. To form the possessive of a singular noun that ends in *s* or the sound of *s*, add *'s* if a new syllable is formed when you pronounce the possessive noun.

her *boss's* name	at *Alex's* recommendation	the *witness's* testimony
Ms. Jones's office	for *Bernice's* neighbor	in *Fritz's* behalf

However, if the addition of an extra syllable would make the possessive hard to pronounce or would sound awkward, simply add an apostrophe (').

Miss Phillips' article	*Mrs. Rodriguez'* husband	*Mr. Hodges'* employer

As illustrated above, always be sure to place the apostrophe after the final letter of the singular noun (*Mr. Hodges'*—not *Mr. Hodge's*).

Compound Nouns. Form the possessive of a singular compound noun by adding *'s* (or an apostrophe only, if the resulting possessive would be hard to pronounce) after the last word in the compound.

sky diver's nerves	*clerk-typist's* duties	*attorney general's* assistant
police chief's car	*grandmother's* clock	*housekeeper's* helpers

Names Followed by *Jr., Sr., M.D.,* and So On. If a name is followed by *Jr., Sr., M.D., Ed.D.,* or a similar term, write the term—not the name—in possessive form. (Note that no comma follows the term when it is in possessive form.)

James Oliver, Jr.'s residence	*Carmen H. Entrialgo, Ph.D.'s* home address

Nouns Interrupted by an Appositive. If two nouns are interrupted by an appositive, write the appositive—not the first noun—in possessive form.

> George, the *clothier's,* sale will be held tomorrow.
>
> Helen, the *beautician's,* shop is on Northern Boulevard.

Two or More Nouns—Separate Ownership. To show separate ownership, write each noun in possessive form.

> *Margaret's* and *Vincent's* families attended the ceremonies.
>
> The fire destroyed *Jones's* and *Smith's* records.

Two or More Nouns—Joint Ownership. To show joint ownership, write only the last name in possessive form.

> We visited *Brown and Wiley's* new offices. (*Brown and Wiley* is one firm.)
>
> *Miss Grier and her assistant's* extension is 6060. (Two people share one telephone.)

☐ PLURAL POSSESSIVES

Follow this procedure for forming the possessives of plural nouns:

1. Change the singular noun to its plural form.

SINGULAR:	lady	son-in-law	woman	child	engineer	typist
PLURAL:	ladies	sons-in-law	women	children	engineers	typists

2. Look at the last letter of the plural noun.

3. If the last letter is not an *s,* add *'s.*

> sons-in-law's   women's   children's

4. If the last letter is an *s,* add only an apostrophe.

> ladies'   engineers'   typists'

☐ SPECIAL SUGGESTIONS

1. To determine whether a noun should be treated as a singular possessive, a plural possessive, or a simple modifier, consider the meaning to be conveyed. Note the following examples:

> The *employee's records* are kept in the personnel department. (This indicates the records of one employee.)
>
> The *employees' records* are kept in the personnel department. (This indicates the records of all employees.)
>
> All *employee records* are kept in the personnel department. (*Employee* is a simple modifier; it tells which records.)
>
> All *employees' records* are kept in the personnel department. (This indicates the records of all employees.)

2. Always follow the style of the official name when writing the name of a publication, an organization, a place, and so on.

American Bankers Association	Times Square
Governors Island	Young Men's Christian Association
Ladies' Home Journal	Harper's Bazaar
Macy's	Readers' Guide to Periodical Literature

3. With the exception of such nouns as those illustrated below, nouns that name inanimate objects should never be written or spoken as possessives. Use an *of* phrase instead.

for *pity's* sake	an *hour's* work	a *day's* pay	a *dollar's* worth
for *conscience'* sake	two *weeks'* work	a *month's* vacation	few *dollars'* worth

Now, note the following:

hood *of the car*	top *of the desk*	a *one-week* vacation	a *three-year* project

4. To determine whether a possessive noun should be singular or plural, do not be concerned as to whether the second noun is singular or plural. Do consider the meaning you wish to convey.

the *owner's* profits	the *owners'* profits
the *supervisor's* statements	the *supervisors'* statements

ASSIGNMENT

○ Worksheets 32, 33, and 34

UNIT 11: Personal Pronouns

One of the most common problems in the use of personal pronouns stems from the fact that these pronouns change form to indicate case—relationship to other words in sentences, clauses, and phrases. Thus this unit presents the forms and uses of personal pronouns in the *nominative case,* the *objective case,* and the *possessive case.*

☐ NOMINATIVE CASE

The Pronouns. The following forms of personal pronouns are in the nominative case:

I	we	you	she	he	it	they

Their Uses. A personal pronoun in the nominative case may be used as:

1. The subject of a sentence or a clause.

I doubt that *he* will cancel the contract, but *you* may disagree. (*I* is the subject of the first independent clause and *you* is the subject of the second independent clause in this compound-complex sentence. *He* is the subject of the dependent clause *that he will cancel the contract.*)

She is a senior vice president of the company. (*She* is the subject of the sentence.)

We believe that *it* is unlikely that *they* will cancel the insurance policy. (*We* is the subject of the sentence. *It* is the subject of the dependent clause *that it is unlikely. They* is the subject of the dependent clause *that they will cancel the insurance policy.*)

31

2. A predicate nominative. Remember that a predicate nominative is a pronoun or a noun that follows a linking verb (*am, be, is, are,* or some other form of the verb *be*) and renames the subject of the sentence or clause in which it appears.

> The three leading candidates are *you, he,* and *she.* (The linking verb is *are. You, he,* and *she* rename or further identify the subject *candidates.*)

> If the matter goes to trial, the losers will be both *they* and *we.* (The linking verb is the verb phrase *will be. They* and *we,* which are joined by the correlative conjunction *both . . . and,* rename or further identify the subject, *losers.*)

3. The complement of the infinitive *to be.* When the infinitive *to be* does not have a noun or a pronoun immediately before it, the pronoun following *to be* must be in the nominative case.

> Would you like to be *she?*   The winner of the contest was thought to be *I.*

☐ OBJECTIVE CASE

The Pronouns. These personal pronouns are in the objective case:

> me   us   you   her   him   it   them

Their Uses. A personal pronoun in the objective case may be used as:

1. The direct or indirect object of a verb. Note that the direct object names the receiver of the action expressed by a verb and that the indirect object tells to whom something was given or for whom something was done.

> The receptionist gave *me* two copies of the new catalog. (*Me* is the indirect object of the verb *gave.* The noun *copies* is the direct object of *gave.*)

> Sandra told *us* that she telephoned *you* before she wrote *him.* (*Us* is the direct object of *told. You* is the direct object of *telephoned. Him* is the direct object of *wrote.*)

> With respect to the order, Carol canceled *it.* (*It* is the direct object of *canceled.*)

2. The object of a preposition. Remember that a preposition is a word, such as *of, for,* or *to,* that connects a following pronoun or noun to a preceding word in a sentence or clause.

> Insofar as the agenda is concerned, I sent a copy of *it* to *him* for *them.* (The prepositions are *of, to,* and *for.*)

> The grateful owner divided the reward between *her* and *me.* (The preposition *between* has two objects, *her* and *me.*)

3. The subject or the object of an infinitive.

> Al asked *me* to help *them.* (*Me* is the subject and *them* is the object of the infinitive *to help.*)

> We wanted to visit *her.* (*Her* is the object of the infinitive *to visit.*)

Give special attention to the following sentences, which illustrate the use of objective-case pronouns with the infinitive *to be.*

> Pat asked *us* to be more cooperative. (Note that there is no noun or pronoun following *to be.*)

> I thought the manager to be *her.* (When a noun immediately precedes *to be,* the pronoun following it must be in objective case.)

> The manager mistook *us* to be *them.* (When a pronoun immediately precedes *to be,* it and the pronoun following the infinitive must be in objective case.)

> Ann mistook *me* to be the manager. (When *to be* is followed by a noun, the pronoun before the infinitive must be in objective case.)

□ POSSESSIVE CASE

The Pronouns. These personal pronouns are in the possessive case:

my   mine   our   ours   your   yours   his   her   hers   its   their   theirs

Their Uses. When using the possessive case of personal pronouns, remember:

1. The possessive forms *my, your, our, her,* and *their* always function as adjectives modifying nouns (including gerunds).

> *Our* offices will be closed next Monday.   *My* complaining didn't help.

2. The possessive forms *mine, ours, yours, hers,* and *theirs* always stand alone as predicate nominatives, subjects, and objects.

> This copy is *yours;* that one is *mine.*   *Theirs* is similar to *ours.*

3. The possessive forms *his* and *its* sometimes function as modifiers (adjectives), and sometimes they stand alone as subjects, objects, and so on.

> Have you met *his* wife? (*His* is used as an adjective modifying *wife.*)

> I was unable to find my keys, but he found *his.* (*His* is used as the direct object of *found.*)

□ SPECIAL SUGGESTIONS

1. When a sentence or a clause has two or more subjects joined by *and, or,* or *nor,* try using each subject by itself with the rest of the sentence.

> *Bob and I* attended the meeting. (*Bob* attended the meeting. *I* attended the meeting.)

> I was there when *you or she* called. (I was there when *you* called. I was there when *she* called.)

2. When a linking verb is followed by a pronoun, mentally put the pronoun in the position of the subject and the subject in the position of the pronoun.

> The owner is *she.* (**THINK:** *She* is the owner.)

> The winners were *you and I.* (**THINK:** *You and I* were the winners.)

3. When a verb or a preposition has a compound object, use the verb or preposition with each object by itself.

> Mrs. McNichols notified *them* and *us.* (**THINK:** *notified them* and *notified us.*)

> The check will be made out to *you* and *her.* (**THINK:** *to you* and *to her.*)

4. Use a pronoun in the objective case before, after, or before and after any infinitive other than *to be.*

> Mr. Anderson wants *us* to help. (The infinitive is *to help.*)

> John offered to write *him.* (The infinitive is *to write.*)

> Miss Norton asked *them* to notify *her* of any changes. (The infinitive is *to notify.*)

When the infinitive *to be* is followed by a pronoun and no pronoun or noun immediately precedes the infinitive, use a pronoun in the nominative case after *to be.*

> Ms. Davis's assistant was thought to be *he.* (**NOT:** *him.* Note that the sentence would make sense if the subject were put after *to be* and the pronoun were made the subject: *He was thought to be Ms. Davis's assistant.*)

When *to be* is immediately preceded by a noun or a pronoun, the pronoun following *to be* should be in the objective case.

> I considered the best manager to be *him.* (Note the noun *manager* before *to be.* **THINK:** *I considered him to be the best manager.*)

5. Be careful to use a pronoun in the nominative case when the verb following it is understood, not stated. This type of situation often arises in sentences that express comparisons.

> You are a better typist than *he.* (**THINK:** You are a better typist than *he is.*)
>
> She is as efficient as either *they* or *we.* (**THINK:** She is as efficient as either *they are* or *we are.*)

ASSIGNMENT

○ Worksheets 35 and 36

UNIT 12: Indefinite Pronouns

☐ DEFINITION

Indefinite Pronoun. An *indefinite pronoun* does not refer to any particular person, place, or thing—it refers to persons, places, or things in general. These are commonly used indefinite pronouns:

someone	each	everything	neither	several	all	many	everyone
somebody	both	everybody	nothing	anybody	one	any	anything
another	some	something	nobody	anyone	few	none	no one

Everyone has *something* to contribute.   *No one* knew *anything* about the offer.

☐ USE

The following comments will help you use indefinite pronouns correctly:

1. Do not confuse such expressions as *any one, some one, any body,* and *every one* with the indefinite pronouns, which are written as one word. In such two word expressions, the first word is an adjective—not a part of a pronoun. In deciding whether to use the one-word indefinite pronoun or the two-word expression, consider the meaning that you wish to convey. Study these examples carefully:

> *Any one* of them will be satisfactory.   *Anyone* could handle that job.
>
> *Every one* of those was damaged in transit.   *Everyone* should read the article.

Generally speaking, the two-word expression is used before an "of" phrase, as illustrated above.

2. Remember that the indefinite pronoun *no one* is always written as two words.

3. Some indefinite pronouns have a possessive, which is formed by adding *'s.*

> no one's   someone's   nobody's   somebody's   one's   anyone's   everyone's

4. The word *other* is sometimes used with *each* when two persons, places, or things are being talked about. Note that when it is necessary to show possession in such instances, the possessive is formed by adding *'s* to *other.* The two words are considered together as one pronoun, but they are written separately.

Margaret and Sue often help *each other* when the workload is heavy.

The two cities compete with *each other* to attract conventions.

Pat and Walt checked *each other's* work.

The two co-workers need *each other's* help almost every day.

5. The word *another* (possessive form, *another's*) may be used with *one* when three or more persons, places, or things are being talked about. Again, the two words are always written separately but are considered as one pronoun.

You, she, and I know *one another* well.

All the stories conflicted with *one another.*

The three of us often check *one another's* work.

Companies often know *one another's* plans for developing new products.

6. The word *else* is often used with some indefinite pronouns, and the two words are always written as two separate words. Note that *'s* is added to *else* when it is necessary to show possession.

Please ask *someone else.*   You should obtain *someone else's* opinion.

Nothing else could be done.   *No one else's* was considered.

7. Avoid such "double negative" constructions as those illustrated in parentheses. They are inappropriate in business communication.

No one did *anything* to help. (**NOT:** No one did *nothing* to help.)

Jeanne did not see *anyone.* (**NOT:** Jeanne did *not* see *no one.*)

8. Remember that some words may be used as indefinite pronouns or as adjectives. When one of these words is used as an adjective, be sure that it agrees in number with the noun or pronoun it modifies.

Some of the members were absent while you were speaking. (Pronoun)

Some members were absent while you were speaking. (Adjective)

This is the best kind. (Pronoun)

This kind is preferred by most people. (Adjective)

ASSIGNMENT

○ Worksheet 37

UNIT **13:** Troublesome Pronouns

☐ *WHO* AND *WHOM*

In informal speech, many people do not make the distinction between *who,* which is the nominative form, and *whom,* which is the objective form; instead, such speakers use *who* whether the pronoun functions as a subject or as an object. In all types of business writing and in all types of formal speaking situations, though, use *who* and *whom* in the ways discussed in this unit.

Who. *Who*, which is in the nominative case, may be used as:

1. The subject of a sentence or clause.

Who is responsible for the delay in shipping the merchandise?

Do you know *who* removed the letter from the files? (*Who* is the subject of the dependent clause *who removed the letter from the files.*)

2. A predicate nominative.

The head of the committee is *who*? (*Who* follows the linking verb *is* and renames the subject of the sentence, *head.* Note that *of the committee* is a phrase modifying *head* and that *committee*, the object of the preposition *of*, is not the subject of the sentence.)

Whom. *Whom*, which is in the objective case, may be used as:

1. The object of a preposition.

By *whom* is Mr. Jeffreys employed? (*Whom* is the object of the preposition *by.*)

With *whom* was Nancy sitting? (*Whom* is the object of *with.*)

2. The direct object or the indirect object of a verb.

We do not know *whom* Allen has sent a copy. (*Whom* is the indirect object and *copy* is the direct object of *has sent.*)

Whom did Miss Emory hire as a replacement for Steve? (*Whom* is the direct object of *did hire: Miss Emory did hire whom as a replacement for Steve?*)

3. The subject of an infinitive.

Marion didn't know *whom* to ask for help. (*Whom* is the subject of *to ask.*)

Whom would you like to be the next mayor? (*Whom* is the subject of *to be.*)

4. The object of an infinitive.

Whom would you like to see? (*You would like to see whom? Whom* is the object of *to see.*)

Whom did you call? (*Whom* is the object of *to call.*)

☐ *WHOEVER* AND *WHOMEVER*

Whoever, which is in the nominative case, may be used in the same ways as *who*. *Whomever*, which is in the objective case, has the same uses as *whom*, as discussed above.

Please write to *whoever* is in charge of the meeting without delay. (*Whoever* is the subject of the dependent clause *whoever is in charge of the meeting*, which functions as the object of the preposition *to.*)

Miss LaCroix may invite *whomever* she wishes. (*Whomever* is the object of *may invite.*)

☐ *WHOSE*

The possessive-case pronoun *whose* is sometimes confused with *who's*, the contraction of either *who is* or *who has*. When in doubt as to whether to use *whose* or *who's*, try using *who is* or *who has*; if either makes sense, use *who's*. If neither *who is* nor *who has* makes sense, use *whose*.

I do not know (?) responsibility it will be to introduce the speaker. (Does *who is* or *who has* make sense? No. Use *whose.*)

I am not sure (?) going to the fair with them. (Does *who is* or *who has* make sense? Yes, *who is* does. Use *who's.*)

☐ PRONOUNS ENDING IN *SELF* OR *SELVES*

Usage Principles. The correct use of pronouns ending in *self* (singular) or *selves* (plural) requires an understanding of these principles:

1. Except when the subject of a sentence is understood to be *you,* a pronoun ending in *self* or *selves* must have a stated antecedent in the sentence in which it appears.

> We must try to help *ourselves.* (The antecedent of *ourselves* is *we.*)
>
> The supervisors *themselves* were at fault. (The antecedent of *themselves* is *supervisors.*)
>
> Have the check made payable to *yourself.* (The subject of the sentence and the antecedent of *yourself* is understood to be *you.*)

2. A pronoun ending in *self* or *selves* may be used as the object of a verb or a preposition, but it may not be used as the subject of a sentence or a clause.

> Ms. Hall bought *herself* a new typewriter. (*Herself,* which refers to *Ms. Hall,* is the indirect object of *bought.*)
>
> Mr. Lynch kept a copy of the contract for *himself.* (*Himself,* which refers to *Mr. Lynch,* is the object of the preposition *for.*)
>
> Miss Thomas requested that *you and I* draft the report. (**NOT:** Miss Thomas requested that *you and myself* draft the report.)

☐ CHOICE OF *WHO* OR *WHOM*

The following procedure will help you choose the correct pronoun, *who* or *whom,* for use in a sentence or clause:

1. If the parts of the sentence or clause are not in their normal order (complete subject first), put them in their normal order. In the following examples, a blank line represents the questioned pronoun (*who* or *whom*).

> _____ will represent your company? (This sentence is in normal order; no change is necessary.)
>
> _____ did you wish to see? (**NORMAL ORDER:** You did wish to see _____.)
>
> Do you know _____ the author of the article is? (**NORMAL ORDER:** You do know _____ is the author of the article.)
>
> We do not know _____ Mr. Johnson will appoint. (**NORMAL ORDER:** We do not know Mr. Johnson will appoint _____.)
>
> _____ do you think will win the grand prize? (**NORMAL ORDER:** You do think _____ will win the grand prize.)

2. Omit all parts of the sentence except those that make up the clause in which the questioned pronoun appears.

> _____ will represent your company?
>
> You did wish to see _____.
>
> _____ is the author of the article?
>
> Mr. Johnson will appoint _____.
>
> _____ will win the grand prize?

3. If the _____ precedes a verb, use *who.*

> *Who* will represent your company?
>
> *Who* is the author of the article? (Do you know *who* the author of the article is?)
>
> *Who* will win the grand prize? (*Who* do you think will win the grand prize?)

4. If the _____ follows a verb or an infinitive (*to* plus a verb), use *whom.*

You did wish to see *whom*? (*Whom* did you wish to see?)

Mr. Johnson will appoint *whom*. (We do not know *whom* Mr. Johnson will appoint.)

☐ REMINDERS

1. When a dependent clause introduced by *who, whoever, whom,* or *whomever* follows a preposition, the entire clause is the object of the preposition. Since the pronoun alone is not the object of the preposition, the form of pronoun to be used depends upon the function of the pronoun in the clause.

There is no question as to *who* was responsible. (*Who* is correct because it is the subject of the dependent clause *who was responsible.*)

Our support will depend upon *whom* they nominate. (*Whom* is correct because it is the object of the verb *nominate.*)

This information should be shared with *whoever* you think needs to have it. (*Whoever* is correct because it is the subject of the dependent clause *whoever needs to have it.* Note that *you think* is a separate dependent clause.)

Many will be pleased with *whomever* the committee nominates. (*Whomever* is correct because it is the object of the verb *nominates.*)

2. *Who* and *whom* are used to refer to people; *which* is used to refer to animals or things; and *that* is used to refer to people, animals, or things.

Your representative, *who* called on me last Wednesday, promised immediate delivery.

Ms. Poliski is the person *whom* you should see.

This horse, *which* is about two years old, will run in the Kentucky Derby next year.

The company, *which* has offices in many major cities, reported record sales last year.

Dr. Langford is the best speaker *that* we have heard in a long time.

Is a dog the best pet *that* a child could have?

The text-editing equipment *that* we would like to purchase is quite expensive.

ASSIGNMENT

○ Worksheets 38 and 39

UNIT 14: Pronoun and Antecedent Agreement

☐ BASIC PRINCIPLE

The basic principle of pronoun and antecedent agreement is this: *A pronoun must agree with its antecedent in person, number, and gender.* To apply this principle correctly, you will need to remember that the antecedent of a pronoun may be a noun, another pronoun, two or more nouns or pronouns, or a combination of nouns and pronouns.

Agreement in Person. If the antecedent is a pronoun that refers to the person or persons speaking (a first person personal pronoun), the pronoun or pronouns that refer to it must be first person.

I will do *my* share of the work tomorrow. (The antecedent of *my* is *I.*)

We should have the order shipped to *us* at *our* new address. (The antecedent of *us* and *our* is *we.*)

If the antecedent is a pronoun that refers to the person or persons spoken to (a second person personal pronoun), the pronoun or pronouns that refer to it must be second person.

I am sure that you will be very happy in *your* new job. (The antecedent of *your* is *you.*)

You may decide to tabulate the results of the survey *yourselves.* (The antecedent of *yourselves* is *you.*)

If the antecedent is a noun or a pronoun that refers to the person(s) or thing(s) spoken about, the pronoun or pronouns that refer to it must be third person.

Elaine knows that *she* will have to make *her* reservations *herself.* (The antecedent of *she, her,* and *herself* is the noun *Elaine.*)

We gave the contractors all the information that *they* need to prepare *their* bids. (The antecedent of *they* and *their* is the noun *contractors.*)

Agreement in Number. The pronoun or pronouns that refer to a singular antecedent must be singular in number. The pronoun or pronouns that refer to a plural antecedent must be plural in number.

Mr. Torrance said that *he* would make the necessary repairs *himself.* (The antecedent of the singular pronouns *he* and *himself* is the singular noun *Mr. Torrance.*)

The members of the committee could not remember parts of the plan *they* had put together *themselves* a few months earlier. (The antecedent of the plural pronouns *they* and *themselves* is the plural noun *members.*)

A compound antecedent that consists of two or more words connected by *and* is almost always plural. In a few instances, though, such a compound antecedent indicates one person or thing and requires the use of one or more singular pronouns to refer to it.

Mrs. Gomez and a member of her staff have made *their* recommendations. (*Mrs. Gomez and a member of her staff,* the compound antecedent, clearly indicates two different people; therefore, the plural pronoun *their* is correct.)

Our vice president and general manager left *his* briefcase at home this morning. (Since there is no article or other word before *general manager,* and since one person could be both *vice president and general manager,* it is correct to use the singular pronoun *his.*)

Agreement in Gender. In many instances, the gender of the antecedent makes it obvious that the pronoun or pronouns used to refer to it must be of a specific gender: masculine, feminine, neuter, or common. For example:

Mr. Albertson told us that *he* always answers *his* telephone *himself.* (The antecedent, *Mr. Albertson,* is obviously masculine; therefore, the masculine pronouns *he, his,* and *himself* must be used.)

Diane said that *she* would answer *her* mail *herself.* (The antecedent, *Diane,* is obviously feminine; thus the feminine pronouns *she, her,* and *herself* are used.)

The shipping clerk took the carton and put *it* on the loading dock. (The neuter pronoun *it* is correct because it refers to the neuter noun *carton.*)

Agreement in gender is not a problem when the antecedent is a plural noun or pronoun, as the third person plural pronouns used to refer to it (*they, them, their, theirs,* and *themselves*) are of common gender.

Many people are still doing *their* holiday shopping. (Since *people* clearly includes both sexes, the pronoun obviously must be common in gender.)

Similarly, the problem of deciding what pronoun to use to refer to a singular antecedent that could be either masculine or feminine is now generally resolved by using both a singular masculine and a singular feminine pronoun, as illustrated below.

Everyone likes to have *his or her* name pronounced correctly. (The antecedent is the singular indefinite pronoun *everyone.*)

Every executive relies on the people who report to *her or him.* (An *executive* may be either a man or a woman; therefore, *her or him* is used.)

Each of us knows that *he or she* must fulfill *his or her* obligations. (*He or she* and *his or her* refer to the singular indefinite pronoun *each,* which is of common gender.)

When the use of such expressions as *he or she* and *her or him* becomes too frequent or awkward, most speakers and writers prefer to use plural antecedents and plural pronouns to refer to them.

All people like to have *their* names pronounced correctly. (The antecedent of *their* is the plural noun *people.*)

Executives rely on the people who report to *them.* (The antecedent of *them* is the plural noun *executives.*)

□ SPECIAL REMINDERS

The following comments and examples will help you avoid a variety of common errors in the use of pronouns.

1. Except when the antecedent is understood to be *you,* pronouns ending in *self* or *selves* require stated antecedents.

Don't be too critical of *yourself.* (The antecedent *you* is understood.)

Unfortunately, problems seldom resolve *themselves.* (The antecedent is *problems.*)

2. Except in a few idiomatic expressions involving the use of *it* and referring to time or weather, all third person personal pronouns (*he, it, she, they, them,* and so on) require stated antecedents. However, the antecedent of such a pronoun need not appear in the same sentence as the pronoun as long as the antecedent was stated in a preceding sentence and the pronoun clearly refers to it.

We have invited Mrs. Albertson to speak at the conference next month. *She* is one of the most highly respected people in *her* field, and we are sure that you will want to hear *her* thought-provoking comments about the roles of women in business and politics. (*Mrs. Albertson* is the person to whom all of the italicized pronouns refer.)

3. Sometimes a phrase that modifies an indefinite pronoun antecedent must be taken into consideration when deciding what pronoun or pronouns to use. Note the following examples, and study them carefully:

Neither of the women has received *her* paycheck this week.

Neither of the envelopes has the correct address on *it.*

Some of the property has lost much of *its* value.

Some of the cities have increased *their* real estate taxes.

One of the cabinets was lying on *its* side.

One of the men forgot to sign *his* timecard.

4. When *each* or *every* modifies a compound antecedent consisting of two or more singular nouns connected by *and,* use singular pronouns to refer to it.

Each man, woman, and child should be able to feel secure in *his or her* own home.

Every husband and wife who studied the policy felt that it provided the types of insurance coverage that *he or she* considered essential.

Every important letter, memo, and report must be filed in *its* proper place.

ASSIGNMENT

○ Worksheets 40 and 41

UNIT 15: Subjects and Word Order of Sentences and Clauses

☐ SUBJECTS

The subject of a sentence or a clause identifies who is speaking, who is spoken to, or who or what is spoken about. In order to avoid errors in subject and verb agreement, which will be discussed in a later unit, you must be able to identify the *complete subject* and determine whether it contains a *simple subject* or a *compound subject.* Further, the ability to identify the complete subject of a sentence or clause will help you determine the word order of a sentence or clause.

Complete Subject.   The *complete subject* of a sentence or a clause names and often describes the person speaking; the person spoken to; or the person, place, or thing spoken about.

Several representatives at the meeting of the Organization of Petroleum-Exporting Countries said *they* were in favor of maintaining present prices.

You and other experienced members of the staff will need to review the procedures.

Simple Subject.   If the complete subject contains only one noun or one pronoun that tells who is speaking, who is spoken to, or who or what is spoken about, that noun or pronoun is the *simple subject.*

Several *representatives* at the meeting of the Organization of Petroleum-Exporting Countries said *they* were in favor of maintaining present prices.

We are pleased to have this opportunity to work with you.

Compound Subject.   When the complete subject contains two or more nouns, pronouns, or nouns and pronouns joined by *and, but, or,* or *nor,* the sentence or the clause has a *compound subject.*

You and other experienced *members* of the staff will need to review the procedures.

Neither the *letters* nor the *memos* have been transcribed yet.

You, Cleo, or *I* should volunteer to assist with arrangements for the conference.

41

☐ WORD ORDER

A sentence or a clause may be expressed in either *normal* or *inverted* word order.

Normal Word Order. When a sentence or a clause is expressed in *normal word order,* the complete subject precedes the complete predicate.

> *Your administrative assistant* told Ms. Richards and me that *you and Mr. Lamb* had submitted your budgets for next year.

Inverted Word Order. If part or all of the predicate precedes the subject, as it usually does in interrogative sentences, the sentence or clause is in *inverted word order.* (Remember that the predicate may contain one or more words that describe the subject. Such predicate adjectives are not part of the subject.)

> Does *either of them* know when the next *train* will leave? (**NORMAL ORDER:** *Either of them* does know when the next *train* will leave.)

> Although *we* cannot be sure of the outcome, *we* think that the negotiations will produce mutually satisfactory results. (**NORMAL ORDER:** *We* think that the negotiations will produce mutually satisfactory results, although *we* cannot be sure of the outcome.)

☐ SUGGESTIONS AND REMINDERS

1. Remember that the predicate of a sentence or a clause may contain one or more predicate adjectives (words that describe the subject) or predicate nominatives (words that rename the subject). Such words are part of the predicate, not the subject.

> *Mark Goodman* is the new secretary of our local school board. (*Mark Goodman* is the complete subject of the sentence.)

> *Mrs. Green* said that *neither she nor you* were too happy about the situation. (*Mrs. Green* is the complete subject of the sentence. *Neither she nor you* is the complete subject of the clause *that neither she nor you were too happy about the situation.*)

2. When a sentence expresses a command, the subject is always *you,* even though the pronoun *you* may not be stated.

> Proofread the transcripts very carefully. (The subject *you* is understood.)

3. The simple subject of a sentence or a clause is never part of a phrase.

> *Both* of them said that *one* of the drivers was seriously injured. (*Both* is the simple subject of the sentence; *one* is the simple subject of the clause.)

4. An entire phrase may be used as the subject of a sentence or a clause.

> *To increase productivity* is management's goal.   *At noon* would be a good time.

> *Your explaining the situation* was what turned a complaint into a compliment.

5. *There* is never the subject of a sentence or a clause.

> There is no *date* on this invoice. (*Date,* not *there,* is the subject of the sentence.)

> I think that there were two *items* missing. (*Items,* not *there,* is the subject of the clause *that there were two items missing.*)

6. An appositive is never the subject of a sentence or a clause.

> We *mechanics* ought to join a union. (*We* is the subject of the sentence. *Mechanics* is an appositive that further clarifies who *we* are.)

> Someone should have notified Miss Rheems when her assistant, *Roy Brown,* became ill. (*Assistant,* not *Roy Brown,* is the simple subject of the clause *when her assistant, Roy Brown, became ill. Roy Brown* is an appositive that clarifies *assistant.*)

7. A name used in direct address is never the subject of a sentence.

Miss Stefano, *you* may be sure that we will contact you again before the end of this month. (The subject is *you*. *Miss Stefano* is a name used in direct address.)

Jerry, please be sure to submit your report directly to Mr. Barker. (The subject *you* is understood. *Jerry* is a name used in direct address—it identifies the person being spoken to.)

ASSIGNMENT

○ Worksheets 42 and 43

UNIT 16: Subject and Predicate Agreement

☐ BASIC PRINCIPLE

The basic principle of subject and predicate agreement is this: *A verb must agree with its subject in person and number.*

First Person Subjects and Verbs. The personal pronouns *I* and *we* are first person. As illustrated below, the verb *be* is unlike other verbs because it has the special first person singular form *am* for use with *I*. Also notice the forms of the verb *write* that are used with each of these subjects, as it is representative of all other verbs.

FIRST PERSON SINGULAR:	FIRST PERSON PLURAL:
I am confident of your success.	*We are* thankful for your support.
I was a secretary at one time.	*We were* in Nebraska last week.
I write many letters every day.	*We write* many job descriptions.
I wrote to Mr. Gomez yesterday.	*We wrote* several reports last month.

Second Person Subjects and Verbs. The personal pronoun *you*, which may refer to one person or to more than one person, is the only second person subject. For purposes of agreement with verbs, however, *you* is always considered plural. Thus, as illustrated below, the second person subject *you* and the first person plural subject *we* require the use of the same forms of verbs, such as *be* and *write*.

SECOND PERSON—ALWAYS PLURAL:

You are eligible for promotion.

You were the best speaker on the program, in my opinion.

You write in an extremely interesting and clear manner.

You wrote more orders for this new machine than anyone else at the convention.

Third Person Subjects and Verbs. All pronoun subjects other than *I, we,* and *you* and all noun subjects are third person. Note the forms of the verbs *be* and *write* that are used with third person subjects on the next page.

THIRD PERSON SINGULAR:	THIRD PERSON PLURAL:
Edith is in the office today.	The *managers are* eager to improve profits.
She was ill yesterday.	*They were* appreciative of our help.
Everyone writes at least a few letters.	*Some write* more memos than letters.
No one wrote to Mr. Dyer last week.	*Many wrote* congratulatory messages.

☐ SITUATIONS REQUIRING SPECIAL ATTENTION

Errors in subject-verb agreement, especially in such situations as those described here, are fairly common.

Subjects Joined by *And*.   As a general rule, a compound subject in which the nouns, pronouns, or nouns and pronouns are connected by *and* requires a plural verb. For example:

Jeff and I are planning to be in Green Bay next month. (**NOT:** *am planning* or *is planning.*)

Florida, California, and Arizona have many popular tourist attractions. (**NOT:** *has.*)

You and your associates know a great deal about each of your competitors. (**NOT:** *knows.*)

However, when the parts of a compound subject refer to one person or thing, the subject requires a singular verb—even though the parts are joined by *and*.

The company's *president and chief executive officer makes* all major decisions. (**NOT:** *make.* In many companies, one person is not only *president* but also *chief executive officer.*)

Bacon and eggs appears on the breakfast menu of most restaurants. (**NOT:** *appear.* The two things can be correctly considered one meal or one item on a menu.)

Also, when the parts of a compound subject are joined by *and* and modified by *each* or *every,* use a singular verb.

Every man, woman, and child in the audience *has* a chance to win a door prize. (**NOT:** *have.*)

Each secretary, receptionist, and typist deserves an opportunity to advance on the job. (**NOT:** *deserve.*)

Subjects Joined by *Or* or *Nor*.   When the parts of a compound subject are joined by *or* or *nor* and each of the parts is singular, use a singular verb that agrees in person with the subject immediately preceding the verb.

Neither *Doris nor I know* the firm's telephone number. (**NOT:** *Neither Doris nor I knows the firm's telephone number.* Note that *know* agrees with *I,* which is first person singular—not with *Doris,* which is third person singular. However, note that *knows,* not *know,* is correct in this sentence: *Neither I nor Doris knows the firm's telephone number.*)

Lucille or Michael has a directory that *she or he consults* frequently. (**NOT:** *Lucille or Michael have a directory that she or he consult frequently.*)

However, when a singular subject and a plural subject are joined by *or* or *nor,* the plural subject should immediately precede the verb and a plural verb should be used.

Neither the *defendant* nor the *defense attorneys have commented* on the star witness's testimony. (**NOT:** *has commented.*)

The *owner* or the *tenants do* an excellent job of keeping the lobby and halls of the apartment building clean. (**NOT:** *does.*)

Collective Nouns as Subjects.   A collective noun that is singular in form requires a singular verb if the persons or things named by the noun are being considered as a unit.

44

The *staff is trying* to eliminate the causes of those bottlenecks in the workflow. (**NOT:** *are trying.* The members of the staff are acting as a single unit, not as separate individuals.)

The *jury has* not *returned* its verdict. (**NOT:** *have returned.* Here, too, the members of the jury are acting as a single unit, not as individuals.)

However, when the persons or things named by a collective noun that is singular in form are being considered as individuals—not as a unit—use a plural verb.

The *staff were arguing* among themselves as to the causes of the bottlenecks. (**NOT:** *was arguing.* The members of the staff are acting as individuals, not as a single unit.)

The *jury have been* unable to agree on the amount to be awarded to the plaintiff. (**NOT:** *has been.* The members of the jury are being considered as individuals, not as a single unit.)

A *Number* and *The Number* as Subjects. When preceded by *the,* the subject *number* requires a singular verb. However, when preceded by *a,* the subject *number* requires a plural verb.

The *number* of candidates *is* unusually large for an off-year election. (**NOT:** *are.*)

A *number* of political leaders *have expressed* support of the President's economic policies. (**NOT:** *has expressed.*)

Quantities, Amounts, and Measurements as Subjects. A subject that expresses a quantity, an amount, or a measurement—whether expressed in figures or in words—is singular and requires a singular verb.

Exactly *$450.86 is* the balance of your account. (**NOT:** *are.*)

Only a *hundred dollars has been collected* so far. (**NOT:** *have been collected.*)

I don't think *8 pounds 4 ounces is* an unusual weight for a newborn infant, is it?

Thirty days is a long time to wait for a reply to an inquiry.

However, when the subject refers to the separate parts of the amount, weight, or measurement, the subject is plural and requires a plural verb.

Thousands of pounds of potatoes *have rotted* in the warehouses.

I think that *30 days have passed* since we received a payment from them.

When a fraction is the subject, use a singular verb if the prepositional phrase following the fraction contains a singular noun but use a plural verb if the phrase contains a plural noun.

One *half* of the building *has been renovated.* (Note the singular noun *building.*)

One *half* of the spare parts *are* rusty. (Note the plural noun *parts.*)

A *fourth* of the work *has been done.* (Note the singular noun *work.*)

A *fourth* of the employees *prefer* to be paid weekly. (Note the plural *employees.*)

Pronouns That Are Singular or Plural. When a pronoun that may be either singular or plural is used as a subject, you must consider what the pronoun refers to in order to decide what verb to use with it. In such instances, the antecedent of the pronoun often appears in a prepositional phrase following the pronoun.

Some of the medicine *has lost* its potency. (The antecedent of *some* is the singular noun *medicine.*)

Some of the figures in this report *are* incorrect. (The antecedent of *some* is the plural noun *figures.*)

All are eager to hear your remarks, Dr. Simpson. (*All* clearly refers to the plural noun *people* or *members* or a similar word referring to persons, but the antecedent is not stated.)

All that some people ever do *is* complain. (*All* means "the only thing" in this sentence.)

45

See the discussion of "Number" in Unit 3 on pages 11–12 for other examples of pronouns that may be either singular or plural.

Subjects Followed by *As Well As* and Similar Expressions. *As well as, in addition to, including, together with, accompanied by,* or a similar expression has no bearing on the number of the subject. The verb must agree with the subject.

Dr. Rayburn, as well as several other physicians, *supports* the proposed legislation.

Mrs. Harris, together with several members of her family, *wants* to visit Puerto Rico.

Several new *employees,* including your secretary, *are* eligible.

Mr. and Mrs. Houston, together with their daughter-in-law, *plan* to spend their vacation in Colorado.

Nouns Plural in Form but Singular in Meaning. A noun subject that is plural in form but singular in meaning requires a singular verb.

Tarpon Springs is a town near Tampa, Florida.

Better Homes and Gardens carries ads of many well-known companies.

That *news pleases* us very much, Miss Grier.

Nouns That Are Singular or Plural. When a noun that may be either singular or plural is used as a subject, consider the meaning to be conveyed.

According to a network official, the *series has* not *been canceled. (Series* is singular; it refers to a TV or radio program broadcast in segments over a period of days, weeks, or months.)

Several new *series have received* excellent ratings. (*Series* is plural. Note the plural modifier *several.*)

See Unit 9, page 27, for examples of other nouns that may be either singular or plural.

☐ SPECIAL REMINDERS

1. The subject of a verb is never part of a phrase; however, an entire phrase may be used as a subject.

The *status* of several projects *is* unknown at this time. (The subject is *status,* not *projects.*)

Correcting errors is part of a typist's job. (The subject is the phrase *correcting errors.*)

2. The subject *you* always requires a plural verb, whether *you* refers to one person or to two or more persons.

You need to have more confidence in yourself. (**NOT:** *You needs to have more confidence in yourself.*)

You deserve most of the credit yourselves. (**NOT:** *You deserves most of the credit yourselves.*)

3. The pronoun *I* is the only first person singular subject. Except when it is used with *am* and *was,* which are forms of the verb *be,* it requires the same form of a verb as a plural subject.

I was ill last night; therefore, *I am staying* at home today.

I have much to do today, but *they have* very little to do. (**NOT:** *I has.*)

4. *Doesn't,* the contraction of *does not,* is used with a singular subject; *don't,* the contraction of *do not,* is used with a plural subject.

He doesn't pay his bills when they are due.

We don't have the correspondence you requested.

5. When *there* appears at the beginning of a sentence or clause, the true subject appears after the verb following *there.* The verb must, of course, agree with the subject.

> There *are* several *ways* to solve the problem. (**NOT:** There *is* several ways.)

> There *is* a simple *solution* to that problem. (**NOT:** There *are* a simple solution.)

ASSIGNMENT

○ Worksheet 44

UNIT 17: Verbs for Relative Pronouns

☐ THE PROBLEM

The verb that is used with *who, that, which,* or another relative pronoun subject must agree in number with the antecedent of the relative pronoun—the word that the entire relative clause modifies. In many instances, there is no problem in identifying the antecedent, determining whether it is singular or plural, and choosing the correct verb for the relative pronoun.

> Ms. Nash is *someone who has* the qualifications. (The antecedent of *who* is *someone,* a singular pronoun. Thus *has,* not *have,* is obviously the correct verb for the relative pronoun *who.*)

> Do you know the names and addresses of two or three *stores that sell* party decorations? (The relative clause *that sell party decorations* modifies *stores,* the antecedent of the relative pronoun *that.* Since the antecedent of *that* is plural, the plural verb *sell* obviously must be used with the relative pronoun subject *that.*)

However, the problem of identifying the antecedent of the relative pronoun subject is more difficult in such sentences as these:

> Louis is one of the people who (*want, wants*) professional recognition.

> Kay is one of those who (*need, needs*) frequent counseling.

> Integrity is only one of the qualities that (*is, are*) needed by people in business.

> Worrying is only one of the things that (*do, does*) not pay dividends.

> Ken is the only one of our customers who never (*complain, complains*) about prices.

> Gus is the only one of our employees who (*has, have*) been ill recently.

☐ THE SOLUTION

1. When the words *the only one* appear before the *of* phrase preceding the relative pronoun subject, use a singular verb with the relative pronoun subject. In this case, the pronoun *one* is the antecedent of the relative pronoun subject.

> Ken is the only one of our customers *who* never *complains* about prices.

> Gus is the only one of our employees *who has been* ill recently.

47

2. When the word *one* or the words *only one* appear before the *of* phrase preceding the relative pronoun subject, use a plural verb with the relative pronoun subject. In this case, the object of the preposition *of* is the antecedent of the relative pronoun subject.

Louis is one of the people who *want* professional recognition. (The antecedent of *who* is *people,* the word that the relative clause modifies. Note that *one* precedes the *of* phrase.)

Kay is one of those who *need* frequent counseling. (The antecedent of *who* is *those.* Note that *one* precedes the *of* phrase.)

Integrity is only one of the qualities that *are* needed by people in business. (The antecedent of *that* is *qualities.* Note that *only one* precedes the *of* phrase.)

Worrying is only one of the things that *do* not pay dividends. (*Things* is the antecedent of *that.* Note that *only one* precedes the *of* phrase.)

ASSIGNMENT

○ Worksheets 45 and 46

UNIT 18: Parts and Tenses of Verbs

☐ PARTS OF VERBS

Verbs are divided into two classes—*regular verbs* and *irregular verbs*—on the basis of how their parts are formed. As you will notice in the following discussion and charts, all verbs other than *be* and a few helping verbs have five different parts that are used by themselves or in combination with other verbs to indicate various tenses or times of actions or states of being.

Regular Verbs. If both the past tense and the past participle parts of a verb are formed by adding *d* or *ed* to the simple present tense, or basic, part of the verb, the verb is classified as a *regular verb*. As illustrated below, it is sometimes necessary to change a final *y* to an *i* before adding *ed*. Most English verbs are regular verbs.

PRESENT	THIRD PERSON SINGULAR	PAST TENSE	PAST PARTICIPLE	PRESENT PARTICIPLE
acknowledge	acknowledges	acknowledged	acknowledged	acknowledging
believe	believes	believed	believed	believing
carry	carries	carried	carried	carrying
delay	delays	delayed	delayed	delaying
expect	expects	expected	expected	expecting
lay (*to place*)	lays	laid	laid	laying
omit	omits	omitted	omitted	omitting
raise	raises	raised	raised	raising
rely	relies	relied	relied	relying

Irregular Verbs. If both the past tense and the past participle are *not* formed by adding *d* or *ed* to the simple present tense, or basic, part of the verb, the verb is classified as an *irregular verb*. The parts of many of the most commonly used irregular verbs are listed in the following chart.

PRESENT	THIRD PERSON SINGULAR	PAST TENSE	PAST PARTICIPLE	PRESENT PARTICIPLE
awake	awakes	awoke	awaked	awaking
become	becomes	became	become	becoming
bid (to offer)	bids	bid	bid	bidding
bid (to command)	bids	bade	bidden	bidding
break	breaks	broke	broken	breaking
bring	brings	brought	brought	bringing
buy	buys	bought	bought	buying
choose	chooses	chose	chosen	choosing
come	comes	came	come	coming
do	does	did	done	doing
drink	drinks	drank	drunk or drank	drinking
drive	drives	drove	driven	driving
eat	eats	ate	eaten	eating
find	finds	found	found	finding
flee	flees	fled	fled	fleeing
fly	flies	flew	flown	flying
freeze	freezes	froze	frozen	freezing
give	gives	gave	given	giving
go	goes	went	gone	going
grow	grows	grew	grown	growing
have	has	had	had	having
know	knows	knew	known	knowing
leave	leaves	left	left	leaving
lend	lends	lent	lent	lending
lie (to recline)	lies	lay	lain	lying
lose	loses	lost	lost	losing
rise	rises	rose	risen	rising
send	sends	sent	sent	sending
set (to place)	sets	set	set	setting
shrink	shrinks	shrank	shrunk or shrunken	shrinking
sit (to seat)	sits	sat	sat	sitting
speak	speaks	spoke	spoken	speaking
spend	spends	spent	spent	spending
stand	stands	stood	stood	standing
steal	steals	stole	stolen	stealing
strike	strikes	struck	struck	striking
sweep	sweeps	swept	swept	sweeping
swim	swims	swam	swum	swimming
take	takes	took	taken	taking
teach	teaches	taught	taught	teaching
tear	tears	tore	torn	tearing
think	thinks	thought	thought	thinking
throw	throws	threw	thrown	throwing
wear	wears	wore	worn	wearing
win	wins	won	won	winning
wind	winds	wound	wound	winding
write	writes	wrote	written	writing

The verb *be* is the most irregular of all verbs. *Be* has eight different parts:

| be | am | is | are | was | were | been | being |

The following helping verbs also comprise a special group of irregular verbs because each of them has but one or two parts. (**NOTE:** When *can* is used in the sense of "to place or store in a container," it is not a helping verb. Also, when *will* is used to mean "to bequeath to others," it is not a helping verb.)

| ought (to) | may | will | shall | can | must |
| | might | would | should | could | |

☐ TENSES OF VERBS

Present Tense.   To show that the time of the action or state of being is now or that something is always true, use the *present tense.*

I *am* eager to hear the results.

You *are* always most helpful.

Juan *is* a conscientious employee.

Several items *are* out of stock.

The sun *rises* in the east.

Some prices *rise* frequently.

If the subject is not the doer of the action, use *am, is,* or *are* plus a past participle. (In other words, write the verb in passive voice.)

I *am helped* by many people.

That magazine *is read* by everyone.

That letter *is written* well.

Our prices *are reviewed* semiannually.

Past Tense.   To show that the action occurred or that the state of being existed sometime before the present time, use the *past tense.*

He *called* me while you *were* away.

Who *took* the message?

I *was* in Detroit last week.

Some of the gifts *were* very expensive.

If the subject is not the doer of the action, use *was* or *were* with a past participle.

Mr. Dean *was invited* by me.

The letters *were written* by Dr. Hansen, but they *were signed* by Ms. Collins.

Future Tense.   To show that the action will occur sometime in the future or that the state of being does not yet exist, use the *future tense.* Except in very formal writing or speech, most people use the auxiliary verb *will* with the basic (simple present tense) form of the verb, regardless of the subject.

You *will be* happy with this new machine.

I *will write* to them tomorrow.

Who *will teach* them?

You *will receive* two copies.

In very formal writing and speech, use *shall* when the subject is *I* or *we* and use *will* with any other subject to show simple future tense.

I *shall be* in the office tomorrow, but Mrs. Davis *will be* in Minneapolis.

We *shall call* the Wilsons next week, but they *will* not *accept* our offer.

To show determination or promise in very formal writing or speech, use *will* when the subject is *I* or *we* and *shall* when the subject is any other word.

I definitely *will cancel* my subscription.

We *will pay* all of your travel expenses.

The annual dues *shall be* $25.

This agreement *shall be* in full force and effect as of the date following the signatures of the parties named below.

If the subject is not the doer of the action, use *will be* or *shall be* (as discussed above) plus a past participle.

His paintings *will be hung* in a museum.

We *will be* (or *shall be*) *delayed* an hour.

Present Perfect Tense.   To show that an action or a state of being began sometime in the past and may continue in the present, use the *present perfect tense.* Form this tense by using *have* or *has* with a past participle.

I *have written* them often.

They *have been* here twice.

He *has called* us several times.

Ms. Evans *has interviewed* many applicants for that position.

If the subject is not the doer of the action, use *have been* or *has been* plus a past participle.

We *have been advised* to invest in real estate by many people.

You *have been chosen* for the panel.

The house *has been painted* several times during the past four or five years.

It *has been frozen* for a long time.

Past Perfect Tense. To show that something began and ended before the present time, use the *past perfect tense*. Form this tense by using *had* with a past participle when the subject is the doer of the action.

All of us *had been* in San Antonio and *had visited* them before they moved into their new home.

Craig *had prepared* his report before he left for Dallas.

If the subject is not the doer of the action, use *had been* with a past participle.

We *had been interrupted* ten times before 11 o'clock this morning.

Future Perfect Tense. To show that the action or state of being will begin and end at some particular time in the future, use the *future perfect tense*. Form this tense by using *will have* (or *shall have*) with a past participle.

On the first of July, I *will have* (or *shall have*) *been* with the same employer for five years.

Mr. Reed *will have talked* with all of the district managers by this time tomorrow.

If the subject is not the doer of the action, use *will have been* (or *shall have been*, as discussed previously) with a past participle.

Most of the apartments *will have been rented* by next week.

Progressive Tenses. To show action in progress or state of being in continuing existence at a particular time, use a present participle as a main verb.

PRESENT PROGRESSIVE TENSE:	I *am being* careful because she *is watching* me.
	They *are listening* because you *are telling* them the truth.
PRESENT PROGRESSIVE TENSE, PASSIVE VOICE:	I *am being considered* for the job.
	You *are being invited* to the seminar.
PAST PROGRESSIVE TENSE:	I *was being* careful because she *was watching* me.
	They *were listening* because you *were speaking* to them.
PAST PROGRESSIVE TENSE, PASSIVE VOICE:	I *was being considered* for the job.
	You *were being invited* to the seminar.
FUTURE PROGRESSIVE TENSE:	All of us *will be paying* our share of taxes.
PRESENT PERFECT PROGRESSIVE TENSE:	We *have been conducting* an informal survey.
	She *has been working* for them at least two years.
PAST PERFECT PROGRESSIVE TENSE:	Some of us *had been waiting* for more than an hour.
FUTURE PERFECT PROGRESSIVE TENSE:	Ed *will have been working* here for five years on April 10.

ASSIGNMENT

○ Worksheets 47 and 48

UNIT 19: Mood and Voice of Verbs

☐ MOOD OF VERBS

The term *mood*, or *mode*, describes the manner in which a verb is expressed. The three moods of verbs are the *imperative*, the *indicative*, and the *subjunctive*.

Imperative Mood. The *imperative mood* of a verb indicates a command or a request.

> *Obey* all traffic regulations; *be* especially careful in school zones. (The subject *you* is understood. Note the use of the verb form *be*.)
>
> Please *sign* both copies of the enclosed contract, *keep* the carbon copy for your files, and *return* the original copy to me for our records. (The subject *you* is understood.)

Indicative Mood. The *indicative mood* of a verb is used for a statement or a question.

> Your order, which *arrived* yesterday, *will be shipped* next Monday.
>
> *Have* you *answered* the letter from Dr. Finch?

Subjunctive Mood. The *subjunctive mood* of a verb indicates a condition contrary to fact, a wish, necessity, or a doubt. The need to use a verb in the subjunctive mood is often signaled by *I wish, if, as if, as though,* or a similar expression.

> Sometimes *I wish* I *were* a movie star. (I am not a movie star.)
>
> *If* it *were* not raining now, I would go outside for a while. (It is raining, though.)
>
> Miss Jenkins acts *as if* she *were* Queen of England. (She obviously isn't, though.)

Note that *if* does not automatically indicate that a verb in the subjunctive mood should be used. If what follows *if* is true or could be true, use *was*.

> *If* Alice *was* angry with me, I knew nothing about it. (She may have been angry with me.)

Also note that a subjunctive verb is used in the dependent clause of a sentence when the main clause contains a verb such as *request, suggest, recommend, move,* or *require*. Be especially careful to use the verb form *be* (not *am, is, are, was,* or some other form of *be*) in such sentences. Note that the number of the subject does not affect the form of the verb used, nor does the tense of the verb in the main clause.

> Some companies require that all orders *be filled* within 24 hours. (NOT: *are filled*.)
>
> We suggest that Maria *be* the one to notify them. (NOT: *is*.)
>
> George recommended that Sara *audit* the accounts. (NOT: *audits*.)
>
> I move that the meeting *be adjourned*. (NOT: *is adjourned*.)
>
> Several people have demanded that the ballots *be impounded*. (NOT: *are impounded*.)
>
> I have suggested that our attorney *meet* with them. (NOT: *meets*.)

☐ VOICE OF VERBS

The term *voice* is used to describe the relationship between an "action" verb and its subject. The two voices of action verbs are *active* and *passive*.

Active Voice. When the subject is the doer of the action, the verb is in *active voice*.

> The auditor *signed* the reports. (*Auditor* is the subject, *signed* is the verb, and *reports* is the direct object of the verb *signed*.)

Miss Pulaski *sent* Joyce a copy of the invoice. (*Miss Pulaski* is the subject, *sent* is the verb, *Joyce* is the indirect object of *sent,* and *copy* is the direct object of the verb *sent.*)

The owners *must make* the necessary repairs. (*Owners* is the subject, *must make* is the verb phrase, and *repairs* is the direct object of *must make.*)

Passive Voice.   When the subject is *not* the doer of the action, the verb is in *passive voice.* A verb in passive voice always includes a form of the verb *be (am, is, are, was, were, be, been, being)* as a helping verb, and the main verb is always a past participle.

The reports *were signed* by the auditor. (*Reports* is the subject; *were signed* is the verb.)

Joyce *was sent* a copy of the invoice by Miss Pulaski. (*Joyce* is the subject; *was sent* is the verb.)

A copy of the invoice *was sent* to Joyce by Miss Pulaski. (*Copy* is the subject; *was sent* is the verb.)

The necessary repairs *must be made* by the owners. (*Repairs* is the subject; *must be made* is the verb.)

ASSIGNMENT

○ Worksheets 49 and 50

UNIT 20: Troublesome Verbs

☐ *LIE* AND *LAY*

Lie.   The verb *lie* means to "rest" or to "recline." When used with either of these meanings, it never has an object.

The books just *lie* on the shelf.	All of us *will lie* in the shade next summer.
A ship sometimes *lies* at anchor.	The folder *is lying* on your desk.
I *lay* in the shade yesterday.	That letter *has lain* on my desk for a week.

Lay.   The verb *lay* means to "put" or to "place." This verb always has an object.

I always *lay* the mail on your desk.	Mark *will lay* the package on the table.
Who always *lays* packages on my desk?	We *were laying* bricks last Wednesday.
Someone *laid* the new floor last week.	They *have laid* more bricks than we have.

☐ *SIT* AND *SET*

Sit.   The verb *sit* means to "rest." It never has an object.

We usually *sit* in the front row.	They *will sit* there for days.
Helen often *sits* behind us.	I *am sitting* at the receptionist's desk.
I *sat* in the last row last night.	We *have sat* beside them many times.

Set.   The verb *set* has many different meanings, such as to "place something somewhere" or to "establish something." When it has such a meaning, *set* requires an object. Note the examples on page 54.

I often *set* the table.   I hope that you *will set* the clock.

Fred usually *sets* a fast pace.   The police *had set* a trap for the thief.

Alice *set* a precedent yesterday.   Marion *is setting* a new sales record.

In such sentences as those below, *set* is used with a meaning that seldom results in its being confused with *sit*.

The sun will *set* at 7:02 p.m. today.   Gelatin desserts *set* quickly.

☐ *RISE* AND *RAISE*

Rise.   The verb *rise* means to "ascend" or to "increase" or to "get up." It does not take an object.

Our costs *rise* frequently.   I think the price *will rise* slightly.

The cost of oil *rises* often.   The value of gold *has risen* sharply.

Taxes *rose* slightly last year.   The value of imports *is rising*.

Raise.   The verb *raise* means to "lift," to "grow," to "increase in amount," and so on. It always has an object.

I usually *raise* the windows.   Your employer *will raise* your salary.

The farmer *raises* cattle.   Dentists *have raised* their fees.

Warren *raised* several questions.   Some cities *are raising* their tax rates.

ASSIGNMENT

○ Worksheets 51 and 52

UNIT 21: Infinitives, Gerunds, and Participles

☐ INFINITIVES AND INFINITIVE PHRASES

Infinitives.   An *infinitive* consists of the word *to* plus a verb. Infinitives are used as nouns, as adjectives, or as adverbs.

Mrs. Lambert announced that she plans *to resign*. (*To resign*, which functions as a noun, is the direct object of the verb *plans*.)

Mr. Packard is the person *to ask*. (*To ask*, which functions as an adjective, modifies the noun *person*.)

Dale and I went *to work*. (*To work* functions as an adverb modifying the verb *went*. *To work* tells where Dale and I went.)

Infinitive Phrases.   Like verbs, infinitives may be modified by adverbs and have subjects, objects, and so on. Thus an *infinitive phrase* (which functions as an adjective, an adverb, or a noun) consists of an infinitive and the word or words that are closely connected to it. Note the examples in the following sentences:

Mr. Hamilton called *to cancel his appointment.* (The infinitive phrase functions as an adverb modifying the verb *called.* It tells why.)

To win the election is every candidate's greatest desire. (*To win the election* functions as a noun; this infinitive phrase is the subject of the sentence.)

Where are the orders *to be processed before we go to lunch?* (This phrase functions as an adjective modifying *orders.*)

☐ GERUNDS AND GERUND PHRASES

Gerunds.   A *gerund,* which is formed by adding *ing* to a verb, is always used as a noun.

Calling may be easier than *writing.*   Who said that *complaining* doesn't pay?

We had heard of Mike's *resigning.*   Her favorite pastime is *reading.*

Gerund Phrases.   Like verbs, gerunds may be modified by adverbs and have objects. Like nouns, they may be modified by adjectives. Thus a *gerund phrase* (which always functions as a noun) consists of a gerund and the word or words that are closely related to it.

Speaking too softly will make it difficult for anyone to hear you.

Writing letters is the most important part of many jobs.

Sending him the memo was a mistake!

Sound planning is necessary if we are to achieve the goal set for us.

☐ PARTICIPLES AND PARTICIPIAL PHRASES

Participles.   When the present participle or past participle part, or form, of a verb is used to modify a noun or a pronoun, it is referred to as a *participle* or as a *participial modifier.* In effect, it is a word that looks like a verb but that functions as an adjective.

The one *standing* is the general manager's administrative assistant. (*Standing* modifies the pronoun *one.*)

Some *advertised* merchandise may not be available at all branch stores. (*Advertised* modifies *merchandise.*)

Does anyone know the value of the *stolen* equipment? (*Stolen* modifies *equipment.*)

Participial Phrases.   A *participial phrase,* which always functions as an adjective, consists of the participle, the adverb or adverbs that modify it, and any other words that are closely connected to it.

Feeling ill, Paul decided to leave work early. (*Feeling ill* modifies *Paul.*)

Being president of the company, Dr. Wren is also a member of the board of directors. (*Being president of the company* modifies *Dr. Wren.*)

We heard someone *singing outside our front door.* (*Singing outside our front door* modifies *someone.*)

Did you see either of the people *injured in the accident?* (*Injured in the accident* modifies *people.*)

The model *chosen by most people* is the one with the extra chrome trim. (*Chosen by most people* modifies *model.*)

1. Always use an objective-case pronoun before, after, or before and after an infinitive except when the infinitive *to be* is not immediately preceded by a noun or a pronoun. When *to be* is not preceded by a noun or a pronoun, use a nominative-case pronoun after it.

Did you ask *them to be* there?   I would like *to be she* for a day.

We asked *them to meet us.*   You may prefer *to write her.*

2. Use a possessive-case noun or pronoun before a gerund.

Tommy's whistling annoyed most of us.   *Your writing* is excellent.

3. Be careful not to confuse a gerund with a participle. Study the following examples carefully:

Several of us saw a stranger *loitering* in the lobby. (*Loitering* is a participle, not a gerund, in this sentence; thus the noun before it is not written in possessive case. We saw a *stranger* who was loitering; we did not see *loitering.*)

The man's *loitering* was suspicious behavior. (*Loitering* is a gerund, not a participle.)

4. Be careful to avoid a "dangling" participle or participial phrase—one positioned so that it modifies an incorrect word.

NOT: *Hanging lopsided on the wall,* many visitors commented about the modern painting. (Here the phrase obviously dangles—it incorrectly modifies *visitors.*)

BUT: Many visitors commented about the modern painting *hanging lopsided on the wall.* (Here the phrase correctly modifies *painting.*)

NOT: The President entered the restaurant *followed by a group of Secret Service agents.* (The participial phrase incorrectly modifies *restaurant.*)

BUT: The President, *followed by a group of Secret Service agents,* entered the restaurant. **OR:** *Followed by a group of Secret Service agents,* the President entered the restaurant. (In each of these sentences, the participial phrase correctly modifies *President,* which is capitalized because it refers to the President of the United States.)

ASSIGNMENT

○ Worksheets 53 and 54

UNIT 22: Adverbs and Adjectives

□ ADVERBS

Adverbs answer questions such as these: How? When? Where? Why? To what extent or degree? These words, most of which end in *ly,* modify verbs, adjectives, other adverbs, and—as discussed in Unit 21—infinitives, gerunds, and participles. Note the following examples:

The negotiations ended *abruptly.* (*Abruptly* modifies the verb *ended.*)

These tomatoes are *unusually* large. (*Unusually* modifies the adjective *large.*)

This machine operates *very efficiently.* (*Very* modifies the adverb *efficiently,* which modifies the verb *operates.*)

We expect the shipment to arrive *soon*. (*Soon* modifies the infinitive *to arrive.*)

Working *haphazardly* results in errors most of the time. (*Haphazardly* modifies the gerund *working.*)

Applied *properly,* the paint will cover most surfaces satisfactorily. (*Properly* modifies the participle *applied.* **NOTE:** The participial phrase *applied properly* modifies the noun *paint* and therefore functions as an adjective.)

☐ ADJECTIVES

Adjectives answer such questions as these: Which? What kind of? How many? Whose? They modify nouns, pronouns, and gerunds.

Attentive listening is *a* sign of courtesy. (*Attentive* modifies the gerund *listening;* the article *a* modifies the noun *sign.*)

Every firm needs *conscientious* workers. (*Every* modifies the noun *firm; conscientious* modifies the noun *workers.*)

Nothing *unusual* occurred *this* morning. (*Unusual* modifies the pronoun *nothing; this* modifies the noun *morning.*)

☐ CHOICE OF ADVERB OR ADJECTIVE

Speakers and writers sometimes have difficulty in deciding whether to use an adjective or an adverb after a verb that pertains to one of the senses (sight, sound, touch, taste, or smell). A verb such as one of the following shows the action of the subject in some sentences and the condition, or state of being, of the subject in others.

look   sound   feel   taste   smell

If the verb expresses an *action* by the subject, use an adverb after it.

The alarm sounded *suddenly.*   The tenants smelled the smoke *immediately.*

When the verb shows *condition* or *state-of-being,* use an adjective after it.

The smoke smells *acrid.*   Your ideas sound *good* to me.

This milk tastes *sour.*   Those gifts look *expensive.*

☐ TROUBLESOME ADVERBS AND ADJECTIVES

Almost* and *most. *Almost* is classified as an adverb meaning ''nearly.'' Nevertheless, *almost*—not *most*—is the correct word to use to modify such pronouns as *all, everyone, everybody,* and so on.

The new forms are *almost* ready to distribute. (*Almost* modifies the adjective *ready.*)

Almost everyone agrees with you. (*Almost* modifies the pronoun *everyone.* **NOT:** *Most* everyone agrees with you.)

Most may be used as an adjective, an adverb, or a pronoun.

Most people agree with you. (*Most* is an adjective modifying the noun *people.*)

Which is *most* nearly correct? (*Most* is an adverb modifying the adverb *nearly.*)

Most of them have been checked. (*Most* is a pronoun used as the subject of the sentence.)

Bad* and *badly. *Bad* is an adjective. *Badly* is an adverb.

Hazel felt *bad* about the errors.   The situation may look *bad* to some people.

The fire damaged the house *badly.*   Was the driver *badly* injured?

***Different* and *differently*.** *Different* is an adjective; *differently* is an adverb.

You may feel *different* about the situation tomorrow. (*Different* modifies *you,* the subject.)

We have a *different* procedure now. (*Different* modifies the noun *procedure.*)

Steve acts *differently* now. (*Differently* modifies the verb *acts.*)

***Good* and *well*.** *Good* is an adjective. *Well* is an adjective when it refers to "good health"; otherwise, *well* is an adverb.

Both of you do *good* work. (*Good* is an adjective modifying the noun *work.*)

Neither of them was in *good* spirits yesterday. (*Good* is an adjective; it modifies *spirits.*)

We felt *good* about the settlement. (*Good,* which is a predicate adjective modifying *we,* is correct. The adjective *good* does not refer to health; it refers to "good spirits or good feelings" about something.)

Carol has not felt *well* for some time. (*Well* is the correct adjective because it refers to health.)

Laura has done *well* in her new job. (*Well* is an adverb; it modifies the verb *has done.*)

***Real* and *really*.** *Real* is an adjective. *Really* is an adverb. (**NOTE:** *Real* is not an appropriate substitute for the adverb *very.*)

This ring has two *real* diamonds. (*Real* is an adjective modifying the noun *diamonds.*)

It was *really* thoughtful of you to call. (*Really* is an adverb modifying the adjective *thoughtful.*)

☐ SUGGESTIONS AND REMINDERS

1. Some adverbs have two acceptable forms. The form ending in *ly* is more formal, and it is more appropriate for business communication.

slow	quick	cheap	direct	fair	loud
slowly	quickly	cheaply	directly	fairly	loudly

Many communities post signs warning motorists to go *slow* in school zones.

We must proceed *slowly* in making such changes as the one Miss Sachs suggested.

2. Never use the pronoun *them* as an adjective. It is not a substitute for *those.*

Please post *those* notices on the bulletin board. (**NOT:** Please post *them* notices.)

3. The placement of *only, also,* or *too* often affects the meaning of a sentence. Therefore, be careful when using these words.

I wrote to them *only* yesterday. (Here, *only* could mean "to them and no one else" or "just yesterday.")

Only I wrote to them yesterday. (No one else wrote to them—only I.)

I *only* wrote to them yesterday. (I didn't call—I only wrote.)

I wrote *only* to them yesterday. (I wrote to them, but I didn't write to anyone else.)

I *also* called Mr. Jeffreys. (In addition to writing to him, I called him. Or, I and someone else called him.)

Also, I called Mr. Jeffreys. (I did something besides call Mr. Jeffreys.)

I called Mr. Jeffreys *also.* (I called Mr. Jeffreys and someone else.)

This letter contains many figures *too.* (It contains figures as well as other things.)

Too, this letter contains many figures. (Maybe the letter contains other things, or perhaps another letter contains many figures just as this one does.)

This letter, *too,* contains many figures. (Another letter contains many figures.)

This letter contains *too* many figures. (It contains an excessive number of figures.)

58

4. Be sure to position modifying phrases and clauses close to the words that they modify. Avoid "dangling" and ambiguous modifiers.

> **NOT:** Bill was sitting on the bench playing the piano when it broke.
>
> **BUT:** When the bench broke, Bill was sitting on it and playing the piano.

5. As a general rule, two or more words that form a one-thought modifier are hyphenated only when they appear before the word they modify.

> Parker's is an *up-to-date* store. **BUT:** Parker's store is *up to date.*
>
> We need a *60-foot* rope. **BUT:** We need a rope *60 feet* long.
>
> They quoted prices in *3-, 5-,* and *10-ton* quantities. **BUT:** They quoted prices in quantities of *3, 5,* and *10 tons.*
>
> It was a *nerve-racking* experience. **BUT:** It was an experience to *rack the nerves.*

Whether an expression such as one of the following appears before or after the word it modifies, do not hyphenate the words.

> real estate   junior college   Wall Street   carefully worded   casually dressed

ASSIGNMENT

○ Worksheet 55

UNIT **23:** Prepositions and Conjunctions

☐ PREPOSITIONS

A *preposition* is a word that combines with one or more noun or pronoun objects to form a *prepositional phrase,* which usually modifies some other word in a sentence. Commonly used prepositions include the following:

in	into	above	for	of	over	against	beside ("by the side of")
to	from	among	off	by	with	through	besides ("in addition to")
up	upon	along	on	at	after	between	but ("except")

> The guest speaker was standing *beside Dr. Swenson.* (*Beside Dr. Swenson* functions as an adverb modifying the verb phrase *was standing.*)
>
> Is anyone *besides Rosemary and him* scheduled to work at the convention exhibit? (*Besides Rosemary and him* functions as an adjective modifying *anyone.*)

Suggestions. The following suggestions will help you use prepositions properly when speaking or writing for a business purpose.

1. Avoid using unnecessary prepositions.

> **SAY:** Where are they going? **NOT:** Where are they going *to?*
>
> **SAY:** Do you know where Jim is? **NOT:** Do you know where Jim is *at?*
>
> **SAY:** The book fell *off* the shelf. **NOT:** The book fell *off of* the shelf.

2. Remember that a word used as a preposition in one sentence may be used as part of a verb or some other part of speech in another sentence. In such situations, the use of a hyphen may or may not be necessary. Consult your dictionary when you are in doubt!

Please do not stand *in* the doorway. (*In* is a preposition, a part of the prepositional phrase *in the doorway*.)

You may be asked to serve as a stand-*in* for Dr. Phillips. (*In* is part of the compound noun *stand-in*.)

Deborah was asked to stand *in* for Mrs. Powell. (*In* is part of the compound verb *stand in*.)

Wesley is a stand-*in* candidate for Mr. Walinsky. (*In* is part of the compound adjective *stand-in*.)

With whom do you plan *to* visit in Toronto? (*To* is part of the infinitive *to visit*.)

We mailed the package *to* your home address. (*To* is a preposition, a part of the prepositional phrase *to your home address*.)

Prepositions in Certain Expressions.   Some writers and speakers are often uncertain as to which preposition should be used with a particular word in a specific situation.

***Angry at* or *about*.**   Use *angry at* or *about* when referring to things.

I don't think that anyone was *angry about* the cancellation of the project.

***Angry with*.**   Use *angry with* when referring to people.

Were you *angry with* your immediate supervisor?

***Comply with*.**   Use *comply with* when referring to requests, directives, and so on.

Few people refuse to *comply with* reasonable requests.

***Conform to*.**   The expression *conform to* is preferred to *conform with*.

These items *conform to* your specifications.

***Differ about*.**   Use *differ about* when people disagree about something.

We *differed about* the best procedure to follow.

***Differ from*.**   Use *differ from* in comparisons.

The prices in the catalog *differ from* those on the invoice.

***Differ with*.**   Use *differ with* when people disagree.

We *differ with* them over the purpose of the committee.

***Different from*.**   Use *different from*, not *different than*, for comparisons.

The model that we received is *different from* the one that we ordered.

***Identical with*.**   Always use *identical with*, not *identical to*.

The price of this one is *identical with* the price of that one.

***In*.**   Use *in* when referring to being within an area.

We have at least a year's supply of those items sitting *in* the warehouse.

***Into*.**   Use *into* when referring to movement from one place to another.

Wesley and I walked *into* the conference room just as the meeting ended.

***Retroactive to*.**   Always use *retroactive to*, not *retroactive from*.

Reports indicate that the pay increase will be *retroactive to* last July 1.

☐ CONJUNCTIONS

A *conjunction* is a word that joins two or more words, phrases, or clauses. *Coordinate conjunctions* (*and, but, or,* and *nor,* for example) and *subordinate conjunctions* are the two main classes.

Usage Pointers. When joining a dependent clause to an independent clause, always use a subordinate conjunction (*when, because, before,* and so on).

Ms. Bennett often speaks too rapidly *when* she dictates to her secretary.

Please study the contract carefully *before* you sign it.

When using coordinate conjunctions (*and, or,* and *but,* for example), conjunctive adverbs (*consequently, therefore,* and *however,* for example), and correlative conjunctions (*either . . . or,* for example), be sure that:

1. The elements joined by the conjunction are grammatically equal. Do *not* use a coordinate conjunction, a correlative conjunction, or a conjunctive adverb to join such grammatically unequal elements as an adjective and an adverb, a dependent clause and an independent clause, and so on.

WRONG: Wayne was assessed a penalty *and because* he didn't pay his taxes on time.

RIGHT: Wayne was assessed a penalty *because* he didn't pay his taxes on time.

2. All the necessary words before and after the conjunction are present.

WRONG: He should but didn't go.

RIGHT: He should *have gone* but didn't go.

3. The elements joined by the conjunction are parallel in construction.

WRONG: He was *either* confused *or* I was.

RIGHT: *Either* he was confused *or* I was.

WRONG: The office is large, airy, and *in a convenient location.*

RIGHT: The office is large, airy, and *conveniently located.*

WRONG: Miss Kreinsen is studying data processing and *to learn business law.*

RIGHT: Miss Kreinsen is studying data processing and *business law.*

ASSIGNMENT

○ Worksheets 56 and 57

UNIT 24: Words Often Confused and Misused

☐ WORDS THAT SOUND ALIKE

The English language contains many words that are often confused and misused because they sound the same, or almost the same, as other words. Such words, including those presented and illustrated in this unit, are *homonyms*.

Accept and except. *Accept* is a verb meaning "to receive with favor; to take what is offered."

Did anyone *accept* your offer?　　It is sometimes difficult to *accept* criticism.

Except may be either a verb meaning "to exclude; to excuse" or a preposition meaning "other than."

Mr. Wong may *except* you from noon-hour duty.　　Everyone was there *except* Peggy.

Ad and add. *Ad* is a short form of *advertisement*. *Add* is a verb meaning "to combine into one sum; to append or attach."

Did you like the two-color *ad*?　　Please *add* this postscript.

Adapt, adept, and adopt. *Adapt* is a verb meaning "to alter; to adjust."

Those plants may *adapt* to this climate.　　We can *adapt* that computer to our needs.

Adept is an adjective meaning "skillful; proficient." *Adopt* is a verb meaning "to take as one's own without change."

Artists are *adept* in choosing colors.　　Should we *adopt* Ruth's plan?

Advice and advise. *Advice* is a noun meaning "suggestions or recommendations concerning a course of action."

The engineers gave us their *advice*.　　What *advice* would you offer?

Advise is a verb meaning "to give advice; to caution or warn."

What did Leslie's attorney *advise* him to do?

Traffic police usually *advise* motorists of dangerous driving conditions.

Affect and effect. *Affect* is a verb meaning "to influence; to pretend."

The new law *affects* intrastate shipments.　　He *affected* a British accent.

Effect may be a noun meaning "the result" or a verb meaning "to bring about."

The *effect* of the fire was disastrous.　　The new plan will *effect* greater productivity.

All ready and already. *All ready* is an adjective meaning "entirely ready." *Already* is an adverb meaning "previously."

Carl is *all ready* to take dictation.　　I have *already* answered his letter.

Capital and capitol. *Capital* is an adjective meaning "most important; most serious" or a noun meaning "money; seat of government." *Capitol* is a noun meaning "a building in which a legislature meets."

Murder is a *capital* offense.　　How much *capital* do you have to invest?

What is the *capital* of Oklahoma?　　Have you seen the dome of the *Capitol* in Washington?

Console and consul. *Console* is a verb meaning "to comfort" or a noun meaning "the control panel of an instrument" or "a cabinet." *Consul* is a noun meaning "a diplomatic representative."

She sat at the *console* as he tried to *console* her.　　I asked the Spanish *consul*.

Council and counsel. *Council* is a noun meaning "an advisory or a governing group." *Counsel* is a verb meaning "to advise" or a noun meaning "a lawyer; advice."

Who is president of the city *council*?　　Who is the plaintiff's *counsel*?

We are members of a trade *council*.　　Did anyone *counsel* you?

***Emigrate* and *immigrate*.** *Emigrate* is a verb meaning "to leave a country." *Immigrate* is a verb meaning "to enter a country."

His family *emigrated* from Cuba.   Many have *immigrated* to Canada.

***Farther* and *further*.** *Farther* is an adverb referring to measurable distance. *Further* is an adjective meaning "additional" or the comparative form of *far*.

I walked *farther* than she did.   You may write them for *further* information.

Both of us must walk *farther*.   We should explore the situation *further*.

***Principal* and *principle*.** *Principal* is an adjective meaning "main; chief" or a noun meaning "sum of money; head of a school."

What is the *principal* reason?   We must repay the *principal* plus interest.

That is the *principal* idea.   Who is the *principal* of the Lincoln School?

Principle is a noun meaning "a rule; a law; a doctrine; a code of conduct."

We didn't understand the *principle*.   It was a matter of *principle* to us.

☐ OTHER WORDS

Certain words are often confused and misused, even though they do not sound alike. For polished speaking and writing, always choose and use the word that conveys the meaning you intend.

***Amount* and *number*.** *Amount* is used to refer to things measured in bulk. *Number* is used to refer to things counted individually.

Canada exports a large *amount* of wheat.

We expect a large *number* of people to attend.

***Anxious* and *eager*.** *Anxious* means "worried; fearful." *Eager* means "enthusiastic; desirous; looking forward to with pleasure."

Parents are *anxious* about their children's safety.

We are *eager* to see your representative.

***As-as* and *so-as*.** For comparisons that are equal, use *as* and *as*. For comparisons that are unequal, use *so* and *as*.

She is *as* tall *as* he.   This ad is not *so* good *as* that one.

***Awful, terrible,* and *very*.** *Awful* means "inspiring awe." *Terrible* means "terrifying; frightening; appalling." *Very* means "exceedingly; truly." Do not use *awful* or *terrible* as a synonym for *very*. (As you will remember, a *synonym* is a word that has the same or almost the same meaning as another word.)

An earthquake is an *awful* event.   The storm was *terrible*.

I had a *very* bad cold.   It is *very* cold today.

***Because* and *reason* (*that*).** Always use *that*, not *because*, after *reason*.

She left *because* she was ill. **OR:** The *reason* she left was *that* she was ill.

***Can* and *may*.** Use *can* to indicate ability or power. Use *may* to indicate possibility or permission.

Our manager *can* resolve the problem.   Margaret *may* appreciate your advice.

Congress *can* override a Presidential veto.   *May* I have an extra week's vacation?

63

Continually and continuously. *Continually* suggests interrupted action recurring over a period of time. *Continuously* indicates uninterrupted action.

We must *continually* improve our skills.   The generators operate *continuously*.

Credible and creditable. *Credible* means "believable"; *creditable* means "worthy of praise."

Do you think the story is *credible*?   Rescuing a pet is a *creditable* act.

Lend and loan. *Lend* is a verb meaning "to grant the use of something." *Loan* is a noun meaning "the temporary use of something."

Please *lend* me $10.   I need a small *loan*.

Less and fewer. Use *less* when referring to bulk or volume. Use *fewer* when referring to things that can be counted individually.

You need *less* help than I.   *Fewer* people attended than we had hoped.

Liable and likely. *Liable* means "legally responsible or obligated." *Likely* means "probable; suitable."

The court held him *liable* for damages.   It is *likely* to rain any minute now.

Mad and angry. *Mad* means "insane"; *angry* means "enraged."

The dog is *mad*.   Miss Albright is *angry* with her secretary.

Per, a, and an. *Per* is a Latin expression meaning "for each." Except in such expressions as *per diem* and *per capita*, use *a* or *an* in ordinary business writing.

The *per diem* allowance is $60.   The speed limit is 55 miles *an* hour.

Provided and providing. *Provided* means "on condition that"; *providing* means "supplying" and takes an object. Do not use *that* after *provided*.

I will attend *provided* you invite me.   *Providing* notebooks is a good idea.

ASSIGNMENT

○ Worksheets 58 and 59

PART THREE

Style in Business Writing

Punctuation, capitalization, and other elements of style greatly affect the general readability of every written message. At the same time, they often determine the meaning of statements, reflect a certain level of informality or formality, and so forth. Thus, as a business writer, you will need to know and be able to skillfully apply the principles of style presented in Units 25 through 31. They are the "rules" that modern business writers use to guide their readers in correctly and easily understanding letters, memos, and other written communications.

UNIT 25: Period, Question Mark, and Exclamation Point

☐ THE PERIOD

After Sentences. Use a period after a sentence that makes a statement or that expresses a command or a polite request.

> We fully agree that conservation of natural resources is important. (Statement.)
>
> Make sure each member of your staff understands these new regulations. (Command.)
>
> Please return the large portion of the statement with your payment. (Polite Request.)

If a request that is phrased as a question requires an action response, not an answer to the question itself, use a period after it.

> Will you be able to help me next Wednesday? (The writer expects a "Yes" or a "No" answer.)
>
> Will you please send us your payment today. (The writer expects a payment.)

NOTE: Some writers prefer to use a question mark after a request that is phrased as a question, even though a period would be technically correct. This departure from

65

the standard rule usually occurs when the writer feels that the reader may consider the request presumptuous.

> Would you please take care of my mail while I'm on vacation. (Technically correct.)
>
> Would you please take care of my mail while I'm on vacation? (Preferable, in the opinion of some writers.)

After Condensed Statements.   Use a period after a condensed statement (elliptical expression), which is usually a word or a phrase used as an answer to a question or as a transitional expression.

> Will you have to contribute to the cost of this new insurance plan? *No.*
>
> *Next, our promotion policy.* To the greatest extent possible, all newly created positions and all managerial vacancies are to be filled by present employees of Deerfield Industries.

Be careful not to confuse a condensed statement with a *sentence fragment.* As illustrated below, a sentence fragment is simply a group of words incorrectly treated as though it were a complete sentence.

> **NOT:** Ms. Gustafson will notify you of the outcome. *Within the next two weeks.*
>
> **BUT:** Ms. Gustafson will notify you of the outcome within the next two weeks.
>
> **NOT:** This may be the greatest bargain. *That we'll be able to offer this year.*
>
> **BUT:** This may be the greatest bargain that we'll be able to offer this year.

With Abbreviations.   Use periods with abbreviations of personal titles, professional titles, academic degrees, seniority terms, and *a.m.* and *p.m.* (**NOTE:** Abbreviations are discussed in greater detail in Unit 30.)

> Mr.   Mrs.   Ms.   Dr.   Prof.   Ph.D.   B.A.   Jr.   Sr.   a.m.   p.m.

With Numbers.   Use a period as a decimal point in amounts of money, percentages, and other amounts consisting of whole numbers plus decimal fractions or simply decimal fractions. Omit *.00* after even amounts of dollars.

> $1,496.64 $78   8.5 percent   1.5 tons   0.75 percent

☐ THE QUESTION MARK

After Sentences.   Use a question mark at the end of a sentence that asks a direct question. As illustrated below, a *direct question* consists of the speaker's or writer's exact words arranged in the order in which they were spoken or written.

> Does the warranty cover the cost of labor as well as replacement parts?
>
> What is the name and address of your present employer?

If a short direct question is added to a statement, set it off with commas and use a question mark at the end of the sentence.

> Joyce has the authority, *doesn't she,* to approve these requisitions?
>
> We should hire a replacement for Mr. Conway immediately, *shouldn't we?*

Be careful to avoid the common pitfall of using a question mark at the end of a sentence that makes a statement about a question.

> Mrs. Koch asked *whether the ad would appear in the next issue of Business Week.* (The direct question that Mrs. Koch asked may have been this: *Will the ad appear in the next issue of Business Week?*)
>
> *What expenses have been incurred so far* is something the accountants can tell us.

After Condensed Questions. Use a question mark after a condensed question, which is usually a word or a phrase that follows a statement.

We haven't received the order you promised to deliver two weeks ago. *Why?*

You said that we could save money by leasing a computer. *How much?*

In a Series of Questions. If a series of brief questions relate to the same subject and verb, use a question mark after each question in the series.

How far is it from Dallas *to New Orleans? to Detroit? to Montreal?*

Should the next branch manager be *Ms. Anderson? Ms. Bushnell? Mr. Symond?*

☐ THE EXCLAMATION POINT

The exclamation point may be used after a sentence, a phrase, or a single word to show strong feeling or emotion.

What an opportunity to increase your income!

Congratulations! I'm sure that your appointment as manager of the Pittsburgh office is something that pleases—but not surprises—all of us.

ASSIGNMENT

○ Worksheets 60, 61, and 62

UNIT 26: Comma and Semicolon

☐ THE COMMA

In Compound Sentences. When the independent clauses in a compound sentence are joined by a coordinate conjunction (*and, but, or,* or *nor*), use a comma before the conjunction unless the clauses are very short.

I received the bill *and* I paid it immediately. (Very short clauses—no comma.)

The council approved the renovation project approximately two years ago, *but* the lack of sufficient funds has resulted in little work on it up to this point.

In a Series. Unless all the items are joined by conjunctions, use a comma after all but the last item in a series of three or more items.

We will need to obtain the approval of *Mr. Delacorte* and *Ms. Powell* and *Miss Miller.* (All items in the series joined by the conjunction *and*—no commas.)

The next conference may be held in *Toronto, Winnipeg,* or *Montreal.* (Note the comma before the conjunction *or* as well as the one between *Toronto* and *Winnipeg.*)

When the series ends with *etc., and so on,* or a similar expression, use a comma before and after the expression. **NOTE:** Never use *and* with *etc.* (*etc.* is the abbreviation of *et cetera,* which means "and so forth.")

Razor blades, shaving cream, and so on, are usually kept near the checkout counter.

We usually buy *notebooks, pencils, etc.,* from a local stationery store.

Do not use a comma before an ampersand (&), which is often used to join parts of a firm name.

Jansen, Finch & Jackson will do the electrical work.

Between Coordinate Adjectives. When two or more adjectives separately modify the same noun, use a comma after each adjective except the last one unless all the adjectives are joined by conjunctions.

Their report contained a *lengthy* and *interesting* but *inaccurate* statement of the firm's financial condition.

Every service complaint deserves *immediate, careful* attention.

Mrs. Melville is looking for a *competent, dependable, personable* assistant.

To determine whether adjectives are coordinate and should be separated by commas, say them in a different order and insert *and* between them. If the result makes sense, use commas to separate the adjectives.

This box contains nothing but *blue wool* sweaters. ("Wool and blue sweaters" doesn't make sense; therefore, no comma is used.)

Passengers on the stalled train escaped to the outside by walking through a *long, dark* tunnel. ("Dark and long tunnel" makes sense; therefore, a comma is used.)

After Introductory Words. Use a comma after *accordingly, consequently, finally, however, nevertheless, otherwise, therefore, yes,* or a similar word used to introduce a sentence or an independent clause within a sentence.

Yes, two companies submitted identical bids; *however,* we think that their doing so was purely coincidental.

Otherwise, we will have no choice but to cancel our order.

Be careful not to use a comma after a word that is an essential part of the sentence. Also note that the comma is usually omitted after the introductory words *hence, thus, then,* and *still.*

However low the cost might be, we cannot afford to remodel the auditorium now. (*However* is not an introductory word; it is a modifier of the adjective *low.*)

Thus no further action will be taken during the remainder of this fiscal year.

After Introductory Phrases. Always use a comma after an introductory infinitive or participial phrase.

To increase productivity, we will need to improve our procedures as well as update our equipment and facilities. (Infinitive phrase.)

Checking meticulously, the auditors discovered several discrepancies in the company's records. (Participial phrase.)

Highly pleased with our progress, Mr. Colombo promised each of us a bonus. (Participial phrase.)

Two sites are being considered, but *to tell the truth,* neither is likely to be selected. (Note that no comma is used between the conjunction and the introductory phrase.)

Use a comma after an introductory prepositional phrase if it is long, if it includes a verbal (gerund, infinitive, or participle), or if it includes a dependent clause.

At the first exit after Trenton, turn right. (Long prepositional phrase.)

By ordering now, you can save at least $50. (Prepositional phrase including a gerund.)

In order to be successful, we must begin the campaign early. (Prepositional phrase including an infinitive.)

For more information concerning the job, please contact Mrs. Weiss. (Prepositional phrase including a participle.)

During the week you were away, Miss Norris asked to be transferred. (Prepositional phrase including a dependent clause.)

Unless omitting the comma would be likely to cause misreading, do not use a comma after a short introductory prepositional phrase.

By June 15 we should have the report ready to distribute.

On the top, soil is usually very fertile. (Comma necessary to prevent misreading.)

When a phrase is used as a subject, do not use a comma after it.

Working at top speed may cause us to make too many errors.

To qualify for a better job is the reason she gave for taking the course.

After Introductory Clauses.   Use a comma after an introductory clause at the beginning of a sentence or at the beginning of an independent clause within a compound-complex sentence.

Before you sign any contract, be sure you read and understand it.

Your representative told me that you would not increase prices again this year, but *when I received my last order,* I noticed some items had gone up nearly 10 percent. (Notice that no comma is used between the conjunction *but* and the introductory clause.)

With Parenthetic Expressions.   Use commas to set off a word, phrase, or clause that interrupts the main thought of a sentence and that is not essential to the meaning or the grammatical completeness of a sentence. As illustrated below, such an expression sometimes qualifies or amends a statement, provides additional information, or contrasts with part of a statement.

You may be sure, *however,* that the matter will be brought to Ms. Hill's attention.

Spending money to repair that truck again would be pointless, *in my opinion.*

Mr. Kovacs, *or maybe it was he and his father-in-law,* owned the Fifth Street Garage.

We think it would be better to meet in Kansas City, *as most of the participants live there.*

The company was founded in 1950, *according to the present owners.*

Ann Simmons, *not Anne Symonds,* is the one who wants to set up a consulting service.

However, do *not* use commas to set off an element that is essential to the meaning or the grammatical completeness of a sentence.

Nothing that Don has read or heard has made any change *in his opinion.*

The city *where the firm has its headquarters* is Seattle.

With Appositives.   Use commas to set off a word or a group of words that is not essential to the meaning of a preceding noun or pronoun (a *nonrestrictive appositive*).

Have you read Mr. Denton's latest book, *The Future of the Americas?* (The appositive, the title of the book, is not essential—he can have but one "latest book.")

One of my customers, *a woman in her early thirties,* bought six bottles of perfume.

If the word or group of words is essential to the meaning or clarification of the preceding noun or pronoun (a *restrictive appositive*), do not use commas to set it off.

We *mechanics* seldom run out of work. (*Mechanics* is needed to clarify who *we* are.)

Have you read the article *"Exploding Management Myths"?* (*"Exploding Management Myths"* is essential to clarify which *article.*)

With Names in Direct Address.   Use commas to set off the name of a person who is being addressed directly.

I believe, *Jim,* that it would be a good idea to discuss the problem with Miss Miller.

Thank you for the help you gave us, *Mr. and Mrs. Bermudez.*

Fay, would you be able to work overtime next weekend?

To Show Omissions.   Use a comma to show the omission of one or more words that can be easily understood from the context of the rest of a sentence.

The green cards are in the top drawer; the blue ones, in the bottom drawer.

With Repeated Expressions.   Use commas to separate words that are repeated for emphasis.

Many, many people contributed to the success of this year's campaign.

With Direct Quotations.   Use commas to set off a direct quotation—the exact words spoken or written by someone else—from the rest of a sentence.

The lawyer said, "I cannot permit my client to accept the proposed settlement."

"I cannot permit my client to accept the proposed settlement," the lawyer said.

"I cannot permit my client," the lawyer said, "to accept the proposed settlement."

With Titles, Degrees, and Seniority Terms.   Use commas to set off titles and degrees that follow the names of persons.

David M. Benitez, *M.D.,* is a member of the mayor's advisory council.

Kathleen Muldoon, *president,* issued a brief statement to the reporters.

The trend is not to use commas to set off the seniority terms *Jr.* and *Sr.* unless it is known that the owner of the name uses a comma before the term. Even if the owner uses a comma, do not use a comma after the term if it is written in possessive form. Note these examples:

P. F. Wilhelms *Jr.* is the principal stockholder of the corporation.

Martin Iannizzi, *Sr.'s* interest is less than 1 percent of the outstanding stock. (Note that Mr. Iannizzi uses a comma before the seniority term; however, no comma is used after the term because it is in possessive form.)

With *Inc.* and *Ltd.*   Do not use a comma before or after *Inc.* or *Ltd.* unless the official name of the firm is written with a comma.

McGraw-Hill, *Inc.,* has its headquarters in New York City.

Time *Inc.* is the publisher of that magazine.

In Dates.   Use a comma before and after the year when it follows the month and day. Also use a comma to separate a day of the week from the rest of a date.

The company began using its new name on *Tuesday,* January 2, *1979,* I believe.

Do not use commas to set off the year in a month-year date.

In June *1978* we sold more than a hundred sets of silverware.

In Addresses.   Always use a comma between the city and the state, but do not use a comma between the state and the ZIP Code. Within a sentence, use a comma after the name of the addressee (if included), the street name, the city name, and the state name unless it is followed by a ZIP Code.

He was in *Albuquerque, New Mexico,* all of last week.

Please send a summary of the results of the survey to *Mr. Thomas Quinn, 6440 Belmore Avenue, Dayton, Ohio 45401* as soon as possible.

Between Consecutive Numbers.   When two consecutive numbers are expressed in figures, use a comma to separate them.

In *1978, 540* full-time employees and 86 part-time employees were on the payroll.

In Numbers.   Use a comma to separate thousands, hundred thousands, millions, and so on, in numbers of four or more digits.

The voters were asked to approve a bond issue of *$8,750,000.*

Do not use commas in numbers that represent years, page numbers, house numbers, ZIP Codes, telephone numbers, serial numbers, and decimal fractions.

in 1980	1140 Main Street	842-9090	7.38575
page 1006	Rockford, IL 61108	US55535788	M4004C53678

With Weights, Measurements, Ages, and So On.   Do not use commas to separate the parts of one weight, one capacity, one age, or a similar expression.

How much does it cost to mail a package weighing *4 pounds 6 ounces.*

According to the label, this bottle contains *2 quarts 5 ounces.*

When the policy was issued, the child was exactly *8 years 4 months 11 days* old.

NOTE: When numbers are used with metric terms, use a space—not a comma—to separate thousands from hundreds, hundred thousands from thousands, and so on.

22 180 km (kilometers)	724 966 m² (square meters)	1 368 742 m³ (cubic meters)

☐ THE SEMICOLON

In Compound Sentences.   Unless the independent clauses of a compound or compound-complex sentence are joined by a coordinate conjunction (*and, but, or, or nor*), use a semicolon to separate them.

We placed the order on March 10; it did not arrive until April 28.

Don is working on the new schedule now; he said that you will receive a copy Friday.

When the independent clauses are joined by a conjunctive adverb (*accordingly, however,* or a similar word), use a semicolon before the adverb and a comma after it.

Please sign and return the memorandum of agreement before March 10; *otherwise,* we shall exercise our option of withdrawing the offer.

When the independent clauses are joined by a coordinate conjunction (*and, but, or, or nor*) and one or both of them contain internal commas, use a semicolon before the conjunction if necessary to prevent misreading. Otherwise, use a comma before the conjunction.

I invited Mary, Herman, and Henry; *and* Carol invited George, Larry, and Cleo. (The semicolon prevents misreading.)

According to Mr. Walker, the break-in occurred late Friday night, *but* it was not reported until 6:45 a.m. Saturday. (A comma is used before the conjunction because no misreading is likely.)

In a Series.   When one or more of the items in a series is punctuated with commas, use semicolons between the items; for example:

The former officers were *Timothy Baldwin, president; Wilma Maedke, vice president;* and *Pat Collins, secretary-treasurer.*

Delegates from *New Orleans, Louisiana; Fort Worth, Texas; Syracuse, New York;* and *Detroit, Michigan,* will have their headquarters in the Hotel Benson.

ASSIGNMENT

○ Worksheets 63 and 64

UNIT 27: Colon, Dash, and Parentheses

☐ THE COLON

After Introductory Expressions.   Use a colon after *these, as follows, the following,* or a similar expression that introduces a series or a list of items.

> You can mix or match your new household appliances by choosing from *these popular colors:* harvest gold, avocado green, burnt orange, and white.

> A few of the many superb stores and well-known restaurants that will gladly accept your new CHARG-IT card are *as follows:*
>
> > Ashland Furniture Company, Northgate Mall
> > Las Dos Hermanas Restaurante, 8446 South Lincoln Avenue
> > Rodgers & Ryan, 2900 West Main Street

Also use a colon after a statement that introduces a long direct quotation or a formal rule or principle.

> *In his February 10 letter, Mr. Martinelli said:* "The enclosed estimate provides a detailed listing of the building materials and supplies and the cost of each item. Please note, however, that it does not include the cost of any electrical or plumbing materials or labor."

> *Be sure to remember this principle:* Speak or write as though you were the listener or reader.

In addition, use a colon after a statement that introduces an explanation or an example. In a situation of this type, the colon generally takes the place of *that is* or *for example.*

> *Only one person can authorize such a large expenditure:* the president of the company.

> *Both researchers report a definite trend:* the number of firms diversifying their operations is increasing.

Between Hours and Minutes.   When clock time is expressed in figures, use a colon to separate hours and minutes. Note the omission of *:00* when time is expressed as an even clock hour.

> The meeting will begin at *9* a.m. and end at *4:30* p.m.

After Salutations.   Use a colon after the salutation of a business letter unless you are using "open style" punctuation for the entire letter. (See page 90.)

> Ladies and Gentlemen: Dear Dr. Guerra: Dear Ms. Wyman: Dear Mr. Loomis:

☐ THE DASH

Before Summarizing Words. Use a dash before *all, these,* or a similar word that follows and summarizes a series at the beginning of a sentence.

Tables, lamps, chairs—*these* are but a few of the hundreds of items now on sale at greatly reduced prices.

Envelopes, paper clips, file folders—*everything* you need is in the stockroom.

NOTE: A typewritten dash consists of two hyphens without space before, between, or after them.

With Parenthetic Expressions Containing Commas. For greater emphasis, use a dash instead of parentheses to set off a parenthetic expression that is punctuated internally with commas. When the expression occurs within the sentence, use a dash before and after it.

A number of sites—*for example, Knoxville, Louisville, and Biloxi*—are being considered for next fall's meeting.

The official—*a member of the city council, according to reliable sources*—allegedly accepted bribes from two construction companies during the past year.

NOTE: When the only comma appearing within a parenthetic expression is the one following *for example, that is,* or a similar introductory phrase or word, it isn't necessary to use dashes or parentheses to set off the parenthetic expression. Use commas unless you wish to emphasize it with dashes or de-emphasize it with parentheses.

One kilometer, *that is, approximately ⅝ of a mile,* is all that will need to be repaved.

In Place of Other Marks. In such situations as those illustrated below, dashes may be used in place of commas, semicolons, colons, and parentheses to give the "set off" material greater emphasis. However, it should be noted that the forcefulness, as well as the effectiveness, of dashes is greatly diminished when they are overused in a letter, memo, or other communication.

Never use a comma, a semicolon, a colon, or a period (unless it is one following an abbreviation) before an opening dash. When necessary, use a question mark or an exclamation point before a closing dash, but do not use a period unless it is one following an abbreviation. Also, do not capitalize the first word of an independent clause set off with dashes unless it is a word that is always capitalized.

The winner—you could be the lucky one!—will receive an all-expenses-paid vacation in Hawaii. (Instead of parentheses.)

Your flight is scheduled to leave O'Hare at 10 a.m.—not 9 a.m.—and arrive at 2:40 p.m. (Instead of commas.)

We have the time—we don't have the money! (Instead of a semicolon.)

There's only one word to describe your plan—brilliant! (Instead of a colon.)

The savings—if there are any—should be passed on to consumers. (Instead of commas.)

☐ PARENTHESES

With References. Use parentheses to set off references to illustrations, charts, diagrams, pages or chapters of books, and similar items.

The diagram (*Figure 5*) illustrates the operation of a thermostat.

Several companies (*see pages 46–49*) contributed $1,000 or more during the past year.

With Enumerated Items. Use parentheses to enclose numbers or letters preceding enumerated items that are not displayed on separate lines.

Please submit receipts for the following: (*a*) hotel or motel room charges; (*b*) plane or train fares; (*c*) automobile rentals; (*d*) entertainment expenses.

In Place of Commas and Dashes. To de-emphasize expressions that are not essential to the meaning or the grammatical completeness of a sentence, use parentheses instead of commas or dashes.

Everyone in Los Angeles (*the team's hometown*) turned out for the victory celebration.

The population of a number of states (*for example, Florida and California*) has grown rapidly during the past few years.

NOTE: The comments concerning the use of other punctuation marks with dashes and the capitalization of material set off by dashes also apply to parentheses. (See page 73.)

ASSIGNMENT

○ Worksheets 65, 66, and 67

UNIT 28: Quotation Marks and Underscores

☐ QUOTATION MARKS

With Direct Quotations. Use quotation marks to enclose a statement that consists of the exact words spoken or written by someone else (a *direct quotation*).

The contract states, "This agreement shall be binding upon the parties hereto, their heirs, successors, assigns, and personal representatives."

"The demand for new housing is not expected to slow down for a while," according to a construction industry spokesperson.

"Although some banks have raised their prime interest rates," replied Mrs. Newton, "we at Second City Savings have no plans to increase ours at this time."

"This year's drive was a tremendous success," reported Mr. Torrance. "Our goal was to collect $50,000, and we received nearly $65,000 in contributions!"

In typewritten material, a long quotation—one consisting of three or more typed lines—is usually indented 5 spaces from the left and right margins, single-spaced, and *not* enclosed in quotation marks.

The third paragraph of the report was changed to read as follows:

While sales volume increased significantly during each of the past two decades, profits after taxes remained at a fairly steady 8 to 10 percent. Thus investors in this particular firm have not fared nearly so well as those in others.

With Titles. Use quotation marks to enclose titles of articles, essays, short poems, lectures, reports, and chapters of books; for example:

Joyce Kilmer's "Trees" is a very familiar poem.

Have you read the article "Information Processing in the Modern Office"?

With Terms and Expressions. Use quotation marks to enclose words that are unusual or special in a technical or trade sense; words introduced by such expressions as *marked, labeled, so-called,* and *signed;* slang or poor grammar that is used purposely; words used humorously or ironically; formal definitions of words; and translations of foreign words and expressions.

Professional typesetters try to avoid "widows." (Printing and publishing term.)

The package was marked "Fragile," but it looks as though someone didn't think it really was. (Word preceded by introductory expression *marked.*)

We soon learned that "there ain't no such thing as a free lunch." (Poor grammar.)

For Quotations Within Quotations. Use single quotation marks (apostrophes) to enclose a quotation within a quotation.

Florence said, "I'll be happy to recite 'Mending Wall' anytime you want to hear it."

With Well-Known Proverbs and Sayings. Do not use quotation marks to enclose well-known proverbs and sayings.

It has been said that an ounce of prevention is worth a pound of cure.

Does anyone really believe that an apple a day will keep the doctor away?

With Indirect Quotations. If a statement does not consist of the exact words spoken or written by someone else, do not enclose it in quotation marks. In many instances, such an indirect quotation is introduced by *that.*

Annabel said that *she would be happy to make all the necessary arrangements.*

I doubt that Harry told anyone *he wouldn't take the job if it were offered to him.*

With Other Punctuation Marks. Always place a comma or a period inside the closing quotation mark; always place a semicolon or a colon outside the closing quotation mark.

"I recommend," Donna said, "that the offer be withdrawn."

Please store the attached papers in the folder labeled "Promotion"; then give it to Ella.

None of these should be marked "Confidential": requisitions, invoices, and purchase orders.

Place a question mark or an exclamation point inside the closing quotation mark only when it applies to the quoted material.

"I'll quit!" she exclaimed.

The interviewer asked, "Why do you want to work for our company?"

Did he say, "Let's forget the whole thing"?

His favorite expression seems to be "Nope"!

☐ UNDERSCORES

With Titles. Underscore the titles of books, magazines, newspapers, pamphlets, long poems, movies, plays, and other literary and artistic works. Such titles are usually set in italics, not underscored, in printed material.

Is our subscription to <u>Time</u> running out?

I wonder whether we have the latest edition of the <u>Standard Handbook for Secretaries</u>.

(**NOTE:** Do not capitalize and underscore *the* unless it is part of the official title.)

With Words. Underscore words referred to as words, words accompanied by definitions, and foreign expressions accompanied by English translations. Such words and expressions are usually set in italics, not underscored, in printed material.

The word notorious certainly isn't synonymous with famous.

The Spanish term amarillo means "yellow" in English.

ASSIGNMENT

○ Worksheets 68 and 69

UNIT 29: Capitalization

☐ FIRST WORDS

Of Sentences. Always capitalize the first word of a sentence or a condensed statement (a group of words used as a sentence).

Gossiping is frequently a means of conveying misinformation. (Sentence.)

Next, the matter of discounts. (Condensed statement.)

Of Direct Quotations. Always capitalize the first word of a direct quotation that is a complete sentence.

The defendant said, "Someone's not telling the truth—and it isn't I."

"If these figures are correct," the director of marketing said, "we should exceed our sales budget by about 8 percent."

Of Displayed Items. Capitalize the first word of each item displayed in a list or an outline.

Please be sure to include these items when you place the next order:
1. Interoffice memo forms
2. Typewriter ribbons
3. Plain bond paper
4. Pencils and pens

Of Statements Following Colons. Do not capitalize the first word of a statement following a colon unless it is a statement that expresses a complete thought (an independent clause). Then, capitalize such a statement only if it is a formal rule or principle, a direct quotation, or a statement introduced by a single word.

The rule is this: Always spell out a number at the beginning of a sentence.

Miss Fong made this observation: "Most employers are complying with these new government regulations."

Note: The information in this report is not to be released to the press.

Of Complimentary Closings. Always capitalize the first word of a complimentary closing.

Sincerely yours,   Cordially yours,   Very sincerely yours,   Sincerely,

☐ TITLES OF PERSONS

Before Names.   Always capitalize a title that precedes the name of a person unless the name is in apposition to the title.

> The proposed reorganization has the approval of *Vice President* H. J. Lee.
>
> We spoke with a *vice president,* J. P. Wharton, about the committee's goals.

After Names.   Except in an address on an envelope or other item, do not capitalize a title that follows the name of a person unless it is the title of a high government official.

> Ms. Laura Lucas, *president* of Bowman Bros., addressed the conference.
>
> John Lawman, *Chief Justice of the United States,* wrote a dissenting opinion.

With *Ex-*, *-Elect*, *Former,* and *Late*.   Never capitalize *ex-*, *-elect*, *former*, or *late* when used with a title.

> This issue contains articles by *ex-Mayor* Alberts and *Senator-elect* Rissner.
>
> Lyndon B. Johnson, *late President* of the United States, lived in Texas.

In Direct Address.   Capitalize any title other than *miss* or *sir* that is used by itself in direct address.

> This policy provides all the protection your family needs, *sir.*
>
> We sincerely appreciate your assistance, *Doctor.*

As Substitutes for Names.   Unless it is used in place of the name of a high-ranking national or state government official, foreign dignitary, or international figure, do not capitalize a title that is used as a substitute for a specific personal name.

> The *President* spoke from the Oval Office of the White House. (Government official.)
>
> The *president* told the stockholders of plans to develop new products. (Company official.)

☐ TITLES OF BOOKS, PAINTINGS, AND SO ON

The two-part rule for capitalizing the titles of books, magazines, newspapers, articles, reports, movies, radio and television programs, songs, plays, paintings, and other literary and artistic works is as follows:

First, always capitalize the first word, the last word, and the first word following a colon or a dash.

Second, capitalize all other words except articles, conjunctions, and prepositions of three or fewer letters.

> Have you seen the movie *A Man for All Seasons* or read the book *For Whom the Bells Toll?*
>
> Did the article "Women in Business—A New Look" appear in *The Wall Street Journal?*

☐ DATES AND HISTORICAL EVENTS

Capitalize the names of the days of the week, months, holidays, and historical events and periods. Do not capitalize the names of seasons or of decades and centuries. **EXCEPTION:** Capitalize decades in such expressions as "the Gay Nineties" and "the Roaring Twenties."

> The first *Monday* in *September* is *Labor Day,* the last of the *summer* holidays.
>
> Didn't the *Industrial Revolution* begin during the *nineteenth century?*

☐ BRAND AND TRADE NAMES

Capitalize all brand and trade names of products except those now used as common nouns. When in doubt, consult a dictionary to determine whether a particular name can be correctly used as a common noun or adjective.

IBM typewriters   Lux soap   Ford trucks   pullman cars   india ink

☐ POINTS OF THE COMPASS

Capitalize *north, south, east, northwest,* and other points of the compass when they are used to designate specific geographic regions, but do not capitalize them when they are used to indicate direction (except in addresses).

The company has a chain of motels operating throughout the *South.*

Our new warehouse is a few miles *southeast* of Indianapolis.

Is your office on *West* Tenth Street?

Also capitalize words derived from points of the compass when they are used to designate people.

The advisory board includes *Northerners, Southerners, Easterners,* and *Westerners.*

☐ SALUTATIONS

Capitalize only the first word, the title, and the name of the person in a salutation; for example:

Dear Dr. Dillon: My dear Mrs. Simms: Dear Juan: Dear Professor Crane:

☐ PLACE NAMES

Capitalize the official and the imaginative names of cities, states, rivers, parks, streets, buildings, and so on.

Chicago, the Windy City   Empire State Building   Mississippi River
Ohio, the Buckeye State   Fifth Avenue   Lincoln Monument

Capitalize *city* only when it is part of the official name of a city; capitalize *state* only when it follows the name of a state.

Oklahoma City   city of Los Angeles   Michigan State   state of Washington
The *city* owns and operates those buses.
Does the *state* actively encourage tourism?

☐ ORGANIZATION NAMES

Capitalize the official names of schools, churches, synagogues, companies, associations, clubs, governmental bodies, and other organizations. Do not capitalize *the* unless it is the first word of the official name. Also, do not capitalize articles, conjunctions, and short prepositions within names.

Washington Carver High School   The Ohio State University
American Federation of Teachers   American Medical Association
House of Representatives   National Broadcasting Company
McGraw-Hill Book Company   First National Bank and Trust Company

Ordinarily, do not capitalize such terms as *company, college, department,* and so on, when they are used alone in place of complete official names. Similarly, do not capitalize *federal* and *government* when they stand alone.

Several executives of the *company* commented about the new regulations issued by the *government.*

Is anything being done at the *federal* or the state level?

☐ WORDS DERIVED FROM PROPER NOUNS

Always capitalize a word derived from a proper noun unless the dictionary or some other authoritative reference (a style manual for writers or an English-usage handbook, for example) indicates otherwise.

Atlantic	Venice	Rome	Pasteur	Italy	Greece
transatlantic	venetian blinds	roman numeral	pasteurized	Italian	Greek

ASSIGNMENT

○ Worksheets 70 and 71

UNIT 30: Abbreviations

☐ PERSONAL NAMES

With the exception of *Saint,* which is usually abbreviated (*St.*) when it is part of a last name, do not abbreviate the name of a person. (Initials, which are written with periods, are not abbreviations.)

George Houston (**NOT:** *Geo.* Houston)   William F. Brinkley (**NOT:** *Wm.* F. Brinkley)

☐ PERSONAL TITLES AND RELATED TERMS

Before Names.   Whether they appear with complete names or with last names only, abbreviate these titles: *Mr., Mrs., Ms.,* and *Dr.*

Mr. Thomas Leland	Mrs. Cleo Sheahan	Ms. Rachel Swartz	Dr. M. J. Paley
Mr. Wong	Mrs. Hendrickson	Ms. Montgomery	Dr. Rasmussen

Write other titles in full when they are used with last names only; abbreviate them when they are used with complete names.

Reverend Sloane	Governor Jenkins	Colonel Helms	Professor Innis
Rev. Edythe Evans	Gov. G. M. Jenkins	Col. H. R. Ash	Prof. Roy Lewis

After Names.   The following are always written in abbreviated form after names: *Esq., Jr., Sr., Ph.D.* and other degrees, and *S.J.* and other names of religious orders.

Julia Hanson, M.D.   P. A. Day, Jr.   Arlene Davis, Ph.D.   Rev. B. J. McBride, S.J.

When writing an abbreviation of an academic degree other than *CPA,* use a period after each part of the abbreviation but do not leave a space between the parts: *B.S., M.A., Ed.D., LL.B., B.Ch.E.,* and so on.

☐ NAMES OF COMPANIES AND OTHER ORGANIZATIONS

Part of a Name. If a company or other organization abbreviates one or more parts of its name, follow the style used by the company or organization itself. If you are uncertain as to whether or not an abbreviation may be used, check the name as it appears in the organization's letterhead or invoice heading, or in some other printed form. Many—but not all—organizations use such abbreviations as these:

Bros. (Brothers) Co. (Company) Corp. (Corporation) Inc. (Incorporated) Ltd. (Limited)

Entire Name. The names of many well-known business firms, labor unions, professional associations, government agencies, and so on, are commonly abbreviated in all but the most formal business writing. Abbreviations of these names, like radio and television station call letters (which are not abbreviations), are written without periods or spaces when they consist of all-capital letters.

NBC (National Broadcasting Company)   AFT (American Federation of Teachers)
ICC (Interstate Commerce Commission)   RCA (Radio Corporation of America)
AMA (American Medical Association)   WCBS (Radio station call letters)

☐ NAMES OF PLACES

Countries. In the names of government agencies, *United States* is usually abbreviated *U.S.;* however, names of countries should not be abbreviated when they appear by themselves in sentences. In addresses, lists, and so on, such abbreviations as *U.S.A.* and *U.S.S.R.* are commonly used.

This report is issued quarterly by the *U.S.* Department of Labor.

They are naturalized citizens of the *United States.* (**NOT:** U.S.)

States. When used within sentences, the names of states should be written in full, not abbreviated. In addresses, tables, and so on, state names are usually abbreviated—often through the use of the two-letter abbreviations devised by the U.S. Postal Service; for example, *AZ* (Arizona) and *MN* (Minnesota).

They recently bought a home in Raleigh, North Carolina. (**NOT:** *NC* or *N. Car.*)

Karen's home address is as follows: 210 East Fourth Street, Fort Worth, Texas 76102. (**NOT:** *TX* or *Tex.*)

Cities. Never abbreviate the name of a city. When used as part of a city name, *Saint* is abbreviated, however: *St. Louis* and *St. Paul.*

Philadelphia (**NOT:** *Phila.*)   Fort Collins (**NOT:** *Ft.* Collins)

☐ MISCELLANEOUS TERMS

Compass Points. Do not abbreviate *south, east, northwest,* or a similar term unless it is used after a street name to designate a section of a city.

8864 *South* 63 Street, *N.E.,* Washington, DC 20019

A.D. and B.C. When used with an important historical date, the abbreviation *A.D.* (representing *anno Domini* and meaning "in the year of our Lord") is written before the year: *A.D. 1776.* The abbreviation *B.C.* ("before Christ") is written after the year: *2000 B.C.*

A.M., P.M., CST, and Similar Terms. Write *a.m.* (the abbreviation of *ante meridiem,* meaning "before noon") and *p.m.* (the abbreviation of *post meridiem,* meaning "after noon") in small letters with periods and no space between the letters. Always use figures—but never the term *o'clock*—with these abbreviations.

We started at *11 a.m.* and finished at *2:45 p.m.* (NOT: *11 a.m. o'clock* or *11 a.m. this morning;* NOT: *2:45 p.m. o'clock* or *2:45 p.m. the following afternoon.*)

Do not abbreviate *noon* or *midnight.* Use either the word alone or write *12 noon* or *12 midnight.*

In sentences and elsewhere abbreviate terms designating time zones when they appear with expressions of clock time. Write the abbreviations in all-capital letters without periods or spaces.

The airlift began at *11 a.m. (CST).*

Illinois, Michigan, and surrounding states are in the *Central Standard Time Zone.*

Weights and Measurements. Do not abbreviate terms pertaining to weight and measurement except when they are used with figures in technical writing, lists, etc.

We bought 4 *gallons* of paint, 2 *pounds* of caulking compound, and 9 *square feet* of screen wire.

What is the equivalent of 100 *kilometers* in miles?

EXCEPTIONS: Such terms as those listed below are often abbreviated:

millimeter, as in *35-mm film*   *Celsius,* as in *48°C*   *Fahrenheit,* as in *88°F*

Days and Months. Except when necessary to save space in tables and lists, do not abbreviate the names of days of the week or of months.

The store will be open *Tuesday* and *Thursday* evenings throughout *August* and *September.*

IOU and SOS. Neither *IOU* nor *SOS* is an abbreviation. Write the expressions in capital letters without periods or spaces.

Business Terms. Such commonly used business terms as those listed below are frequently abbreviated, especially in lists, invoices, memos, and reports.

c.o.d. *or* COD (cash on delivery)   P.O. (post office)
f.o.b. *or* FOB (free on board)   e.o.m. *or* EOM (end of month)
PR (public relations)   R&D (research and development)

ASSIGNMENT

○ Worksheets 72 and 73

UNIT **31:** Numbers

□ GENERAL RULES

Numbers Beginning Sentences. Spell out a number that begins a sentence.

Six floors of this building have been rented to a Japanese firm.

Fourteen hundred municipal workers will be affected by these budget cutbacks.

Numbers 1 Through 10. Write the numbers *1* through *10* in words; use figures for numbers over *10*. **NOTE:** Use figures for numbers referred to as numbers, as in the preceding sentence and in the heading of this rule.

> We have received only *nine* or *ten* responses so far.
>
> At least *150* people were waiting to enter the store when it opened this morning.
>
> I'm not sure whether this is a *1* or a *7*, are you?

Related Numbers. Express related numbers in the same way. If some should be written in words and others in figures, write all of them in figures.

> *Eight* of the *twenty-five* offices on this floor are occupied by attorneys. (**NOT:** *Eight* of the *25* offices on this floor are occupied by attorneys.)
>
> We plan to hire *14* secretaries, *2* typists, and *6* clerk-typists to work in those *two* departments. (The number of departments is not related to the other numbers.)

Consecutive Numbers. When two numbers occur together, write one number in words and the other in figures. Ordinarily, spell out the number that will make the shorter word.

> You can get *four* 2-liter containers of soda for the price of *three* during this sale. (**OR:** You can get *4* two-liter containers of soda for the price of *3* during this sale.)
>
> Several contractors bid on the construction of the *16 twenty*-story apartment buildings.

Fractions. When a fraction stands alone, write it in words. Use a hyphen between the numerator and the denominator unless either or both of those parts of the fraction must be written with a hyphen.

> The measure must be approved by a *two-thirds* majority.
>
> If exposed to heat, this bolt will expand at least *twelve thirty-seconds* of an inch. (The denominator, *thirty-seconds*, must be written with a hyphen; thus there is no hyphen between the numerator and the denominator of this fraction.)

Also, do not use a hyphen between the parts of a fraction when it is used in the manner illustrated by the following sentence.

> *One half* of the room was painted white; the *other half,* blue.

Mixed Numbers. Write a *mixed number* (a whole number plus a fraction) in figures.

> The Greenlees sold their farm for nearly *4½* times the amount they paid for it.

Indefinite Numbers. Always write indefinite numbers in words, not in figures or in a mixture of figures and words.

> This ad should draw *hundreds* of inquiries. (**NOT:** *100s.*)
>
> I think *several thousand* copies of the brochure have been mailed. (**NOT:** *several 1,000* or *several 1000.*)

☐ SPECIAL RULES

Dates. When the day follows the month, write the day in figures without the ordinal ending *st, d* (*nd* or *rd*), or *th*.

> Your salary increase is retroactive to *July 1.*
>
> Mr. Rivera has been our corporation counsel since February 1, 1980.

When the day precedes the month or stands alone, write it in figures with an ordinal ending or in words.

Was Miss Richards in Jacksonville on the *24th of August?* (OR: *twenty-fourth.*)

Do you think we can complete this project by the *8th?* (OR: *eighth.*)

Unless you are referring to a class graduation year or a well-known year in history, don't use an apostrophe and two figures to represent the year.

When people talk about the *blizzard of '88,* they obviously mean *1888.*

The plaque was donated by the *class of '79.*

Time of Day.   Always use figures with the abbreviations *a.m.* and *p.m.* For time on the hour, omit *:00* except in a tabulation where other times are given in hours and minutes.

You may pick up your tickets between *10 a.m.* and *5:30 p.m.* next Friday.

Use either figures or words—but never *a.m.* or *p.m.*—with *o'clock.*

We should plan to meet around *2 o'clock* this afternoon. (OR: *two o'clock.*)

Centuries and Decades.   Any of the styles illustrated below may be used for centuries and decades.

Everyone is supposed to wear a costume representative of the *1800s.* (OR: *eighteen hundreds* or *nineteenth century.*)

Some of the women thought it would be more fun to dress like the flappers of the *'20s.* (OR: the *twenties,* the *1920s,* or the *nineteen-twenties.*)

Except in such expressions as "the Roaring Twenties" and "the Gay Nineties," do not capitalize the names of decades.

Addresses.   Use figures for all numbers in addresses except the numbered street names *One* through *Ten* and the house number *One.* Do not use the abbreviation *No.* or the symbol # in an address.

The real estate agent tried to rent us an apartment at *One Fifth Avenue.*

In case you would like to write to Ms. Kowolski, her address is as follows:
8800 East 98 Street, Apt. 404
St. Paul, MN 55104

Unless a word such as *East* or *North* separates the house number and the street-name number, use an ordinal ending with the street name: *2430 11th Avenue, 134 21st Street,* and *20 102d Circle.*

Money.   Use figures and the word *cents* for an amount under a dollar and figures with the $ sign for an amount of a dollar or more. Omit *.00* with even dollar amounts except in a tabulation where some amounts are in cents only or in dollars and cents.

Six dollars is the price of each ticket. (Number beginning a sentence.)

The balance of *$400* may be paid in monthly installments of *$66.40.*

This hotel bill shows a miscellaneous charge of *75 cents.*

When an amount under a dollar is related to other amounts of a dollar or more, though, follow the style illustrated below.

How long has it been since eggs cost *$.45* a dozen or milk cost *$1.10* a gallon?

Ages.   Spell out an age given in years only, unless it is used as a significant statistic in a news release, a résumé, or a letter pertaining to employment.

Sharon's youngest son will be *twelve years* old next week. (The age is not a significant statistic in this sentence.)

E. J. Ruskin, *28,* has been appointed vice president of Ruskin & Ruskin, Inc. (Age included in a news release.)

For an age in any combination of years, months, and days, use figures.

When I began working here, I was exactly *24 years 8 months 12 days* old.

Percentages.   Express a percentage in figures with the word *percent.*

Approximately *80 percent* of the work has been completed.

You were fortunate to obtain a mortgage at *9.5 percent* interest.

The difference was less than *0.6 percent.* (**NOTE:** For clarity, use a *0* before the decimal point when the percentage is less than 1 percent.)

The symbol % should be used only in technical material and in tabulations. When used, it must be repeated with each percentage: *6%, 7.5%,* and *8.2%.*

Time Related to Payment Terms.   Use figures for periods of time related to discount terms, loans, and similar terms.

You will receive a discount of 2 percent if you pay within *10 days.*

The full amount of the loan must be repaid within *6 months.*

If we do not receive payment within the next *30 days,* we will turn the account over to our attorneys for collection.

Size, Serial, and Similar Numbers.   Use figures for size, serial, part, model, style, and similar numbers. Capitalize *serial, model,* and so on, and—when used—the abbreviation *No.* before such a number.

Would *Model 40* be an acceptable substitute?

The enclosed check is in payment of *Invoice 4024.*

Measurements.   Use figures for weights, dimensions, and other measurements that have a technical significance.

This package weighs *2.2 kilograms.*

According to the label, this bottle contains *1 quart 4 ounces.*

The living room measures *4 by 6.3 meters.*

ASSIGNMENT

○ Worksheets 74, 75, 76, and 77

PART FOUR

Business Letters, Memos, and Reports

The ability to write letters, memos, reports, and other types of messages that produce the desired results is a skill that every employer seeks – and usually recognizes and rewards quickly and generously! In business, industry, and government, almost everything of any significant importance that takes place involves at least some written communication. Thus, regardless of the job title you hold, you are almost certain to have numerous opportunities to apply the techniques and principles of business writing that are presented in Units 32 through 45.

UNIT 32: Letter Parts and Placement

The four major sections of a business letter are the *heading, opening, body,* and *closing.* In the following discussion, the required and optional parts in each section are presented in the order in which they normally appear.

☐ THE HEADING

In almost all business letters, the heading consists of a printed *letterhead* and a typewritten *date line.* For a personal-business letter, such as a letter of application for a job, the heading generally consists of a typewritten *return address* and a *date line.*

Letterhead. Almost every company uses stationery with a printed letterhead that includes the firm's name, address, and telephone number. Sometimes the letterhead contains the addresses of branch offices, the company's slogan, and other information that will be useful not only to the reader in responding to the message but also to the firm in creating a favorable impression.

Date Line. The date line consists of the month, day, and year—with the month written in full, not abbreviated or represented by figures. Both of the following styles are acceptable, but most writers prefer the "business style."

BUSINESS STYLE: December 12, 198–   **MILITARY STYLE:** 12 December 198–

If you are using standard-size stationery (8½ by 11 inches) or A4 stationery (210 by 297 millimeters—about 8¼ by 11¾ inches), type the date on line 15 or on the third line below the letterhead, whichever is lower on the page.

Return Address or Typewritten Letterhead. If you are writing a job-application or other personal-business letter, use plain paper and include a single-spaced return address. Arrange the city, state, and ZIP Code as the last line, and position the date immediately below it on line 15.

For a business letter on plain paper, include a typewritten letterhead. Starting at a point that will permit you to type the date on line 15, arrange the information in three or four horizontally centered lines.

TYPEWRITTEN LETTERHEAD:

STERLING PRODUCTS COMPANY
9900 Richards Avenue
Norwalk, Connecticut 08657
(203) 555–1234

February 16, 198–

RETURN ADDRESS:

Apartment 22-J
9408 Casco Street
Freeport, ME 04033
March 10, 198–

☐ THE OPENING

The opening section normally consists of an *inside address* and a *salutation*. However, it sometimes includes a *personal* or *confidential notation* and an *attention line*.

Personal or Confidential Notation. If the message is of a personal or confidential nature, type *Personal* or *Confidential* in all-capital letters or in underscored capital and small letters on the second line below the date—starting at the left margin.

Inside Address. The inside address, which consists of the name and address of the person or company to whom you are writing, usually begins on the fifth line below the date line, at the left margin.

Mr. Bernard J. Nance
Director of Marketing
Wharton Industries, Inc.
2480 North Second Street
Bethesda, Maryland 20014

Dana Corporation
3636 Linden Avenue
Stamford, CT 06904

Ms. Lucy Hall, President
Hall & Larson, Inc.
6666 Overlea Boulevard
Toronto M6H IA4
CANADA

If the address includes a title of position, type it either on the same line as the person's name or on a separate line—whichever results in better balance.

When writing to a person, use either a courtesy title (*Miss, Mrs., Ms.,* or *Mr.*) or a professional title (*Dr.* or *Prof.,* for example), not both, with the name.

INCORRECT: Mr. Anthony Petkus, M.D.   CORRECT: Anthony Petkus, M.D.
Dr. Anthony Petkus, M.D.   Dr. Anthony Petkus

Attention Line. When writing to a company, you may direct your letter to a specific person (by name or by title) or department by typing an attention line on the second line below the inside address. Instead of using an attention line, many writers now include the appropriate information in the inside address.

ATTENTION: Sales Manager   Attention of the Sales Manager
ATTENTION: MISS WILMA STONE   Attention Personnel Department

86

Salutation. On the second line below the inside address or, if used, the attention line, type an appropriate salutation. Do *not* consider an attention line, if used, when deciding what salutation to use. If you are writing to a person, the salutation you select will depend upon the relationship between you and the addressee and the general circumstances under which you are writing.

LETTER TO COMPANY:	Ladies and Gentlemen:
	Gentlemen: (*If firm is composed of men only.*)
	Ladies: (*If firm is composed of women only.*)
LETTER TO PERSON:	Dear Pat: Dear Mr. Fong: Dear Ms. Kearn: Sir:
	Dear Madam or Sir: Dear Sir: Dear Madam: Madam:

☐ THE BODY

The basic part of the body of a business letter is the *message,* or text. This section sometimes includes a *subject line.*

Subject Line. If you wish to give the reader advance notice of what the letter is about, type a subject line on the second line below the salutation. Note that the word *subject* may be omitted. Especially in law firms, the Latin term *In Re* or *Re* is often used in place of *Subject.*

SUBJECT: Account No. 577-17-176   CHANGES IN DISCOUNT POLICY
SUBJECT: PRICE CHANGES   Subject: Selection of Factory Site

Message. The message, or text, of the letter begins on the second line below the salutation or, if used, the subject line. If at all possible, arrange the message in at least two paragraphs and use single spacing, with one blank line between paragraphs. If the message is very short, use double spacing for *all* parts of the letter and remember to indent the first line of each paragraph 5 or 10 spaces.

When the letter is too long to fit on one page, continue the message on a second sheet of plain paper of the same quality and color as the letterhead sheet. On the seventh line from the top of the second and each subsequent continuation page, if any, type the name of the addressee, the page number, and the date in one of these *continuation-page heading* arrangements:

Dr. J. R. Bennett   2   July 15, 198–

Mrs. Maureen Hanley
Page 2
September 20, 198–

Three or four lines below the heading, resume typing the message. If it is necessary to divide a paragraph, leave at least two lines on the preceding page and carry at least two lines to the continuation page. For a paragraph of three or fewer lines, carry over the whole paragraph. Never divide the last word on a page or the last word in a paragraph.

☐ THE CLOSING

The closing section typically consists of the *complimentary closing,* the *writer's identification,* and *reference initials.* It may include an *enclosure notation,* a *cc notation,* a *mailing notation,* a *postscript,* and other notations.

Complimentary Closing. On the second line below the message, type a complimentary closing that is appropriate to the general tone of the message; for example:

Sincerely yours,	Yours very sincerely,	Sincerely,	Respectfully yours,
Cordially yours,	Very cordially yours,	Cordially,	Yours very truly,

Company Signature. Many writers consider a company signature superfluous, especially when it appears in a letter written on letterhead stationery. If used, the name of the company should be typed in all-capital letters on the second line below the complimentary closing.

Sincerely yours,	Yours very truly,	Very sincerely yours,
BULLARD'S, INC.	CLARKE BROS.	WEBBER PRODUCTS COMPANY

Writer's Identification. The writer's identification usually consists of the name and title of the writer; however, it sometimes includes the name of a department or division of the company. This information usually appears on the fourth line below the complimentary closing or, if used, the company signature. If the writer is a woman who prefers a particular courtesy title, she should include that title with her typed name or (in parentheses) with her signature.

Cordially yours,	Sincerely yours,	Yours very truly,
David O'Dwyer	D. L. Hale, Manager	Ms. Evelyn M. Torres
General Manager	Accounting Department	Senior Vice President

Reference Initials. The reference initials, which are usually typed on the second line below the writer's identification, may consist of the writer's and the typist's initials, the typist's initials only, or the full name of the writer (if it does not appear in the writer's identification) and the typist's initials.

URS:TYP	URS/TYP	URS:typ	URS/typ	typ	U. R. Reiter:typ

Do not use reference initials for a letter you write and type for yourself.

Enclosure Notation. If a check, contract, or other item is to be enclosed with the letter, type an enclosure notation on the line below the reference initials.

URS:TYP	typ	URS/TYP	typ	URS:typ	
Enclosure	Enc.	Enclosures (2)	Enc. 2	Enclosures:	Check
					Contract

Carbon Copy (cc) Notation. If you wish the addressee to know that you are sending a copy of the letter to someone else, type a *cc* notation on the line below the reference initials or, if used, the enclosure notation.

cc: Miss Thelma Ashford	cc Dr. Barker	CC Mrs. Swanson
		Mr. Gorbea

Blind Carbon Copy (bcc) Notation. If you do not wish the addressee to know that you are sending a copy of the letter to someone else, use a *bcc* notation. Obviously, this notation is never used on the original copy of the letter; it appears in the upper left-hand corner of the carbon copies (or photocopies) only.

bcc: Ms. Mary Kohn	bcc Mr. Peterson	BCC: Prof. Edwin F. Booth

Mailing Notation. If the letter is to be sent special delivery or by certified mail, registered mail, messenger, or a similar means, type an appropriate mailing notation on the line below the *cc* notation (or whatever notation you used last). An acceptable alternative is to type the mailing notation on the second line below the date, starting at the same point as the date.

SJH:emj	cc: Mr. Conti	January 28, 198–
REGISTERED MAIL	SPECIAL DELIVERY	CERTIFIED MAIL

Postscript (PS).   If an addition is made to the message of the letter, type a postscript starting on the second line below the mailing notation (or whatever notation you used last). If two additions are made, use *PS:* or *PS.* for the first one and *PPS:* or *PPS.* for the second one. If you indent the paragraphs in the message, indent the first line of the postscript; otherwise, begin it at the left margin. **SUGGESTION:** Reserve the use of postscripts for information that you wish to highlight, not to overcome faulty planning of the content of the message itself.

PS: Remember—this special introductory rate expires April 1!

PS.   Effective February 1, our address will be 810 Broadway—no change in ZIP Code.

☐ LETTER PLACEMENT

In the preceding discussion, the vertical placement and the internal spacing of letter parts were indicated. By following those guides and the margin-setting instructions that follow, you should have no difficulty in appropriately and attractively positioning the letters that you write on standard-size stationery, which measures 8½ by 11 inches, or on A4 stationery, which measures 210 by 297 millimeters (approximately 8¼ by 11¾ inches).

Side Margins.   Estimate the number of words in the message of the letter. Then determine the length of writing line that should be used, as indicated in the following table. Whatever writing-line length is used, center it horizontally on the paper. If you are using standard-size stationery and the horizontal center of the paper is at 50 on the scale of your typewriter, the margins will be those indicated in the chart (to make it unnecessary to use the margin-release key frequently, add 5 spaces to the desired ending point for the right margin, as is done below).

WORDS IN BODY	LENGTH OF WRITING LINE		MARGIN SETTINGS	
Up to 100	PICA:	40 spaces	PICA:	30 and 75
	ELITE:	50 spaces (*rounded off*)	ELITE:	25 and 80
100–200	PICA:	50 spaces	PICA:	25 and 80
	ELITE:	60 spaces	ELITE:	20 and 85
Over 200	PICA:	60 spaces	PICA:	20 and 85
	ELITE:	70 spaces (*rounded off*)	ELITE:	15 and 90

Top Margin.   The depth of the letterhead, of course, determines the top margin of the first page. On each continuation page, leave a top margin of six blank lines (resume typing on the seventh line).

Bottom Margin.   The bottom margin of every page but the last should be from six to nine blank lines. The last page may have a much deeper margin.

ASSIGNMENT

○ Worksheets 78 and 79

UNIT 33: Letter Styles and Stationery

☐ ARRANGEMENT STYLES

The parts of a business letter may be arranged in a number of styles or formats, the most frequently used of which are briefly discussed below.

Full-Blocked Style. In the *full-blocked style,* all parts of the letter begin at the left margin. This style is also known as the "extreme block" style.

Blocked Style. The *blocked style* is also widely known as the "modified block style with blocked paragraphs." In this arrangement the date line, complimentary closing, and writer's identification usually begin at the horizontal center of the page; however, the date line is sometimes positioned to end at or near the right margin. All other parts begin at the left margin. (See the letter on page 98.)

Semiblocked Style. The *semiblocked style* is very similar to the blocked style, except that the first line of each paragraph is indented 5 (sometimes 10) spaces from the left margin. This arrangement is also known as the "modified block style with indented paragraphs." (See the letter on page 116.)

Simplified Style. The *simplified style* was originated by the Administrative Management Society. This arrangement is very similar to the full-blocked style—but it has these distinctive features:

1. It never includes a salutation or a complimentary closing.

2. It always includes a subject line—without the word *subject.* The subject is always typed in all-capital letters, with two blank lines above and below it, between the inside address and the message.

3. It always includes the writer's name in the writer's identification, which is typed in all-capital letters and is always preceded by four blank lines and followed by one blank line.

☐ PUNCTUATION STYLES

Only two punctuation styles are widely used today: the *open* and the *standard* (or "mixed") styles.

Open Style. In the open punctuation style, no punctuation mark appears at the end of any line above or below the message section unless the last word in the line is abbreviated.

Standard Style. In the standard, or "mixed," punctuation style, a colon follows the salutation and a comma follows the complimentary closing.

☐ ADDRESSING ENVELOPES

In addressing an envelope for a letter that you write, follow these steps:

1. If the envelope does not have a printed return address, type your name and address in the upper left corner. Start on the third line from the top and about five spaces from the left edge; use single spacing.

2. If an attention line or personal or confidential notation is necessary, type it on the ninth line from the top of the envelope or at least two lines below the return address, about five spaces from the left edge.

3. If a mailing notation is necessary, position it to end about five spaces from the right edge, on the same line as the attention line or other notation.

4. Slightly more than halfway down and slightly less than halfway across the envelope, type the name and address of the addressee. Always use single spacing and block the address. Note that the last line of the address should always consist of the city, state, and ZIP Code. The state name may be written in full (*Michigan*), abbreviated in the traditional manner (*Mich.*), or abbreviated in the style developed by the U.S. Postal Service (*MI*).

☐ STATIONERY

Letterhead.   Almost every business office, government organization, and professional person uses high-quality stationery with a professionally designed and printed letterhead. Although tinted paper is not uncommon, white stationery is by far the most popular in business offices. While a wide variety of sizes is available, the standard size (8½ by 11 inches) is the most commonly used for general business correspondence.

Some executives use *monarch* (7¼ by 10½ inches) stationery. *Baronial* stationery (5½ by 8½ inches) is also fairly popular among executives and other writers, especially for short letters.

Officials and employees of government offices and agencies frequently use *official* stationery, which measures 8 by 10½ inches.

The metric sizes of stationery are the A4 and the A5. The A4 measures 210 by 297 millimeters (approximately 8¼ by 11¾ inches); it is the nearest metric equivalent of standard stationery. The A5 measures 148 by 210 millimeters (approximately 5⅞ by 8¼ inches); it is the nearest metric equivalent of baronial stationery. There are no metric equivalents for monarch and official stationery.

Remember that a letterhead sheet should never be used for a continuation page. If a letter is too long to fit on one page, use a plain sheet of paper that matches the letterhead sheet in color, size, and quality for the second and each succeeding page.

Envelopes.   Of the seemingly countless sizes of envelopes available, the four most commonly used sizes are as follows: 6½ by 3⅝ inches and 9½ by 4⅛ inches (for standard-size letterheads); 7½ by 3⅞ inches (for monarch stationery); and 5¹⁵/₁₆ by 4⅝ inches (for baronial stationery).

The metric sizes of envelopes are the DL, C6, and C7/6. The DL, which measures 220 by 110 millimeters, is the nearest metric equivalent of the No. 10 envelope (9½ by 4⅛ inches). The C6 measures 162 by 114 millimeters; the C7/6, 162 by 81 millimeters.

ASSIGNMENT

○ Worksheets 80 and 81

UNIT 34: Basic Principles of Effective Writing

☐ EFFECTIVE BUSINESS WRITING

Many writers feel that if a letter, memo, report, or other type of communication produces the results it was intended to achieve, it is an example of effective business writing. As a general rule, such a guide for measuring the effectiveness of writing is as good as any, provided the writer gives thoughtful attention to all the results that a communication produces and to the manner in which he or she achieves those results. Consider the following portion of a letter, for example:

Dear Madam or Sir:

Thanks a lot for your recent order. We sure do wish we could sent them four bed spreads you asked for, but we can't do that because we don't have the information we need to do it.

You see, like a lot of other people who order things by mail, you failed to tell us what size you need for your beds. As you know, I'm sure, these things come in four different sizes: twin, full, queen, and king. By the way, being as how were not a speciality store, please be sure to remember that we don't stock none of them far-out shapes and sizes like is used in someplaces.

We have a great reputation for promptness, but when people makes mistakes and then bad mouths us for what they done themselves, its hard to keep. As you can seen, you can help us help you and us by giving us the size you want at the bottom of this letter and returning it to us in the enclosed envelope that don't require no postage stamp. Thanking you in advance for your cooperation, we remain,

Sincerely yours,

Quite obviously, all of us would agree that such a letter is an example of extremely *in*effective business writing—even if the person receiving it were to provide the requested information. The accusing and patronizing statements, the grammatical errors, the general tone of the message—almost everything about the letter violates some important principle of effective business writing.

☐ BASIC PRINCIPLES

1. Clearly define your purpose in writing. Whether the purpose is to request information about a product, to provide information that the reader has requested, to order merchandise, or to satisfy some other need, carefully consider exactly what it is before you begin to write. Most of what you say in your message should be directly and clearly related to the main purpose of the message.

2. Keep your reader in mind, as he or she is the person who will make the final decision as to whether or not your message produces the results you want. In saying what you have to say, use the *you* approach—but remember this approach sometimes requires the use of *I* or *we, me* or *us,* and other first person pronouns—not simply *you, your,* and *yours.* Note the following example of the true *you* approach:

NOT: You didn't indicate either the size or the quantity of envelopes you need; therefore, you can't expect us to ship this part of your order to you right away.

BUT: Immediately upon receiving your order, we shipped everything except the envelopes. In order that we may send them to you with the least possible delay, would you please let us know the size and quantity that you would like to have.

3. Decide what *tone* is best suited to the subject of your message, your purpose in writing, and your reader. If you are writing a letter to someone that you know quite well and are asking that person to serve as a consultant for a project that you are working on, you probably will use a warm, friendly tone. However, in writing to warn a delinquent customer that it's no longer a matter of "will you pay" but "you must pay or face the consequences," you would use a very formal but courteous tone.

4. Use words that mean what you want to say and that help to establish the tone that you select. Then use the words in a grammatically correct manner. Avoid expressions that are likely to antagonize (*you failed, you neglected*) or bewilder your reader.

5. Avoid trite, outmoded, hackneyed expressions.

6. Organize your message in a logical, forceful, forward-flowing manner—from sentence to sentence and from paragraph to paragraph. Attract the reader's attention at the outset and hold it to the end of the message.

7. Express your thoughts concisely, completely, and courteously.

8. When you have said everything that needs to be said, stop! Some writers yield to the temptation to pad out their messages by summarizing everything they have said or by using a closing paragraph that fades into nothingness.

☐ OBJECTIONABLE EXPRESSIONS

When speaking or writing in business, avoid using any word or phrase that is overworked, outmoded, stilted, pompous, legalistic, or meaningless. The following are among the expressions that you should avoid:

Along these lines; on the order of.   These expressions are wordy substitutes for *like* or *similar to.*

As per.   Use *according to, as indicated, as requested,* or a similar expression instead of this legalistic phrase.

As to; with regard to.   Instead of using either of these expressions to introduce a subject, simply begin discussing the subject.

At an early date; at your earliest convenience.   If you can't give a specific date or time, say *soon, today, next week,* or something similar.

At hand; on hand.   Don't use either of these ancient phrases.

At this time; at the present time.   Say *now, today,* or *at present.*

Attached please find; attached hereto; enclosed herewith.   Just say *attached is, we are enclosing, the enclosed letter,* and so on.

Awaiting your answer; looking forward to hearing from you.   Don't end a letter or any other business communication with a weak participial closing.

Beg.   Don't *beg to inform* or *beg to tell* anyone anything.

Due to the fact that.   This is the long way of saying *because* or *since*.

Duly.   Don't use this legalistic expression in ordinary communications.

Favor; communication.   Both words are poor substitutes for *letter, memo, report,* and so on. *Favor,* in the sense indicated here, is archaic.

For your information; as you know.   More often than not, these are tactless, patronizing expressions.

Free of charge.   In business, it's just plain *free* if it's *free of charge*.

Hereby; heretofore; herewith.   These are outmoded and unnecessary.

I wish to thank you; may I ask.   Don't *wish* and *thank* or *request permission* and then *ask* in the same breath. Just thank or ask.

In advance of; prior to.   Say *before*.

In compliance with your request.   Just say *as you requested*.

In due course; in due time.   Both are indefinite and meaningless. Omit them.

In re; re.   Don't use these Latin legal expressions in the message of a letter or a report.

In receipt of.   The fact that you are *in receipt of* something is usually obvious. Omit the phrase or say *thank you for*.

In regard to; with regard to.   Both are wordy ways of saying *about* or *concerning*. Always choose the concise expression in any situation.

In the amount of.   Say, for example, *check for $10* and save three words.

In the event that.   If one thing depends upon another, say *if*.

Our Miss James.   Miss James, or anyone else, may work for us—but she doesn't belong to us. Say *Miss James, our receptionist* (or *our receptionist, Miss James*).

Party.   Except in a contract, don't use *party* for *person* or for the name of a person.

Pursuant to.   Do not use this legalistic expression.

Said.   Don't use this verb as an adjective (*said agreement, said request*).

Same.   Do not use *same* as a substitute for a noun or a pronoun.

Thank you again.   One *thank you* in any message is enough.

Thank you in advance.   Thanking anyone for anything in advance is presumptuous. Doing so is likely to antagonize the reader or listener.

The writer; the undersigned.   Use the pronoun *I* or *me*, whichever is correct in the particular situation.

ASSIGNMENT

○ Worksheets 82, 83, 84, and 85

UNIT 35: Request Letters and Acknowledgments

☐ WRITING A REQUEST LETTER

Background.   A *request letter* is written to ask for something: information, a catalog or a price list, a product sample, a pamphlet, or a similar item. Such a letter is generally very easy to write, as illustrated by the following request for a booklet:

Ladies and Gentlemen:

Will you please send me a free copy of *How to Set Up an Information Processing System*, which was mentioned in your advertisement in this month's issue of *The Business Journal*.

Although we are a comparatively small organization, we have a fairly large volume of correspondence and other paperwork. Thus this booklet will be most helpful to us in deciding whether to install a different system for handling our written communications.

Sincerely yours,

Writing Suggestions.   When you write a request letter, keep the following points in mind. They will help you achieve the results you want.

1. Define exactly what your need is before you start to write. Before you write to ask for information, you will find it especially helpful to jot down the question or questions that you will need to ask your reader in order to obtain the information or item that you need.

2. Keep your request reasonable, especially when asking for free materials or information. If your reader is likely to wonder why you are making a particular request, briefly state your reason.

3. If your request is prompted by an advertisement, give the title and publication date of the magazine or newspaper, for example. Every organization is very much interested in the effectiveness of its advertising, and you will be doing the reader a service by providing such information.

4. State your request in simple, courteous language. Be especially careful to avoid demands and commands; long, involved sentences; patronizing statements; and so on. After all, your reader will be doing you a favor by filling your request—and often gaining only your goodwill by doing so.

5. Make it easy for your reader to determine and to provide quickly and accurately what you want. If you are requesting several items or asking several questions, for example, display them in a numbered listing. If the reader is to provide information in letter form and is unlikely to gain anything by filling your request, enclose a self-addressed, stamped envelope. Doing so frequently will increase your chances of getting a prompt reply.

6. Express appreciation in some way—but don't thank the reader in advance. "Thank you," "thank you in advance," or a similar expression is considered inappropriate because it tends to obligate the reader. At least some readers view such an expression as an indirect demand for them to do something.

ASSIGNMENT

○ Assume that you are the secretary to Evelyn Beardsley, a partner in the law firm of Ryan, Beardsley & Stokes in your city, and that she has encouraged you to "look into the possibility of replacing your manual typewriter with a 'memory' typewriter." Write a letter to Business Equipment Manufacturers, Inc., 9909 East Broadway, New York, New York 10004, asking for literature about their newest machines.

○ Assume that you are the director of marketing of Brentwood Industries, a manufacturer of sports equipment and a member of the Sporting Goods Manufacturers Association. Your firm has not exhibited its products at previous conventions of the association, but you would like to convince the president of your company that doing so would be a good idea. Write a letter to Mr. Thomas Reilly, director of exhibits for the association, at 4404 Wildwood Road, Terre Haute, Indiana 47811, asking for information about (1) the time and place of the next convention, (2) the cost of exhibit space, (3) everything else that you think you may need to know. Remember to ask only those questions that you can reasonably expect Mr. Reilly to be able to answer.

☐ WRITING A SIMPLE ACKNOWLEDGMENT

Many companies that receive numerous requests for catalogs, pamphlets, and similar materials use preprinted postcards or brief form letters (preprinted letters that may or may not need to be personalized by adding the customer's name and address, the date, the title of the booklet, and similar "fill ins" that vary from one situation to another). If you need to write a simple acknowledgment, all you need to do is express appreciation for the request, identify whatever you are sending, and, in general, attempt to gain goodwill.

ASSIGNMENT

○ Assume that you work in the Customer Relations Department of Business Equipment Manufacturers, Inc. Write a simple acknowledgment letter to send with the literature requested in the first of the preceding assignments.

☐ WRITING A DETAILED REPLY

Answering some requests requires a substantial amount of time and effort. For example, you may need to consult other members of your organization to obtain answers to some questions—or to get permission to release information that you may have yourself. The important thing is to reply to every question or important point that the writer has raised in his or her letter to you.

In some instances, writing a detailed reply gives you an opportunity to "sell" your company's products or services. In answering a request for literature pertaining to a product, for example, it generally is appropriate to point out some feature of the product, to offer to have a representative call on the prospective customer, or to give the name and address of a local dealer.

Dear Mrs. Logan:

Thank you for your request for information concerning our new line of MAR-BEL floor coverings. We are confident that you will find the enclosed brochure helpful in choosing just the right patterns and colors for your home.

After examining this brochure, you undoubtedly will want to see these beautiful, durable tiles for yourself. You can do so at your convenience by visiting The Colonial Home Improvement Center at 104 Salem Drive in Northport.

                              Sincerely yours,

ASSIGNMENT

○ Assume that you, not Mr. Thomas Reilly, are the director of exhibits for the Sporting Goods Manufacturers Association mentioned in the second of the preceding assignments. Write a detailed response to the request for information about the time and place of the next convention, the cost of exhibit space, and so forth.

○ Worksheet 86

UNIT 36: Sales Letters

☐ BACKGROUND

A *sales letter* is developed for the specific purpose of selling a product or a service. Especially in large organizations, the preparation of such letters is the responsibility of members of the marketing department. In many instances, such a letter is a form letter—one of which hundreds or thousands of copies are made for mailing to customers or prospective customers. Sometimes, each copy of the letter is personalized through the addition of the addressee's name and address, the use of the person's name in the salutation, and perhaps the insertion of the person's name somewhere in the message, or text, of the letter. Thus, through the use of memory typewriters and text-editing typewriters, it is very easy to give each copy of the letter the appearance of having been written and produced solely for the person receiving it.

   To write a successful sales letter, you must first:

1. Acquire a thorough knowledge of the product or service you are selling and know its strengths and weaknesses, especially as compared with those of your competitors' products or services.

2. Obtain all the information you can about the group of persons or the individual to whom you are writing. For example, is the group composed of home owners or apartment dwellers? What is the income level of the group? The answers to these and a number of other questions must, of course, relate to the product or service you are attempting to sell—and they will have an important bearing on what you say and how you say it.

3. Select the feature or features that you wish to stress about your product or service.

4. Choose the best appeal or appeals to use in leading your reader to buy your product or service. Such appeals include thrift, comfort, safety, prestige, and status. The appeal or appeals that you use must, of course, be suited to whatever it is you are selling and to whomever you are writing.

5. Time your message so that it will have the greatest impact on your reader. Some products and services are in seasonal demand (lawn furniture, garden equipment and supplies, home decorating services, and so on); others are in constant demand (auto repair services and household appliances, for example).

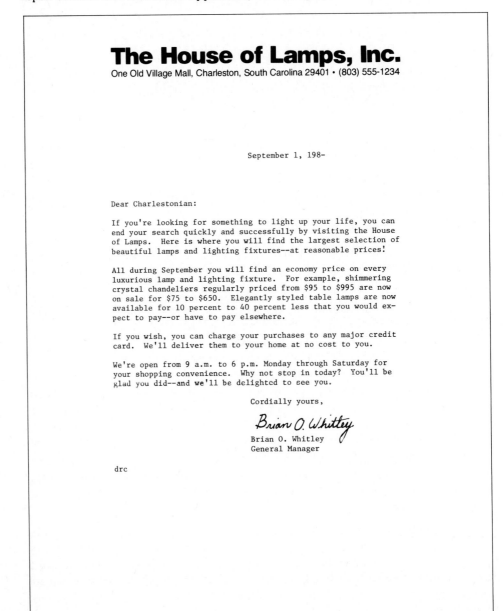

The House of Lamps, Inc.
One Old Village Mall, Charleston, South Carolina 29401 • (803) 555-1234

September 1, 198-

Dear Charlestonian:

If you're looking for something to light up your life, you can end your search quickly and successfully by visiting the House of Lamps. Here is where you will find the largest selection of beautiful lamps and lighting fixtures--at reasonable prices!

All during September you will find an economy price on every luxurious lamp and lighting fixture. For example, shimmering crystal chandeliers regularly priced from $95 to $995 are now on sale for $75 to $650. Elegantly styled table lamps are now available for 10 percent to 40 percent less that you would expect to pay--or have to pay elsewhere.

If you wish, you can charge your purchases to any major credit card. We'll deliver them to your home at no cost to you.

We're open from 9 a.m. to 6 p.m. Monday through Saturday for your shopping convenience. Why not stop in today? You'll be glad you did--and we'll be delighted to see you.

Cordially yours,

Brian O. Whitley

Brian O. Whitley
General Manager

drc

☐ WRITING SUGGESTIONS

When writing a sales letter, keep in mind that your letter must do these four things in order to produce the results you want:

1. Gain the reader's attention.

2. Arouse the reader's interest.

3. Create a desire for the product or service.

4. Motivate the reader to act.

Gaining Attention. Writers have used countless devices to gain their readers' attention, including unusual letter formats, gadgets and coins attached to letters, startling questions and statements, endorsements of other customers, quotations of famous persons, well-known proverbs, and handwritten notations. Whatever means of gaining attention you choose to use, be sure that it is related in some way to the product or service you are selling. Here are some examples that you could use under certain circumstances:

> How would you like to sit in the shade summer after summer? (OK for a letter selling shade trees and shrubbery to home owners in a new subdivision, for example.)

> It's the littlest thing that counts! (OK for a letter selling a pocket calculator, for example.)

Arousing Interest. Before the impact of the attention-getting device wears off, you need to make some statement that will at least partly answer the reader's "what's this all about" question and set the stage for the real selling that is to follow. To arouse the reader's interest, then, you will want to introduce the basic appeal of your letter (comfort, convenience, thrift, prestige, or whatever) or, if you introduced it in your attention-getting opener, to expand upon it.

> How would you like to sit in the shade summer after summer? That's the dream of most of us—and it's one that we can make come true for you! All you have to do is choose from our large selection of trees and watch us go to work to ensure that you can spend those hot summer days outdoors in cool comfort.

Creating Desire. As the preceding example illustrates, you can sometimes begin to create a desire for the product or service at the same time you arouse the reader's interest in your product or service. Your approach may be to appeal to your reader's emotions or to his or her reason. If you choose to make your appeal through reason, you will want to describe whatever you are selling in a logical, concrete manner and point out the specific benefits to your reader. If you choose to make your appeal through emotions, you will want to take a more abstract, colorful approach toward putting your reader in whatever emotional state you wish. Note the last sentence in the preceding example.

Motivating Action. In one way or another, almost everything in a sales letter is designed to motivate action on the part of the reader. However, at the end of your letter, you should make a clear-cut statement of the action you expect him or her to take—and make it as easy as possible for the reader to take that action. Note the closing of the letter on page 98 and the following example.

> For further information, simply sign and return the enclosed card—today. There is no obligation on your part.

○ You are the sales-promotion specialist of Valley-Mont Development Corporation, a firm that builds and sells new homes priced at $40,000 and up. Make up all the details concerning the kind of homes available (including their location), the type of persons to whom the letter would be sent, and so on. Then write a sales letter that will achieve your and your employer's objectives.

○ You are the owner of a travel agency that you recently opened in a nearby community. The number of people using your agency to book their airline reservations for business and personal travel, to plan their vacations (you have a number of tour packages to offer), and so on, has not reached the level you would like. Write a letter designed to sell your agency's services.

○ Worksheet 87

UNIT 37: Order Letters and Acknowledgments

☐ ORDER LETTERS

Background. The purpose of an *order letter* is to request merchandise or services. Such a letter represents an offer to buy something on terms that are understood between the buyer and the seller or that are stated in the letter or elsewhere. Letters of this type are most often written by an individual or a small business. Companies that place a great many orders almost always use printed forms known as *purchase orders,* and many individuals and firms use printed order forms provided by suppliers of products and services. Typically, then, an order letter is written only when a purchase order or an order form is not available. Note the letter on page 101.

Writing Suggestions. When writing an order letter, be sure to include complete and accurate information about each product or service. Arrange the information in a manner that will make it easy to read and understand. Otherwise, the reader may be unable to process your order promptly and correctly.

When you order merchandise, give special attention to such details as these: catalog numbers, part numbers, style numbers, quantities desired, descriptions of items, unit prices of articles, total cost of the merchandise, sales taxes, discounts, method of payment, method of shipment, desired delivery date, and delivery address.

ASSIGNMENT

○ Assume that you are the owner of (*your name*) Gift Shop. Write a letter in which you order four different items from Delmar Distributing Company, One Chase Avenue, Miami Beach, Florida 33140. Compose a letterhead, using your own address—and make up all the information necessary to identify each of the items you order. Remember that you want Delmar to process your order quickly and accurately.

○ As the manager of The Clover Leaf Inn, located in your city, you have spoken with Kurt Keister, an independent building contractor, about installing a new ceramic tile floor in the lobby. He offered to provide the tiles you selected and all the other materials necessary and to do the work for $1,875. Write a letter accepting his offer and ordering the work to be done this month. Provide all the necessary details.

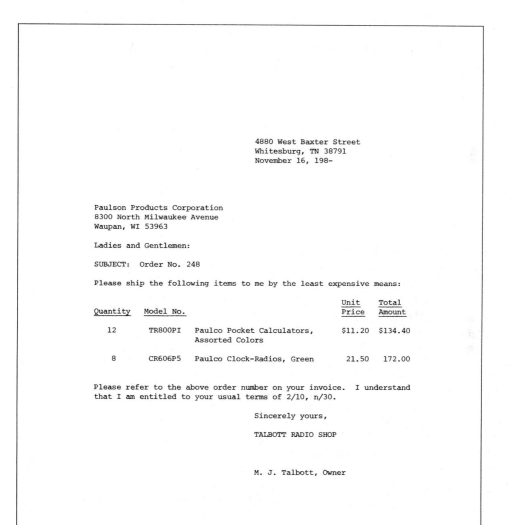

4880 West Baxter Street
Whitesburg, TN 38791
November 16, 198-

Paulson Products Corporation
8300 North Milwaukee Avenue
Waupan, WI 53963

Ladies and Gentlemen:

SUBJECT: Order No. 248

Please ship the following items to me by the least expensive means:

Quantity	Model No.		Unit Price	Total Amount
12	TR800PI	Paulco Pocket Calculators, Assorted Colors	$11.20	$134.40
8	CR606P5	Paulco Clock-Radios, Green	21.50	172.00

Please refer to the above order number on your invoice. I understand that I am entitled to your usual terms of 2/10, n/30.

Sincerely yours,

TALBOTT RADIO SHOP

M. J. Talbott, Owner

☐ ORDER ACKNOWLEDGMENTS

Background.   Some companies use form letters, postcards, or individually prepared letters to acknowledge all orders immediately upon receiving them. Many others acknowledge orders only if they cannot process the orders as soon as they arrive, as when merchandise is out of stock temporarily or when an item is no longer available, for example. Writing acknowledgments of orders is obviously a good practice that builds goodwill and pays dividends in repeat business.

Writing Suggestions.   When writing an order acknowledgment letter, identify the order and state exactly how it is being handled. For example, if all or part of an order is out of stock and cannot be shipped by the date requested, state the reason for the delay and indicate when the customer can expect to receive it. You can always use an order acknowledgment letter as a means of building goodwill—and in some instances, as a means of promoting some other product or service.

Dear Mrs. Lopez:

We appreciate your recent order for two of our Model B600 Benlux portable mixers. This model is an extremely popular one—so popular, in fact, that we are temporarily out of stock! Thus we regret that there will be a slight delay in shipping your order.

We expect a new shipment by the end of this week, Mrs. Lopez, at which time we will rush your mixers to you. To ensure that you will receive your mixers by the end of this month, we will send them by Special Delivery—at no extra cost to you.

It is always a pleasure to serve you, and we look forward to handling all your future orders promptly.

Cordially yours,

ASSIGNMENT

○ One of the items ordered from the Delmar Distributing Company (see the preceding assignment) is no longer available. As a correspondent in the Customer Services Department of Delmar, write an appropriate acknowledgment letter. In doing so, you may find it appropriate to suggest that your firm could supply a similar item as a substitute.

○ Worksheet 88

UNIT 38: Claim and Adjustment Letters

☐ CLAIM LETTERS

Background.   The volume of business transactions, the number of possibilities for error in connection with many of those transactions—these and other factors make it almost impossible for any organization to have a perfect record in its dealings with all of its customers or clients. As a customer or as a representative of a company that is a customer, you may receive the wrong merchandise, damaged products, a seriously delayed shipment, an incorrect invoice or statement of account, or a product or a service that does not turn out the way you had expected. Whatever the situation may be, you probably will have to write a letter in which you make a claim against the supplier of the product or the service. Note the following message:

Ladies and Gentlemen:

SUBJECT: Account No. 343–28–607

On your August 31 statement of my account, you indicated a balance due of $182.40. However, if you will check your records carefully, I am sure you will find that the correct balance is $58.40, including $4.60 in interest.

This statement does not credit me for the $75 payment I made on August 12. For your convenience, I am enclosing a photocopy of the receipt I obtained from a cashier in your credit office.

All other transactions shown on this statement appear to be correct. Would you please send me a corrected statement as quickly as possible. Immediately upon receiving it, I will send you a check for the balance of my account.

Sincerely yours,

Writing Suggestions. When writing a claim letter:

1. Explain carefully and tactfully what your complaint is. Describe the condition of the merchandise when you received it, the error that was made in filling your order, or whatever grievance you may have.

2. Give all the details the reader of your letter will need in order to process your claim: date of order, order number, method of shipment, delivery date, the product or service involved, and so on.

3. Indicate whatever loss or unusual inconvenience you have experienced as a result of your reader's error—or perhaps the error of someone else, such as a delivery firm, involved in the transaction. Don't exaggerate!

4. State what you consider to be a fair adjustment, and show confidence that your claim will receive prompt and favorable attention.

5. Don't lose your temper! If you are angry, cool off before you write. If you were to receive the following claim letter, what would your reaction be?

Dear Sir or Madam:

Thanks to you, I've had a migraine headache since 3 o'clock yesterday afternoon—that's exactly two hours after your delivery truck pulled out of my driveway. No wonder you call that refrigerator you talked me into buying a frost-free Spring Line. The thing doesn't even get cool, let alone cold. However, it does make a real mess—or I should say that it did, because I unplugged it when I saw that huge puddle of water it was making in the corner of my beautiful kitchen.

I don't think I need to tell you that I want that thing out of my kitchen and out of my house now. Also, I don't think I need to tell you that I'm not going to pay you a penny, let alone $650, for a useless piece of junk. So get somebody over here to pick it up tomorrow morning.

Sincerely yours,

ASSIGNMENT

○ Assume that you have just received a coat you ordered from a mail-order firm and discovered that it has what appears to be a cigarette burn on the sleeve. Since you're not a smoker, you know that you didn't cause the damage. Write a claim letter in which you provide all the details necessary. Will you send the coat back with the letter? Will you keep the coat if the company will agree to lower the price significantly?

○ You have your own apartment, and you have just returned from vacation. As a matter of fact, you were away the entire month of August. In going through your mail, you find a statement from the utility company showing charges of $36.40 for gas and electricity usage in August as well as an unpaid balance of $48.06 for July. You have a canceled check to prove you paid the July bill. Write an appropriate claim letter.

☐ ADJUSTMENT LETTERS

When you receive a claim or complaint letter of any kind, you will need to confirm the facts of the situation and answer the letter promptly. Whether your investigation shows that the customer is right, that you and your company are right, or that both the customer and you and your company are partly right, you should write a letter that:

1. Shows the customer that you understand the problem.

2. Tells the customer exactly what you have done, are doing, or will do to resolve the matter.

3. Contains no accusations, negative words, or other expressions that are almost certain to wipe out any chance of regaining the customer's goodwill.

4. Ends with a positive statement that will help you and your company regain the goodwill and retain the business of the customer.

Granting an Adjustment. If the customer has made a valid claim or complaint, you have a very easy job ahead of you. All you have to do is cheerfully and unreservedly grant the customer's request for an adjustment.

> Dear Mrs. Tanner:
>
> As you said in your May 4 letter, you did indeed order a Diamond washer with the loading door on the top—not the front—of the machine. We very much regret the mix-up and the inconvenience that it has caused you.
>
> You will receive your brand-new top-loading Diamond washer on Friday of this week, Mrs. Tanner, at which time our delivery people will pick up the other machine.
>
> Our thanks and cordial best wishes to you.
>
> Sincerely yours,

Granting a Partial Adjustment. When your investigation of a claim or a complaint shows that the customer is partly right and that you and your company are partly right, you obviously will need to write a letter in which you propose a compromise settlement. For example:

Dear Mr. Lopez:

Thank you for your March 8 letter concerning the living room furniture you purchased from us on January 16 of this year. We have checked our records and found a sales slip signed by you indicating that the furniture was in good condition when it was delivered. However, we realize that a quick visual inspection would be unlikely to reveal a defect in the upholstery fabric.

As much as we would like to exchange both the chairs and the couch, as you suggested, we find that we will be unable to do so. The reason is that our standard warranty does not apply to merchandise sold at lower than its regular price.

However, we would be happy to send a service representative to your home to inspect the couch, which you indicated was the only item with any serious defect. Then, if our representative finds that the damage is not the result of ordinary wear, we will be happy to re-cover the seat cushions with a matching fabric for the cost of the fabric alone.

The head of our service department will phone you on March 16, Mr. Lopez, to arrange for a representative to call at your home. At that time, we hope to hear from you that this proposed solution meets with your approval.

Sincerely yours,

Refusing an Adjustment. If the customer is entirely at fault, you generally will have no choice but to refuse to make an adjustment. Writing a "no" letter is not an easy task because you must first develop your case very carefully and then get your "no" answer across clearly—but very, very tactfully.

Dear Mr. Wilton:

Thank you for your letter of September 10. We very much regret that the Handy-Dandy jigsaw you purchased from us in August has not met all your expectations.

As you indicated, Mr. Wilton, a portable tool of this type provides completely trouble-free service when used for a wide variety of purposes. However, as you discovered, it is too light in weight and limited in power to handle a variety of heavy jobs, such as those described in the owner's manual accompanying each Handy-Dandy jigsaw.

As much as we would like to exchange the jigsaw or refund the purchase price to you, the terms of the warranty covering the jigsaw leave both you and us in a difficult position. Consequently, we have no alternative but to suggest that you have someone at a local repair shop inspect your saw and determine whether or not it can be repaired to your satisfaction.

We hope that you'll stop in to see us the next time you are in the vicinity of our store, Mr. Wilton—and that you'll be able to tell us that your Handy-Dandy jigsaw is back in perfect working condition.

Sincerely yours,

ASSIGNMENT

○ As an employee of Stafford Department Store, you receive the claim letter requesting a corrected statement of account (see page 103). The letter is from Ms. Cheryl Rizzo, who has correctly stated the circumstances surrounding her claim. Write her an appropriate letter (make up the missing information).

○ Respond to one of the claim letters you wrote in the preceding assignment.

○ Worksheet 89

UNIT 39: Credit Letters

☐ THE USE OF CREDIT

Manufacturers, wholesalers, retailers, banks, individuals—all are either directly or indirectly users of credit. Business firms borrow money to operate and to purchase goods and services from various suppliers, for example. Similarly, of course, individuals borrow money from banks, open charge accounts with department stores, and use credit cards for travel and other expenses. Thus, without credit, the economic activities of private individuals, companies, and government organizations would be greatly reduced.

Although credit is such a large and highly important part of our economy, it is especially significant that losses from bad debts are extremely small. One of the major reasons is that people are basically honest and place a very high value on a good credit standing. Another, of course, is that credit is not granted on a hit-or-miss basis: every applicant for credit, whether an individual or an organization, is thoroughly investigated before the privilege of "buying now and paying later" is granted.

☐ CREDIT REQUESTS

Background. Requests for credit, especially those by individuals, frequently involve filling out a credit-application form that calls for information concerning employment, income, assets, and so on. In many instances, an in-person interview is also a part of the process of obtaining credit. In others, the request for credit is made by letter. Regardless of the procedure when you apply for credit, your objectives are to assure the person or firm to whom you are applying that you are of good character and that you have the financial resources and capacity to repay the loan (whether it is in the form of merchandise or services or money) according to specified terms.

Writing Suggestions. When you write a credit-request letter, you should:

1. State your reason for requesting credit—to buy a car, to finance additional education, or to redecorate your home, for example.

2. Indicate the amount of credit you would like to obtain and the payment terms you would like to arrange.

3. Provide complete and accurate information about your income: the name and address of your present employer, your job title, your salary, and the period of time you have been in your present job. It is also a good idea to give the names and addresses of former employers, if any—especially if you have been with your present employer for only a year or two.

4. Give your present home address and telephone number, and indicate whether you rent or own your own home. State how long you have lived at your present address, and if it is a fairly short time, give your previous address.

5. Indicate the number of dependents, if any, that you have.

6. List all your outstanding debts. Give the name and address of each creditor, the full amount you owe, and the amount you pay weekly or monthly on the debt.

7. Give the names and addresses of two or three character references (not relatives)—but list them only after you have obtained the permission of each person to do so.

8. If possible, give several credit references—names and addresses of banks, stores, credit card companies, or other businesses that you have dealt with on a credit basis. Be sure to include the name and address of the bank with which you do business (such as the one with which you have a checking or savings account).

9. Anticipate that the firm will extend credit to you and that the association will be mutually rewarding and satisfying.

10. Offer to provide any additional information that the firm may need in connection with your request for credit.

Note the following example of a letter to the credit manager of a wholesale auto parts distributor:

Ladies and Gentlemen:

For the past year I have owned and operated the Pleasant Valley Auto Repair Shop, buying parts and supplies on a cash basis from local dealers. To achieve greater economy and convenience in purchasing materials, I would like to open an account and establish a credit line of $2,000 with your company. From talking with other repair shop owners, I understand that your customary terms are 2/10, n/30.

Now that I have become established in Pleasant Valley, I have been averaging approximately $3,000 a month from the auto repair shop, which I opened with a loan from the Pleasant Valley National Bank. The current balance of that loan is $3,650, and my monthly payment is $400. I have no other outstanding debts.

For the past two years, my wife and I have lived at 2880 Federal Street, which is almost directly across the street from my shop. The monthly rent on our apartment is $325, including utilities. My home phone number is 555-8849.

In addition to the Pleasant Valley National Bank, you may wish to contact the following persons, who have given me permission to use their names as references: Ms. Gladys Fitzsimmons, Dean of Students, Hardin County Community College; and Mr. Franklin Flynn, 1680 North 12 Street. Both are here in Pleasant Valley.

Should there be any additional information that I may be able to furnish in connection with this request, please let me know. I am looking forward to beginning a long and mutually profitable business relationship with you.

Sincerely yours,

ASSIGNMENT

○ Assume that you have yourself and one dependent to support on a monthly income of $1,000. The rent on your apartment is $275 a month, including utilities, and you have a few installment payments totaling $150 a month. You would like to buy some sporting goods equipment and household items that cost a total of $280 from Sears & Wards, a mail-order house. You do not have a credit-application blank; therefore, you decide to write a letter to ask for charge-account privileges. Make up all the information necessary to write a complete and convincing credit-request letter.

☐ CREDIT-APPROVAL LETTERS

It is a very simple matter to approve credit by letter. Good news requires few words. All the customer looks for is the "Yes." The rest of the message is simply in the interest of gaining the customer's goodwill—and business, of course.

> Dear Miss Hamagaki:
>
> It is a pleasure to tell you that your application for charge-account privileges at Mott Brothers has been approved.
>
> The enclosed card, which you should sign immediately and keep in your possession at all times, is your personal key to convenient shopping at our main store in Greenbrier Plaza as well as in all our suburban branches. Should your card be lost or stolen, please notify us immediately by writing to the address above or by calling us at 555-4500.
>
> All of us are delighted to have you as a member of Mott's family of happy, thrifty charge customers. We look forward to the pleasure of serving you soon—and often!
>
> Sincerely yours,

☐ CREDIT-REFUSAL LETTERS

When writing a credit-refusal letter, you need to use all the tact and writing skill at your command. You should express sincere regret, explain the reason for the refusal, and yet leave the applicant with a feeling of goodwill toward you and your company. No matter what you say or how you say it, the applicant undoubtedly will be disappointed. But if you give all the details concerning the rejection in a friendly but firm manner, the customer probably will not be offended.

> Dear Mr. Finchley:
>
> Thank you for applying for credit with our company. We have reviewed your application very carefully and found you to be a person of high integrity and excellent reputation. Thus it is very difficult for us to have to tell you that we feel it would not be in your best interest for us to extend you credit at this time.
>
> Within the next few months, Mr. Finchley, we are confident that you will reduce your current monthly obligations to a level that would make it easy for you to assume the responsibility of repaying a loan of the size you requested. At that time, we hope that you will contact us again, as we would welcome the opportunity to be of service to you then.
>
> Many of our customers have told us that the enclosed booklet has been extremely helpful to them in getting the most out of their income and in applying for a loan at Citizens Bank and Trust Company. We hope that it will be of assistance to you also.
>
> Cordial best wishes.
>
> Sincerely yours,

ASSIGNMENT

○ You are the credit manager of Atlantic Auto Parts, Inc., 3600 Second Avenue, your city and state. Study the credit-request letter on page 107, and decide whether you will grant Mr. Thomas Bryant's request for an open charge account with a limit of $2,000. Your company's credit terms are 2/10, n/30, in case you decide to grant the request.

○ Write a credit-approval or a credit-refusal letter in response to the credit-request letter you wrote to Sears & Wards in the preceding assignment. Provide all the details needed to make your reply complete in all respects.

○ Worksheet 90

UNIT 40: Collection Letters

For a variety of reasons, a few organizations and individuals become unable to pay their accounts as promised when they obtained credit. When this happens, of course, the need for collection letters arises. While every company has its own policies and procedures, many companies develop and use a series of letters that includes *reminder letters, discussion letters,* and *ultimatum letters.* The premise of each letter is that a delinquent customer will pay if reminded regularly and with increasing insistence.

☐ THE REMINDER LETTER

Background. Most companies that grant credit bill their charge customers on a regular cycle. Typically, at the end of each 30-day period, a charge customer receives an itemized monthly statement that shows the date, kind, and amount of each purchase, the date and amount of each payment received, the balance at the end of the previous billing cycle, interest or service charges, the new balance, the amount and date of the payment due, and so on. If the customer does not make payment until near the end of a certain period, often 30 days or less beyond the due date, the company probably will pay little attention to the overdue account. However, failure to pay by the end of that "grace period" usually results in a letter (or other type of reminder notice, such as a duplicate statement marked "Overdue") reminding the customer that payment is past due.

June 20, 198–

Mr. C. R. Billings
9977 Boxwood Avenue
Riverside, NJ 08370

Dear Mr. Billings:

Did you forget something last month? It seems that you must have, as we have not received your regular monthly payment of $45.60!

If your payment is already in the mail—or if you have sent us a check in payment of the balance of $368.85—please accept our thanks and disregard this notice. Otherwise, would you please send us your check for $45.60 today.

Better still, stop in this week and take advantage of the countless bargains we are now offering for every member of the family.

Sincerely yours,

Marcia Mullins
Credit Department

Writing Suggestions. When writing a reminder letter, give it the appearance of a routine letter—one sent to *all* customers. In the letter:

1. Remind the customer that payment is past due.
2. Restate the amount due.
3. Provide the customer with an excuse for not making payment on time.
4. Show that you still value and solicit the customer's business.

ASSIGNMENT

O Mr. Jesse B. Gavin, of 1224 Kennedy Boulevard in a city near your home, opened a charge account with Goodrich & Company, Inc., six months ago. At that time he signed an agreement requiring a minimum payment of $30 plus carrying charges on purchases up to $500. The same day that he opened his account, he bought $368.74 worth of clothing and sports equipment, but he has made no purchases since then. He made the first five monthly payments on time, but last month's payment is now 45 days overdue. As credit manager of the store, write him an appropriate reminder letter. **NOTE:** In actual practice, of course, the store would add carrying charges to the unpaid balance at the end of each billing period. Ignore the addition of such charges and consider the balance to be $218.74.

☐ THE DISCUSSION LETTER

Background. If a delinquent customer does not respond to a reminder letter within a reasonable period of time (often two to four weeks), the company will then send a discussion letter. The main purpose of this letter is to collect the money due. However, if the customer is unable to pay for some reason, the second purpose is to encourage the customer to stop in or write or call and explain the difficulty in fulfilling his or her obligation to pay.

July 21, 198–

Mr. C. R. Billings
9977 Boxwood Avenue
Riverside, NJ 08370

Dear Mr. Billings:

In reviewing our records, we were surprised to find that we have not received a payment from you since April 20. The balance of your account is now $374.38, including carrying charges—and payments totaling $91.20 are overdue.

To you, $91.20 (or $374.38) may seem an insignificant amount, Mr. Billings. However, I am sure you will agree that we must rely upon you and all our charge customers to meet obligations promptly and fully.

If there is some reason why you cannot bring your account up to date now, please write or call or stop in to see me so that we can discuss the matter and continue your present good credit rating. Otherwise, may we expect to receive your check within 10 days.

Sincerely yours,

Marcia Mullins
Credit Department

Writing Suggestions. When writing a discussion letter to a delinquent customer:

1. Restate the amount due.

2. Express surprise that no payment has been received.

3. Ask the customer to tell you why you have not received payment.

4. Appeal to the customer's sense of fair play, and indicate that the customer's credit rating may be adversely affected if payment is not received promptly.

Since a good credit rating is an extremely valuable asset, the possibility of losing it is enough to make most people meet their obligations immediately after receiving a discussion letter.

ASSIGNMENT

○ The reminder letter that you wrote to Mr. Gavin about a month ago (see the preceding assignment) has produced no results—neither a payment nor a response. Now, write him a discussion letter.

☐ THE ULTIMATUM LETTER

Background. If the discussion letter does not produce results within a couple of weeks or so, a serious new problem arises. Should the delinquent account be turned over to a collection agency, or would it be better to write the customer another letter? Most companies take the letter route to collection and resort to collection through an agency only if the ultimatum, or urgency, letter fails in its mission. Collection by an agency is unpleasant and expensive—for both the company and the customer.

August 6, 198–

Mr. C. R. Billings
9977 Boxwood Avenue
Riverside, NJ 08370

Dear Mr. Billings:

Our records show that you have not made a payment on your account since April 20 and that you have not responded to our previous requests for payment. Since we have not received payment or heard any explanation from you for more than 90 days, we must inform you that the balance of your account, $380 (including carrying charges), is now due us.

As we are sure that you do not wish to lose your credit rating, we are reluctant to enforce payment of your long overdue account. However, we shall have no alternative but to place your account in the hands of our attorneys if we do not receive your check for $380 by August 16.

Very truly yours,

Marcia Mullins
Credit Department

Writing Suggestions. When you write an ultimatum letter, state your message in a courteous but cool and formal manner.

1. Review your efforts to bring about a settlement—and indicate that all of them were ignored.

2. State that the balance of the account is due and indicate exactly what the full amount is.

3. Appeal again to the customer's fear of losing his or her good credit rating, a loss that would be of serious consequence.

4. Demand that payment be made by a specific date, and indicate that the account will be turned over to an attorney or a collection agency if the deadline is not met.

ASSIGNMENT

○ None of your efforts to reach a settlement with Mr. Gavin (previous assignments) have been successful. Write him an ultimatum letter, as his account is more than 90 days overdue.

○ Prepare a list of questions concerning credit and collection procedures and practices that you would like to have answered. Then discuss with your instructor the possibility of inviting a representative of a local bank, department store, or other firm to address your class and answer your and the other class members' questions.

○ Worksheet 91

UNIT **41**: **Public Relations Letters**

☐ SOCIAL-BUSINESS LETTERS

Background. During the course of your business career, you will have many opportunities to write letters that have no purpose other than to build good relations with co-workers and "outside" people whom you have met in the course of performing your own job and with whom you have developed an almost personal friendship. Such letters may be prompted by job promotions or employment anniversaries, for example, and they frequently come very close to being social correspondence of the type you would write to close personal friends. Here is an example of a social-business letter, one that you could write on your company's letterhead stationery.

Dear Lorraine:

Congratulations! I just heard that you have been named Director of Marketing Services. You certainly have earned the promotion, and I join everyone else in wishing you outstanding success in your new position.

Fortunately, we shall still have the opportunity to work together—and I want you to know that you can count on my enthusiastic support. Good luck!

Sincerely,

Writing Suggestions.   Writing a social-business letter should always be a purely voluntary action. Never write out of a sense of duty or obligation, as doing so would defeat the purpose of such correspondence. When you do write:

1. Give attention to your relationship to the person whom you are writing, and adjust the tone of your message accordingly. If you are a supervisor or manager writing to someone who reports to you, you most likely would write a different letter than you would if your role and the reader's role were reversed, for example.

2. Consider the circumstances of the occasion that prompts you to write, and limit your comments accordingly. If it is an occasion that evokes regrets or sadness, express your thoughts sincerely and briefly.

3. Choose the most appropriate stationery. In many instances, plain paper is the best choice—and it is never inappropriate. Be discreet in using company stationery.

☐ GOODWILL LETTERS

Goodwill is that intangible something that keeps people coming back to a particular company when they could just as easily go somewhere else for the products or services they need and buy. Goodwill is an extremely important asset to every firm— so important that when a business is sold, a value is placed on goodwill and the buyer pays accordingly. Thus building, maintaining, or expanding goodwill is an important part of almost every writing project that you undertake, and it is the sole reason for writing a great many letters. Ultimately, of course, goodwill letters help to sell products and services—but they are not true sales letters. The main objective of a goodwill letter is generally one of the following:

1. To offer to be of service.

2. To capitalize on a special occasion.

3. To express appreciation for business already received.

Service Letters.   The typical sales letter says, "Please buy"; the typical service letter says, "Let us be of service to you." The main reason for writing a service letter, therefore, is to describe your company's range of services. Such a letter is usually directed to prospective customers, customers whose charge accounts have become inactive, new residents of a community, newly married couples, or others who have one particular thing in common.

> Dear Mr. and Mrs. Stefano:
>
> All of us at National Bank and Trust Company take great pleasure in welcoming you and your family to Midland Park. We are confident that you will find living and working in "The Flower Capital of the South" a wonderful experience in every respect.
>
> Within the very near future, Mr. and Mrs. Stefano, you undoubtedly will want to select a bank that is able and willing and eager to provide you with a wide variety of financial services. At National Bank and Trust Company you will find whatever types of banking services you may need: checking accounts, savings accounts, small loans . . . .
>
> Too, you will find everyone at National Bank and Trust Company happy to see you and pleased to be of service to you. Why not stop in soon so that we may become acquainted?
>
> Cordially yours,

ASSIGNMENT

○ You are the owner-operator of The Letter Shop, and in addition to selling a wide range of stationery items, you do offset printing work. Write a letter that you could send to prospective customers.

Special Occasion Letters. Another type of goodwill letter is often prompted by a holiday, the beginning of a new season, the arrival of new merchandise, the offering of a new service, an anniversary, or a similar occasion. Any occasion of this type is a wonderful opportunity to remind customers of the event—and of you and your company. When writing a letter of this type, stress the occasion and what it means to your reader.

Dear Mr. and Mrs. Robertson:

We just couldn't pass up this golden opportunity to congratulate you on your fiftieth wedding anniversary. It is a joyous occasion, and we wish you many, many more years of happiness and good health.

Fred, Anne, Shirley—all of us at Wright Jewelers who have gotten to know you so well over the years count you among our very special friends. Needless to say, we hope to have the pleasure of congratulating you in person within the very near future.

Cordially yours,

ASSIGNMENT

○ Since you have just opened a food-catering service in your community, you are understandably eager to ensure its—and your—success. It's the first of December, and you feel that the coming holidays offer you a special opportunity to do so. Write a letter that you could send to prospective customers.

Appreciation Letters. Who doesn't like to feel appreciated? Anyone who has done something for you or for your company most certainly will appreciate your taking the time to say "thank you." As illustrated below, a thank-you letter should be written in a friendly tone and avoid pressure of any kind on the reader.

Dear Mrs. Wheeler:

This is just a note to express our sincere thanks to you for the many orders you have placed with us during the past year.

We hope that this year has been a most successful one for you personally—and for Wheeler's Garden Shop. Please accept our sincere best wishes for a happy and prosperous New Year.

Cordially yours,

ASSIGNMENT

○ At your invitation, Dr. Lauren McCloskey gave a one-hour talk entitled "Business and Education—Partners for Progress" at a conference you chaired for your local Jaycees Club last night. Filling in all the details you think appropriate, write the speaker a thank-you letter.

○ Worksheet 92

UNIT 42: The Application Letter

□ BACKGROUND

An application letter—the letter you write to apply for a job—probably will be the most important kind of letter you will ever write. And since most people change employers several times during their business careers, the chances are quite good that you will need to write such a letter a number of times. Your first job, as well as each of those that follows, is almost certain to involve some writing—and most employers look upon an application letter as an excellent indicator of an applicant's writing and other communication skills.

Writing an application letter, which is usually accompanied by a résumé, is the most important beginning step in your campaign to get a job. Its main purpose is to get you an in-person interview with the prospective employer. If the letter is weak, your chances of getting an interview are likely to be nil. However, if the letter is a good one, you can be reasonably certain that you will be granted an interview. Thus when you write an application letter and a résumé to send along with it, remember that several others probably will be doing the same thing for the same reason and that only those who can demonstrate that they have the qualifications for the job will make the employer want to follow up with an in-person interview.

□ PLAN OF THE LETTER

The general plan of an application letter matches that of a sales letter fairly closely; thus, with minor modifications, the principles and techniques of writing a sales letter apply to writing an application letter. When writing an application letter, the "prospect" to whom you are selling is the employer. The "product" you are selling consists of your knowledge, your skills, your personality—everything about you that will enable you to perform the job to the satisfaction of the employer. As a result, you must understand the employer's needs, know the specific requirements of the job you are seeking, and know what you have to "sell." After you have compiled and studied all of this information, you will want to plan your application letter so that it will:

1. Attract the reader's attention. Some writers have used startling or gimmicky opening statements successfully. If you do, make sure that your opening statement is unlikely to "fall flat." As a general rule, you will be on much safer ground if you rely on the neatness and overall attractiveness of your letter to make an attention-getting impression.

2. Interest the reader in you as a prospective employee. Let your letter show that you have self-respect and self-confidence. Never appeal to an employer's sympathy, apologize for asking for a job, or pat yourself on the back for being such a great person (let the employer discover that!). Show that you know something about the prospective employer's company, if you do, and that you know the general requirements of the job—which you should.

3. Make the reader want to hire *you*. Show that you have all the skills and other qualifications required to perform the job for which you are applying. Present your qualifications in relation to the requirements of the job. Look at the situation from the

115

reader's point of view: emphasize "what I can do for you," not "what can you do for me?" Don't be afraid to use the pronoun *I,* but don't overdo it. Remember that the *"you* attitude" involves a great deal more than sprinkling *you, your,* and *yours* all through your message.

4. Lead to a personal interview.

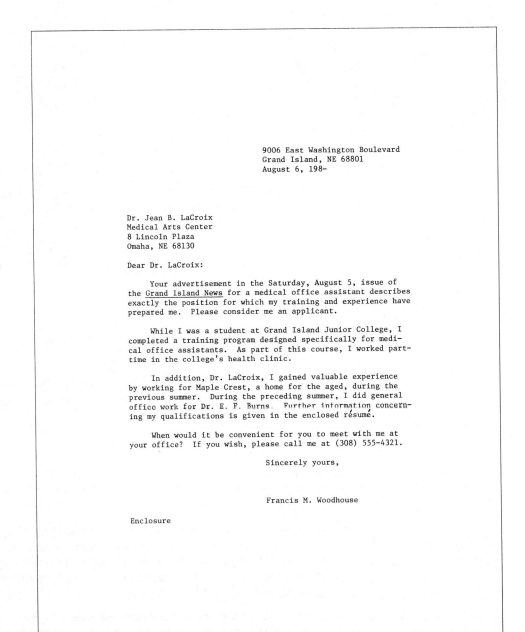

9006 East Washington Boulevard
Grand Island, NE 68801
August 6, 198–

Dr. Jean B. LaCroix
Medical Arts Center
8 Lincoln Plaza
Omaha, NE 68130

Dear Dr. LaCroix:

    Your advertisement in the Saturday, August 5, issue of the <u>Grand Island News</u> for a medical office assistant describes exactly the position for which my training and experience have prepared me. Please consider me an applicant.

    While I was a student at Grand Island Junior College, I completed a training program designed specifically for medical office assistants. As part of this course, I worked part-time in the college's health clinic.

    In addition, Dr. LaCroix, I gained valuable experience by working for Maple Crest, a home for the aged, during the previous summer. During the preceding summer, I did general office work for Dr. E. F. Burns. Further information concerning my qualifications is given in the enclosed résumé.

    When would it be convenient for you to meet with me at your office? If you wish, please call me at (308) 555-4321.

        Sincerely yours,

        Francis M. Woodhouse

Enclosure

☐ ORGANIZATION OF THE LETTER

When writing an application letter, you may find it helpful to view it in sections—opening, middle, and closing. Remember, though, that all three sections make up one forward-moving, smooth-flowing message: the unity of the whole message is basic. In addition to studying the following, closely examine the application letter on page 116.

The Opening Section. In the opening paragraph, state that you are applying for a particular job or for a specific type of work. Your reader will appreciate the fact that you know what you want to do. Further, the reader will appreciate not having to waste time trying to determine what your letter is all about. In this paragraph, you may feature your most outstanding qualification for the job.

> Please consider me an applicant for the position of administrative assistant that you advertised in today's *Morning Star and Register.* I have just completed a two-year business administration program at *Rockland Community College* and feel that I am fully qualified for this position with your company.

If someone suggested that you apply for a job and if mentioning that person's name would be likely to help you achieve your objective, obtain the person's permission to mention his or her name and consider starting your letter in a manner similar to this:

> Ms. Myra Gifford, a member of your information processing staff, has told me that you may soon have an opening for an advertising copywriter.

Or you may want to consider opening your letter with a question. If you decide to use this approach, be sure to follow the question with a statement that directly relates to—and at least partly answers—it.

> Does your company have an opening for someone who can type 80 words a minute for ten minutes without error? If so, I would like to prove to you that I am the person for that job.

The Middle Section. In the middle paragraphs of your letter, you will need to elaborate on your opening paragraph and emphasize the highlights of your education and of your experience (if you have work experience). Again, relate the discussion to the requirements of the job. Refer the reader to the enclosed résumé for additional information. If you wish, indicate why you would like to work for the reader's company in particular.

The Closing Section. In the closing paragraph, request a personal interview. Make it easy for the reader to grant your request by enclosing a self-addressed postcard or by stating the telephone number where you can be reached during business hours. If the employer is some distance away, you might use a closing paragraph similar to the one that follows.

> I am planning to be in Richmond on September 20 and 21. Would it be possible for you to grant me a personal interview on either of those days? Your notifying me by returning the enclosed postcard would be very much appreciated.

NOTE: If you have little or no work experience, stress your educational qualifications. Mention any special scholastic achievements or honors; describe courses you have taken to prepare yourself for the particular kind of job; list extracurricular activities and hobbies. If you have part-time work experience, be sure to mention it—even if it is not directly related to the job for which you are applying.

○ Choose a "Help Wanted" ad from a local newspaper and write a letter of application. Be sure to choose an ad dealing with a job that appeals to you—and a job for which you are qualified. Assume that you will enclose a résumé.

○ Worksheet 93

UNIT **43**: The Résumé

☐ BACKGROUND

As you probably have noticed in "Help Wanted" ads, most employers ask for a statement of an applicant's background before granting an in-person interview. This compact statement of all significant aspects of a job applicant's education, experience, and so on, is often called a *résumé;* however, it may be referred to in advertisements and elsewhere as a *personal data sheet, a fact sheet,* or a *qualifications summary,* for example. Like the application letter that the résumé typically accompanies, the purpose of the résumé is to help the applicant get a personal interview.

By carefully planning and preparing your résumé, you can avoid cluttering your application letter with numerous details that would interfere with its lively, readable "sales presentation." Further, you can present all the appropriate background information about yourself in a greatly condensed, well-organized, easy-to-understand, attractive format—probably on one page! As illustrated on page 119, you should divide your résumé into various sections, each with an appropriate heading; also you should be consistent in the form and phrasing of statements, but you need not use complete sentences. Also note that almost any attractive layout is acceptable; the one illustrated here is but one of several that are commonly used and recommended by personnel specialists.

☐ ORGANIZATION

A résumé is usually divided into these main sections: *heading, objective, education, experience, personal data,* and *references.* The education, experience, and personal data sections may be presented in any order, depending on what you want to stress.

Heading. The *heading* consists of your name, address, and telephone number. This information may be centered or positioned at either side of the page.

Objective. Since your résumé and application letter may become separated, state your specific job *objective* immediately below the heading.

Education. List first the school you attended most recently. Do not list schools other than high schools and colleges, technical schools, and similar post-high school institutions. Give the name and address of each school; the title of the degree granted, if any; the date of graduation; the subject or subject areas in which you specialized. Also include, under subheadings if you wish, scholastic honors, extracurricular activities, and offices held. If you do not have work experience, stress your education.

Résumé

Francis M. Woodhouse
9006 East Washington Boulevard
Grand Island, Nebraska 68801
Telephone: (308) 555-4321

POSITION SOUGHT: Medical Office Assistant

EXPERIENCE: Grand Island Junior College Health Clinic, Grand Island,
                 Nebraska. January 198- to June 198-. Worked part-time
                 in conjunction with Co-Op Training Program. Duties in-
                 cluded assisting regular staff members in the prepara-
                 tion and filing of various medical records.

                 Maple Crest, Box 888A, Route 1, Grand Island, Nebraska.
                 July 198- to September 198-. Duties consisted of light
                 office work and occasional assistance in the care of ge-
                 riatric patients. Supervisor: William Baines, R.N.

                 E. F. Burns, M.D., Suite 400, One Nebraska Street, Grand
                 Island, Nebraska. July 198- to September 198-. Duties
                 consisted of typing, transcribing, filing, and similar
                 office work.

EDUCATION: Grand Island Junior College, 3600 Campus Circle, Grand
                 Island, Nebraska. Awarded Associate in Arts degree upon
                 completing two-year course. In second year, completed
                 courses in medical dictation and transcription and medi-
                 cal office procedures as part of special Medical Office
                 Assistant Training Program, which also included part-time
                 work in the college's health clinic.

                 Carson Senior High School, 1200 Grand Island Boulevard,
                 Grand Island, Nebraska. Graduated with honors in June
                 198-, upon completion of college preparatory curriculum.

REFERENCES: Dr. Louise M. Leland, Coordinator of Business and Office
                 Education, Grand Island Junior College, 3600 Campus Cir-
                 cle, Grand Island, Nebraska 68801.

                 Mr. Morton L. Sanders, 7733 Grange Road, Grand Island,
                 Nebraska 68801.

                 Ms. Lucy Daley, 8462 West Lincoln Terrace, Grand Island,
                 Nebraska 68801.

Experience.   List your work *experience* in reverse chronological order—most recent employer first. Give the name and address of each employer; the starting and ending dates of your employment with each firm; the title of your job with the firm; a description of your job duties; the name and title of your supervisor; and, if you wish, your beginning salary and your ending salary. Unless your experience consists entirely of part-time work, be sure to account for any gaps in your employment history.

If there is a time lapse between your graduation from school and your first job or between two jobs because of military service, set up a separate section headed "military service." Indicate your dates of service, your rank at the time of separation or discharge, and a brief description of your military duties. Also, include the names of any military schools you attended and the titles of the programs in which you were enrolled.

Personal Data.   Although you may provide any *personal data* you wish, you need not provide any. You may decide to provide nothing more than height, weight, and a general statement concerning your health.

References.   Under this heading, you may simply indicate that the names of *references* will be provided upon request. Or you may list the names, addresses, and telephone numbers of at least two people who can vouch for your character. If they are professional people, give their titles and business addresses and telephone numbers. Never list a person's name as a character reference without first obtaining permission to do so.

ASSIGNMENT

○ Prepare a résumé for yourself.

○ Worksheet 94

UNIT 44: Other Employment Letters

Before and after you get a job, you will need to write at least a few other types of employment letters. These include *reference-request letters, follow-up letters, letters of acceptance or refusal,* and—perhaps at one or more points—a *resignation letter.* In addition, of course, you may need to write reference letters for others and letters accepting resignations of employees reporting to you, for example. Several of these other types of employment letters are briefly discussed in this unit.

☐ REFERENCE-REQUEST LETTERS

Before listing a person's name as a character reference in your application letter or in your résumé, write a short letter in which you:

1. Request permission to use the person's name as a reference.

2. Provide a few details concerning the job for which you plan to apply.

3. Express appreciation for any assistance the person may give you—but do not literally thank the person in advance. Note the following letter:

Dear Dr. Albertson:

While I was a member of your medical office procedures class at Grand Island Junior College, you thoughtfully offered to serve as a reference when I applied for a job. Would you be willing to grant me that favor now?

Upon returning from vacation at the end of July, I plan to submit an application to some medical facilities and doctors' offices in this area as well as in Omaha. While I would enjoy working here in Grand Island, I would very much like to gain the experience of living and working in Omaha.

Upon receiving your written permission, Dr. Albertson, I shall list your name on my résumé. Any assistance you may give me would be deeply appreciated.

Cordially yours,

☐ FOLLOW-UP LETTERS

Immediately after a personal interview, write a follow-up letter to thank the interviewer for the time and courtesy extended to you. Under certain circumstances, you can also use this letter to provide additional information concerning your qualifications for a job, to return the firm's application form, or to submit samples of your work.

Dear Dr. LaCroix:

Thank you for taking the time to talk with me this afternoon. I very much enjoyed meeting you and the other members of the Medical Arts Center staff.

It is my understanding, Dr. LaCroix, that you will notify me of your decision by the end of next week. As indicated during our discussion, I am willing, able, and eager to begin working for you as your medical office assistant immediately.

Sincerely yours,

☐ LETTER OF ACCEPTANCE OR REFUSAL

If you are offered a job and decide to accept it, write a letter in which you acknowledge the offer and state your acceptance of it. Reassure the employer that you are the right person for the job. Indicate your eagerness to begin work and state when you can report to work (if a definite date was established during the interview, confirm it).

If you are offered a job and decide not to accept it, courtesy and business ethics demand that you write a friendly, tactful letter of refusal. Identify the job by title, give the reason for not accepting it, and express your appreciation for the time and courtesy extended to you as well as your thanks for the job offer, of course.

☐ RESIGNATION LETTERS

Should you decide to resign from a job, the businesslike thing to do is to give your employer at least two weeks' notice (in some situations, a month's notice is customary) and to write a letter of resignation to your immediate supervisor. In writing the letter, show a positive attitude. Briefly discuss your reason for leaving the job—but never make statements that may haunt you later (your next employer will want to know why you left your previous job and may contact your present employer for information about you). Give the date on which your resignation is to become effective. Regardless of the circumstances, express your appreciation for at least one or two things related to your present employment.

121

○ Write the following employment letters, assuming that each letter stems from the application letter and résumé you wrote earlier: (1) a reference-request letter, (2) an interview follow-up letter, (3) a letter of acceptance or refusal, and (4) a thank-you letter to one of your character references.

○ Worksheet 95

UNIT 45: Memos and Reports

☐ INTEROFFICE MEMOS

Background. The *interoffice memorandum,* often called an *interoffice memo* or simply a *memo,* serves as the principal form of written communication within a business, government, or other type of organization. Executives, managers, supervisors, secretaries, accountants—all members of an organization write memos to one another, but they do *not* use memos as substitutes for letters when communicating with people outside the organization. Unlike a letter, a memo does not have an inside address, a salutation, an attention line, or a complimentary closing. Instead, a memo is typically a printed form with "guide words" in the heading that tell the writer or the typist where to insert such fill-in information as the name of the addressee, the name of the writer, the subject of the message, the date, and any other data that may be necessary within a particular organization to ensure the speedy delivery of the memo to the correct person. (Note the guide words in the headings of the memos on pages 123 and 125.)

Interoffice memos are frequently used to announce staff meetings, employee promotions, vacation schedules, and so on; issue instructions; transmit other documents; provide information in the form of informal reports; summarize and confirm the results of departmental meetings and of the major points of discussions between employees. In most companies, the general practice is to "put it in writing if it's important" rather than to rely on memory.

Writing Suggestions. Writing a memo requires consideration of essentially the same factors as those involved in writing a letter—but, at least in some instances, from a somewhat different perspective. Here are some suggestions:

1. Consider your job level in relation to that of the person to whom you are writing. Some companies pride themselves on their highly informal, everybody-on-a-first-name-basis atmosphere; others do not. Unless you are absolutely certain that it would be completely acceptable to do otherwise, for example, show the appropriate degree of deference to a person who is at a significantly higher job level (perhaps starting with a courtesy title before the person's name in the *To* line of the heading).

2. Gear the tone of your message to the subject you are writing about as well as to the person to whom you are writing. For example, if you are writing to a subordinate about a procedure that he or she is to follow in performing a particular task, you may want to be quite "emphatic"—but not discourteous—in discussing it.

```
                                                                    ╱VIDEOX╲
        Interoffice Memorandum                                     ╱   V    ╲

    TO:  Mr. Carlos Noriega          FROM:  Kay Collins

 SUBJECT:  Vacation Advance           DATE:  June 16, 198-

        Would it be possible for me to obtain three weeks' vacation pay in advance?
        If so, Mr. Noriega, I should appreciate receiving the check by July 11, as I
        shall be on vacation from Monday, July 14, through Friday, August 1.

        Your approving this request would be very much appreciated.

                                      KC
```

3. Stick to the subject of your memo (don't mix several different topics in the same memo). Identify the subject in the heading, and get into it immediately in the first paragraph. If your memo is a follow-up to a previous memo or a request from the reader, for example, it is usually a good idea to make whatever brief reference is appropriate at the outset.

4. Organize your message in a manner that is easy to follow, easy to read, and easy to understand. Make it possible for your reader to get from the beginning to the end of your message without having to stop at one or more points in between or, perhaps, go back to the beginning in order to understand the ending.

5. State your thoughts clearly, correctly, and concisely. Avoid convoluted expressions, inaccurate information, poor grammar, and so on, as well as words and statements that do nothing more than fill up space. You will save yourself and your reader a great deal of time—one of the main objectives of a memo. Numbering statements or questions or presenting information in tables or charts is frequently a good idea.

6. Indicate what, if anything, your reader is to do in connection with your message in the closing paragraph. Be specific not only about the expected action but also about the time of the action, if appropriate.

Format. As indicated previously, most firms use printed forms for memos. When using a form similar to the one shown above, all you have to do is fill in the information indicated in the heading, space down three or four lines, and type the message (with single spacing); then type your initials below the message. If someone is typing the memo for you, that person's initials should appear two lines below your initials, at the left margin. Do not include your job title with your name in the *From* line or with your initials. If you wish, sign the memo or initial it, but note that neither is essential. If something is attached to or enclosed with the memo, an enclosure notation should appear below the typist's initials.

If you are using plain paper instead of a printed form, all you need to do is center the title *Interoffice Memo* an inch or so from the top of the paper; set margins for a 60-space pica or 70-space elite writing line; space down three or four lines and type (double-spaced) the guide words *To, From, Subject, Date,* and whatever others you may need with the appropriate fill-ins after them; space down three or four lines and type the rest of the memo in the same way you would if you were using a printed form.

ASSIGNMENT

○ Assume that you are interested in enrolling in one of your firm's in-service training courses, which is conducted from 5 to 7:30 p.m. on Tuesdays and Thursdays for a period of six weeks. You feel that taking the course would help you in your work and that you may be able to get your supervisor to approve your enrolling in the course under the company's tuition-refund plan. Write a memo to your supervisor (make up the names and all the other details).

☐ BUSINESS REPORTS

Purpose. In every business, employees at almost all job levels frequently must submit as well as receive information about a wide variety of subjects and activities in order to perform their duties successfully. Thus one of the most vitally important communications in the business world is the business report, a communication prepared primarily to provide complete, accurate information about expenses, production, sales, advertising, customers, or some other subject related to the operations of a company.

Writing Suggestions. The following suggestions will help you handle most of your report-writing assignments successfully:

1. Collect all the data you need to provide in the message of your report before you begin to write, and be sure that it is complete and accurate. Incomplete or inaccurate data about sales, the condition of office equipment, employee turnover, or any other subject can lead the person receiving your report to make an unwise, if not disastrous, decision.

2. Organize the data you have collected so that you can present the clearest, most concise, and most readable report possible. When you can, arrange information in tables, charts, graphs, or lists rather than paragraphs.

3. Check the files to see if they contain reports similar to the one you have been asked to write. If they do, you should be able to use one of them as a model or general guide.

4. Consider the reader of your report and the subject about which you are writing in deciding what tone to give your report. Under most circumstances, the "you and I" approach is preferable to the "writer and reader" approach. However, always be sure to gear your report—in *all* respects—to your reader, and remember that someone other than the person to whom you are writing may see it and read it also. Supervisors and managers often request reports, read them, and pass them along to others up the line.

5. Keep your report as short as possible. Remember that you are writing for one basic purpose: to provide information about a particular subject. Therefore, unless you have been requested to do so or are reasonably certain that your reader will welcome your doing so, do not editorialize, inject personal opinion, or state your own conclusions or recommendations, for example.

---

inter-office memorandum

To	Ms. Karen Keating	From	Anthony Russo
Company	Book	Company	Corporate
Dept. or Pub.	Executive	Dept. or Pub.	Personnel
Floor or Branch	6	Floor and Ext. or Branch	2, Ext. 2046
Subject	Participation in Training Programs	Date	February 8, 198-

As you requested in your January 16 memo, I have completed an analysis of the enrollment of members of the Data Processing, Office Services, and Marketing Departments in corporate-sponsored training programs during the previous year.

	Department			
Title of Course	Data Processing	Marketing	Office Services	Totals
Accounting Fundamentals	22	8	12	42
Business Writing	12	36	24	72
Effective Listening	8	24	15	47
Giving a Talk	4	18	20	42
Refresher Shorthand	1	1	22	24
Refresher Typing	8	14	31	53

This enrollment is approximately 10 percent higher than that during the previous year (280 versus 254).

AR

jng

6. Prepare your report in the format that you feel is best suited to your reader and to the subject about which you are writing. To the greatest extent possible, most business writers use memo forms, such as the one illustrated previously. Occasionally, though, you may need to prepare a report in a manuscript format and include a title page, a contents page, and other special pages; if so, the best procedure is to consult a writer's handbook or other reference.

ASSIGNMENT

○ Using a recent issue of your local newspaper, study the "Help Wanted" ads and prepare a report that shows the various types of business and office jobs available to qualified applicants, the number of jobs of each type (accountant, secretary, sales representative, and so on), and the salary range for each type of job. Address your report to your instructor.

○ You know several people working for companies that have flexible work hours—that is, they can decide what hours they will work on any given day, but they must put in 35 hours during each Monday-through-Friday period. You and your co-workers feel that your office should adopt a similar policy, and you have studied several magazine and newspaper articles on the subject of "flexible work hours" as well as talked to people with firsthand experience with this type of work schedule. Write an unsolicited report (one not requested by the person to whom you are writing) to the general manager of your company. Remember that you may want to make some specific recommendations at the end of your report. However, you decide for yourself what you want to include.

○ Worksheet 96

PART FIVE

Other Business Communication Skills

Communication is a two-way process that involves the sending and the receiving of a message. Thus writing without reading would be a pointless exercise, as would speaking without listening. In business, industry, and government all four communication activities—writing, reading, listening, and speaking—typically occupy much of the time of every employee.

UNIT 46: Reading, Listening, and Speaking in Business

☐ **READING**

Importance.   Memos, letters, reports, professional journals, computer printouts—all types and forms of written communications come across the desk of individual employees in business, industry, and government in increasingly large numbers. As you will discover on the job, the importance and urgency of the materials that you receive will vary widely, and you undoubtedly will develop the technique of scanning before reading as a means of coping successfully. Even with scanning as a means of deciding what does or does not require careful reading, though, you probably will find that the need to read will place a heavy demand on your time. Consequently, you will not be surprised to find that many businesses and other organizations conduct or participate in training programs designed specifically to help employees increase both their reading speed and their reading comprehension. Quite obviously, then, the more proficient you become in reading now, the better prepared you will be for your chosen career.

The responsibility for the reading aspect of communication is one that the writer and the reader of a message share. When you write, for example, your reader will expect you to construct and present your message in a manner that will enable him or her to quickly, easily, and correctly understand everything you have said. In effect, he or she will expect you to know and to apply all the principles of English grammar, usage, and style and the techniques of writing that you studied and practiced in this course. (These principles and techniques are essentially nothing more than tools that the writer uses to help the reader.) If you have developed and presented your message from the receiver's point of view, then, you should be able to expect your reader to quickly and accurately grasp the meaning of what you have said and to react or to respond in whatever manner you intended. Thus effective reading and effective writing stem, at least to a large extent, from a thorough knowledge and practical application of a common set of basic language-usage principles and techniques.

Suggestions.   The following steps, which you can easily take on your own, may be helpful to you in increasing your reading speed and comprehension. If you feel that either aspect of reading skill poses a serious problem for you, you should, of course, consult your instructor or someone else qualified to provide you with professional assistance.

1. Have your eyesight checked to be sure that you do not have a physical impairment that makes reading a "real chore" for you. If reading for any length of time results in eyestrain or a headache, you obviously will find reading neither an enjoyable nor a very productive activity. Developing poor vision is frequently such a gradual process that many of us have the problem before we realize it; thus the solution lies in periodic visits to an optometrist or ophthalmologist.

2. Control, to the extent that you can, the physical conditions under which you read. Most people find it extremely difficult to read with speed or comprehension when, for example, the lighting is too dim or too bright, the temperature is too low or too high, the room is poorly ventilated, distracting noises are coming into the room, or the chair being used is uncomfortable (or too comfortable).

3. Scan the material before you actually begin to read it. In this way, you will gain a good impression of the organization of the material and know what the most significant points are likely to be. Thus scanning will help you read not only much faster but also more productively.

4. Read in logical thought units, not word by word. By developing the ability to read in phrases, you'll do more than cut down on eyestrain—you'll also read faster and remember more of what you read.

5. Use such "signals" as punctuation and capitalization not only as guides to grouping thought units but also as aids for properly interpreting or comprehending the material you are reading.

6. Try to determine the meaning of an unfamiliar word by considering the context in which it is used. When surrounding sentences coupled with the sentence in which the word appears do not provide the general meaning of the word, though, be sure to consult your dictionary. Doing so will decrease your speed, of course, but it will increase your comprehension of the material.

7. Gear your reading speed to the type of material you are reading and to your purpose for reading it. For example, if you are reading a memo that sets forth procedures that you will be expected to remember and to follow in doing something later, you obviously will read it at a different speed than you would read an announcement of someone's promotion or transfer to another job. At the same time, you probably will make a greater effort to fully comprehend a communication that is of special significance to you than you would to understand and remember something that is of incidental or casual interest. As you gain on-the-job experience, you probably will develop the habit of simply scanning a number of items of the "casual interest" type.

8. Measure your present reading speed and attempt to increase it without sacrificing complete comprehension. Take any piece of copy that you wish, count the actual number of words in it, and time yourself as you read it. To determine your reading speed, simply divide the number of words in the article by the number of minutes you took to read it. At regular intervals, repeat the process—but use different selections that are of about the same length and general difficulty as the one you used the first time. If you "push" yourself to read a little faster each time, you will increase your speed and be able to maintain the faster rate without experiencing any difficulty.

9. Reinforce your understanding of what you have read by pausing from time to time to recast the writer's statements into your own words—but pause at a logical "stopping place," not midparagraph, for example. Or, when doing so would be appropriate, make written notes concerning important points covered in whatever you are reading—again pausing and doing so at logical points in the copy you are reading. Both procedures will help you increase your reading comprehension and assist you in remembering important details much longer.

10. Develop the "reading habit." Reading, like typing or swimming or any other skill, requires deliberate and frequent practice if it is to become one in which you are truly proficient. Newspapers, books, magazines, correspondence—the greater the variety of materials you read, the more skillful you will become. In addition to increasing your reading skills and your knowledge of a variety of subjects, you most likely will find—as many people have found—your spelling, vocabulary, and other basic communication skills improving simultaneously without devoting any special or unusual amount of attention to them.

ASSIGNMENT

○ Select an article containing 1,000 words or so and use it to determine your present reading speed. (See item 8, above.) After you have determined your reading speed, give the article to someone and have that person ask you questions based on the information it contains. In other words, measure both your present reading speed and your present reading comprehension. At fairly regular intervals (perhaps weekly), repeat the process and note the improvement in your reading skills.

☐ LISTENING

Importance. To everyone in business, listening—*hearing with understanding*—is at least as important as reading. In some respects, listening skill is more important than reading, writing, or speaking: we spend most of our communication time listening to others. Indeed, to those engaged in many kinds of work, the ability to listen—not simply to hear—is the key to successful job performance. Can you imagine, for example, the fate of a sales representative who fails to *listen,* not simply to hear, when customers and prospective customers speak? Not at all surprising, then, is the fact that many business and other organizations provide listening-improvement courses for their employees or offer tuition-refund programs to encourage their employees to participate in such courses offered by educational institutions.

Suggestions. Here are a few suggestions that you may find helpful in improving your listening skills. If you feel that a physical impairment may be hindering your ability to hear, you should, of course, consult someone professionally qualified to assist you.

1. Prepare yourself to listen if you know in advance what the speaker's subject is to be—as is generally the case when someone is to make a formal presentation and you are to be a member of his or her audience. Read about the subject, and talk with others about it. In this way, you'll be better equipped to assess what the speaker has to say about a particular subject.

2. Look—not stare—at the person who is speaking. The speaker's facial expressions, physical gestures, and other elements of "body language" reinforce—and often add unstated meaning to—what he or she is saying.

3. "Look" for expressions that the speaker uses to signal important points, examples that he or she uses to illustrate various points, and so forth. In addition, of course, actually look at charts and other visual aids that the speaker may be using to reinforce or explain important statements and key points in his or her message.

4. Concentrate as intently as possible on what the speaker is saying. Try to "tune out" distracting noises or things that may be happening around you, for example. Giving the speaker your undivided attention is not only the courteous thing to do—it is also one of the best things you can do to help you get the most out of what someone has to say.

5. Use "spare time" to mull over what the speaker has said. Like everyone else, you can listen at a much faster rate than anyone can talk. Therefore, since every speaker is certain to pause briefly from time to time during a presentation, you will have several opportunities to reflect upon what you have heard. However, don't become absorbed in a silent debate with the speaker or become so involved in thinking about something already said that you miss hearing and understanding other statements.

6. Take notes—if appropriate—while you are listening. In doing so, though, write only the key points, and recast them in your own words. At all costs, avoid the temptation to write—in your own words or in those of the speaker—everything that is said. Remember that it's the "wheat," not the "chaff" that's mixed with it, that is worth recording and remembering!

ASSIGNMENT

○ Have someone select and read to you an article that you have not previously read. Then, have that person ask you questions about the content of the article. Be sure the person asks you meaningful questions about key points—not questions about relatively unimportant details. Your success in answering such questions correctly will give you an immediate, practical, and fairly accurate measure of your ability to hear with comprehension. Keep practicing until you develop the ability to listen, not simply to hear!

☐ SPEAKING

Importance.   The ability to speak effectively is obviously a very important asset to everyone, but it is especially important to those whose work brings them into contact with people outside the organization for which they work: receptionists and marketing representatives, for example. At the same, it is an essential skill for managers, supervisors, executives, and others who must make either formal or informal presentations to other members of their organizations at meetings and conferences. Thus business and other firms and organizations, like educational institutions, frequently hire highly qualified instructors to teach their employees the principles and techniques of giving oral presentations.

Suggestions.   Here are some basic steps that you can easily take on your own to assist you in improving your speaking skills. Practice them often—and, if possible, enroll in a public speaking or other course geared specifically to your needs and interests, especially if the career for which you are preparing will require better-than-average skill in speaking.

1. Give special attention to the pronunciation of words. If necessary, consult the dictionary to determine whether or not a particular pronunciation is considered acceptable—and remember, as pointed out earlier in this course, that the pronunciation of a word may depend upon how it is used as a part of speech. (For example, note the difference in pronunciation between *record* as a noun and *record* as a verb.) Many errors in pronunciation stem from adding or omitting letters or syllables and from placing the stress on an incorrect syllable.

2. Enunciate each of the sounds in a word clearly and distinctly. Avoid running words together; for example, say ''what do you''—not ''whatcha.''

3. Vary the pitch and the volume of your voice as you speak. Such changes will help you give emphasis to parts of sentences and make what you have to say more interesting and meaningful to your listeners.

4. Vary the rate at which you speak. Avoid speaking too rapidly, too slowly, or in a singsong manner. An unvarying rate of speaking, like an unvarying pitch or volume, makes it very difficult for your audience to concentrate on or to understand what you are saying. Don't let the way in which you speak overshadow what you are saying!

5. Use a cassette player to record and listen to your voice. Better yet, if you have access to a videotape recorder, have someone tape you as you deliver a short speech. In addition to analyzing your own strengths and weaknesses, have others listen to and watch you and then solicit their constructive criticisms.

ASSIGNMENT

○ As you read the following sentences aloud, give special attention to the pronunciation of the italicized words.

Is the cost of running these *advertisements concurrently comparable* to that of running them *separately?*

You are *quite* right, Mrs. Bright!—she kept *quiet* about her *diet.*

An *athlete's* running for Congress is not at all *incongruous.*

○ As you read the following sentences aloud, enunciate all the sounds clearly and distinctly—and avoid running words together.

We are going to go, but wouldn't you know it would have to snow?

Cecil Simmons said Susan Sullivan saw Cecilia Simpson selling seashells at the seashore.

Peter Piper promptly picked, pickled, and packed a peck of peppers.

○ Prepare and, if possible, deliver a 3- to 5-minute talk on a subject with which you are thoroughly familiar.

Identifying Sentences, Clauses, and Phrases

Decide whether each of the following groups of words is a *sentence* or a *sentence fragment* (a group of words that expresses an incomplete thought and that incorrectly begins with a capital letter and ends with a period, a question mark, or an exclamation point). Indicate your decision by circling *S* (for *sentence*) or *SF* (for *sentence fragment*).

1. The convenience and ease of saving through a payroll-deduction plan.   1. S SF

2. Whose signature appears on the purchase order sent to that company?   2. S SF

3. Plans to install a closed-circuit television system next spring.   3. S SF

4. Print or type your new address on the label from a recent issue.   4. S SF

5. Although neither of them was aware of the firm's merger proposal.   5. S SF

6. To reach a mutually satisfactory settlement is the negotiators' goal.   6. S SF

7. Carefully studied the proposal before issuing a statement about it.   7. S SF

8. As long as you have a strong interest in the matter!   8. S SF

9. Early last week notified the head of the department of the shortage.   9. S SF

10. That solution to the problem may be the best one for all concerned.   10. S SF

Indicate whether each group of words is a *phrase*, a *dependent clause*, or an *independent clause* by placing a check mark (√) under the appropriate heading.

	PHRASE	DEPENDENT CLAUSE	INDEPENDENT CLAUSE
11. while you were attending the meeting in Pittsburgh	11. _____	_____	_____
12. should receive an answer before next Wednesday	12. _____	_____	_____
13. it's a matter of special concern to local residents	13. _____	_____	_____
14. that Ms. Navarro will become a member of the board	14. _____	_____	_____
15. making such a large investment at this time	15. _____	_____	_____
16. among the provisions of the proposed agreement	16. _____	_____	_____
17. to ensure the success of any business venture	17. _____	_____	_____
18. shown in the chart on page 16	18. _____	_____	_____
19. your assistance will be very much appreciated	19. _____	_____	_____
20. after you have met with the members of your staff	20. _____	_____	_____

2 Classifying Sentences

Underline the dependent clauses (if any) in the following sentences. Then indicate whether each sentence is *simple, compound, complex,* or *compound-complex* in structure by writing the appropriate classification in the space provided.

1. Mr. Torres plans to interview several applicants while he is in Jacksonville next week.

1. _____

2. Please invite both of them to the reception.

2. _____

3. The deadline for completing the project is next Friday; however, I doubt we will meet it.

3. _____

4. Jack told me that he had volunteered to help you.

4. _____

5. The loss amounts to thousands of dollars.

5. _____

6. We invited Ms. Lange to be this year's speaker, but she was unable to accept.

6. _____

7. Mrs. Royce and I recommended several changes.

7. _____

8. George received a copy, but I did not.

8. _____

9. One of our customers in San Antonio noticed the defect.

9. _____

10. When you see Paul, you should ask him about it.

10. _____

Classify each of the following sentences according to its function by writing *declarative, interrogative, imperative,* or *exclamatory* in the space provided. Then insert the appropriate punctuation mark at the end of the sentence.

11. Miss Hale has worked for us about four years

11. _____

12. That's no bargain

12. _____

13. The increase will be retroactive to June 1

13. _____

14. Will you please call or write us next week

14. _____

15. How many companies have submitted bids so far

15. _____

16. Be sure to file your tax return by April 15

16. _____

17. When the shipment will arrive is anyone's guess

17. _____

18. Do you think there is an acceptable alternative

18. _____

19. Lisa asked why the meeting had been canceled

19. _____

20. Would you be willing to take such a risk

20. _____

3 Composing Subjects

In the space provided, write an appropriate subject to make each numbered item a complete sentence. Compose a different subject for each one, and avoid using one-word subjects.

1. _____ reported record sales last month.

2. _____ will meet you at the airport.

3. _____ should be stored in a safe place.

4. _____ seemed interested in the project.

5. _____ may run for reelection next year.

6. _____ attended the convention in Dallas.

7. _____ issued several new directives.

8. _____ will be considered carefully.

9. _____ may be interested in that job.

10. _____ amounted to more than $100.

11. _____ contained a few errors.

12. _____ received a copy of the annual report.

13. _____ increased significantly last month.

14. _____ should have notified us of the change.

15. _____ arrived nearly an hour late.

16. _____ conducted the survey for us.

17. _____ must be willing to take some risks.

18. _____ wanted to settle the claim out of court.

19. _____ lived in Connecticut for several years.

20. _____ had hoped for a greater reduction in taxes.

21. _____ obtained a home-improvement loan last week.

22. _____ offered to work overtime last weekend.

23. _____ should be completed soon.

24. _____ gave us some very good advice.

25. _____ may be eligible for a refund.

4 Composing Predicates

In the space provided, write an appropriate predicate to make each numbered item a complete sentence. Compose a different predicate for each one, and avoid using one-word predicates.

1. The new president of the company _____

2. Each of us _____

3. Most business executives _____

4. Copies of our new price list _____

5. My co-workers _____

6. Those who submit their applications early _____

7. Use of the metric system _____

8. A great deal of time and effort _____

9. The effects of inflation _____

10. Shorthand and typing _____

11. Many large companies _____

12. Mrs. Baker's recommendations _____

13. The winner of the contest _____

14. Next year's convention _____

15. The manager of our word processing department _____

16. Newspapers and magazines _____

17. Many political leaders _____

18. Some members of the committee _____

19. Success _____

20. The members of the jury _____

21. The agenda for the meeting _____

22. Steps to control costs _____

23. Every manager _____

24. The use of credit cards _____

25. The company's regional offices _____

5 Classifying Nouns

Draw a line under each *common noun* in each of the following fragments. For each *proper noun*, draw three short lines under each letter that should be capitalized.

1. a report by mark on the work done

2. may work on the staff of *business week*

3. paid the interest on bill's account

4. interest us in moving to kansas city

5. purchase stock at a reasonable price

6. to report on the work every business week

7. will mark the spot on fifth avenue

8. to account for an increase in may or june

9. are moving to a city in kansas next fall

10. confirm the price of every purchase

Circle *C* if the italicized word is a *collective noun* or *G* if it is a *gerund*. If it is neither a collective noun nor a gerund, draw a line through the letters *C* and *G*.

11. plaster falling off the *ceiling*　　　C　G

12. surprised by Sam's *resigning*　　　C　G

13. recommendation of the *committee*　C　G

14. tied a *string* around the carton　　C　G

15. are *typing* the agenda now　　　C　G

16. several people in the *audience*　　C　G

17. at the *meeting* last Wednesday　　C　G

18. for each member of the *staff*　　　C　G

19. customers *claiming* refunds are　　C　G

20. the opinion of the *majority* is　　　C　G

Indicate whether the italicized noun is *singular* or *plural* in number. Circle *S* (for *singular*) or *P* (for *plural*). If the noun may be either singular or plural, circle both letters.

21. of special interest to *employees*　　S　P

22. at a place near *Palm Springs*　　　S　P

23. clothing for young *children*　　　S　P

24. in behalf of the *stockholders*　　　S　P

25. the *benches* in the waiting room　　S　P

26. saw the *deer* in the national park　S　P

27. thought that you or *Ms. Jones*　　S　P

28. the *attorneys* for the plaintiff　　S　P

29. the *procedures* to be followed　　S　P

30. each of the *photocopies*　　　　S　P

Indicate the gender of each italicized noun. Circle *M* (for *masculine*), *F* (for *feminine*), *N* (for *neuter*), or *C* (for *common*).

31. a successful *secretary*　　M　F　N　C

32. a qualified *doctor*　　　M　F　N　C

33. the number of *wives*　　M　F　N　C

34. any new *company*　　　M　F　N　C

35. that *Louise* would ask　　M　F　N　C

36. the *car* belonging to Lois　M　F　N　C

37. our *manager,* Mr. Hill, is　M　F　N　C

38. every qualified *woman*　M　F　N　C

39. the *committee* will issue　M　F　N　C

40. some *paint* we ordered　M　F　N　C

6 Correcting Errors in Noun Usage

Underline each error in noun usage, and write the necessary correction in the space provided. If all the nouns in a sentence are correct, write *OK*.

1. The engineer submitted several reccommendations.   1. _____

2. Our offices are in this new sky scraper.   2. _____

3. How many stamps were on those two envelops?   3. _____

4. Businesses, as well as individuals, pay taxs.   4. _____

5. Most stores and restaurants accept credit-cards.   5. _____

6. All employees' timecards are stored by the time clock.   6. _____

7. Most jobs offer opportunitys for advancement.   7. _____

8. We appreciate the assistance of our coworkers.   8. _____

9. Co-operation is essential to the success of the plan.   9. _____

10. Is education of greater importants than experience?   10. _____

11. The maintainance of the equipment is not a problem.   11. _____

12. How much commission did the stock broker collect?   12. _____

13. I think miss day will accept the assignment.   13. _____

14. Your appointment is scheduled for 9 oclock.   14. _____

15. This machine is worth $50 on a trade in.   15. _____

16. What is your supervisors' name and telephone number?   16. _____

17. Good judgement is a requirement for success.   17. _____

18. Herman's company is a manufacturer of hardwear.   18. _____

19. Both volumns are on sale in the bookstore.   19. _____

20. The company's work force wants a shorter workweek.   20. _____

21. Most of the brochure was devoted to advertizing.   21. _____

22. We should hold the next conference in atlantic city.   22. _____

23. Their representative has an apointment to see you.   23. _____

24. Management often uses the technique of brain storming.   24. _____

25. Construction of more facilitys is underway.   25. _____

138

7 Using Your Dictionary

Everyone whose work involves the use of language, especially in its written form—secretaries, executives, typists—knows the importance of using the dictionary. This most frequently used reference provides information that all of us need—at least occasionally!—about spelling, word division, pronunciation, definitions, and other matters of word usage.

Using the Dictionary to Confirm the Correct Spelling. One of the words in each numbered line below is incorrectly spelled. Draw a line under that misspelled word, and write the correct spelling in the space provided.

1. correspondence   garantee   statement   purchase   1. _____
2. elimanate   operator   practice   coverage   2. _____
3. equipment   handled   simular   annual   3. _____
4. planning   choice   varius   notice   4. _____
5. managment   expense   receipt   current   5. _____
6. valuable   percent   freight   intrest   6. _____
7. untill   writing   referred   submitted   7. _____
8. complete   payed   either   minimum   8. _____
9. corporation   goverment   across   original   9. _____
10. repersentative   necessary   cannot   accept   10. _____

Using the Dictionary to Confirm Word Division. A one-letter syllable at the beginning or end of a word cannot be separated from the rest of a word, nor can a one-syllable word be divided. Leave a syllable of at least two letters at the end of a line, and carry to the beginning of the next line at least one syllable of three letters (or two letters and a punctuation mark). Keeping these points in mind, draw a line between the letters to indicate *each* acceptable division point in the following words; for example:

avail|able

11. sincerely   attention   committee   convenience   opportunity
12. whether   through   reference   brochure   excellent
13. cordially;   warehouse   quantity   effect   description
14. inventory   computer   really   inquiry   explanation
15. practical   mortgage   decision   pleasure   throughout

Using the Dictionary to Confirm Pronunciation. The way in which a word is used as a part of speech is sometimes indicated by a change in pronunciation or syllabication—or both—instead of by a change in spelling. In other instances, the same types of changes occur when a prefix (a word beginning) or a suffix (a word ending) is added to a word to form a derivative (a new word). In each of the following words, insert a stress mark (') to indicate the end of the syllable that receives the strongest emphasis when the word is pronounced. If each syllable in the word receives equal emphasis, do not insert a stress mark.

16. refer	reference	confer	conference	address (*n*)	address (*v*)
17. origin	original	console (*n*)	console (*v*)	associate (*n*)	associate (*v*)
18. convert (*n*)	convert (*v*)	object (*n*)	object (*v*)	preferable	prefer
19. conduct (*n*)	conduct (*v*)	conductor	confide	confident	confidential
20. famous	infamous	expose (*v*)	expose (*n*)	ordinary	extraordinary

Using the Dictionary to Confirm Definitions. Four of the words in each line are related in meaning. Draw a line under the one word in each line that is not related in meaning to the others.

21. meticulous	careful	meritorious	scrupulous	punctilious
22. gratuitous	essential	supererogatory	unnecessary	superfluous
23. colossal	huge	enormous	immense	miniscule
24. efficacious	effective	effluent	efficient	productive
25. supersede	replace	supplant	displace	overdo

Using the Dictionary to Find Other Information. Examine the various front and back sections of your dictionary, as well as the main word list, to see what kinds of information each section contains. Then answer each of the following questions, using a complete sentence for each answer.

26. Where are the Endicott Mountains? _____

_____

27. In what states is there a city named Kansas City? _____

_____

28. Who was Leon Victor Auguste Bourgeois? _____

_____

29. What does the expression *verbatim ac litteratim* mean? _____

_____

30. From what Spanish word is the word *mirador* derived? _____

_____

140

8 Identifying Antecedents of Pronouns

Underline the antecedent of each italicized pronoun; then draw an arrow from the pronoun to its antecedent. Note the example (0). Remember that the antecedent of one pronoun may be another pronoun.

0. Ann and Ken expressed *their* approval of the plan *that* Sue outlined in *her* memo.

1. Mrs. Keating asked Mr. Quinn, *her* assistant, to keep accurate records of all expenses.

2. The Kellys were able to sell *their* home before *they* moved to Los Angeles last month.

3. I think that you and I will have *our* part of the work done before the deadline.

4. Every manager knows that *he* or *she* must have the support of *his* or *her* subordinates.

5. These cartons of apples should have shipping labels attached to *them*.

6. The owner of the garage said that the truck needed to have a lot of work done on *it*.

7. You may prefer to discuss the matter with Dr. Stefano *yourself*.

8. We were unable to recover *our* losses, but other home owners recovered *theirs*.

9. Louis believes that the leading candidates are *he* and Margaret Williams.

10. Fernandez & Gonzalez gave *its* employees *their* vacation pay at the end of June.

11. Mr. Hamagaki, do *you* know someone *whom* you could recommend to serve as a mediator?

12. According to the mayor, the city is doing all *it* can to keep *its* expenses under control.

13. I think both copies are *yours*, Miss Steinberg.

14. We have already returned two shipments of refrigerators with dents in *them*.

15. *Some* of the speakers appeared to contradict *themselves*.

16. Larry told me that the general manager asked *him* to put *his* proposal in writing.

17. Ms. Jackson gave Jennifer instructions to do *her* work before *she* starts yours.

18. The owners have indicated that *they* will make all the necessary repairs.

19. I would appreciate your considering *my* request for a full-time assistant.

20. All were highly pleased with the bonuses *their* employers gave *them* last year.

9 Recognizing Properties of Pronouns

Identify the case of each italicized pronoun by circling N (for *nominative*), O (for *objective*), or P (for *possessive*). Base your answer on the way the pronoun is used in the sentence.

1. We asked *everyone* to help.   N O P
2. *You* have our endorsement.   N O P
3. Who was with *her?*   N O P
4. I think that *you* should go.   N O P
5. *Whose* folder is this?   N O P
6. This copy is for *you.*   N O P
7. No one knew *our* names.   N O P

8. Several need *your* help.   N O P
9. *Who* approved the ad?   N O P
10. I saw *her* new office.   N O P
11. *She* will not attend.   N O P
12. *He* knew all the answers.   N O P
13. *It* rained very hard.   N O P
14. *Their* address is here.   N O P

Draw one line under each pronoun that is *singular* in number and two lines under each pronoun that is *plural* in number. Ignore pronouns that may be either singular or plural.

15.	everything	all	several	them	yourself	those	someone	some
16.	themselves	her	no one	whom	nobody	which	myself	each
17.	everybody	one	herself	these	himself	whose	nothing	that
18.	ourselves	who	itself	few	anyone	they	everyone	both
19.	something	our	what	mine	yours	many	theirs	she
20.	yourselves	I	oneself	him	this	their	most	its

Draw one line under each *first person* pronoun and two lines under each *second person* pronoun. Ignore the others (they are, of course, third person).

21.	him	who	you	ours	both	those	my	all	me	I	its	they	their	none
22.	hers	she	her	mine	your	theirs	us	our	we	it	his	them	yours	he

Draw one line under each *feminine* pronoun, two lines under each *masculine* pronoun, and three lines under each *neuter* pronoun. Ignore the pronouns that are of common gender.

23.	she	him	themselves	ourselves	herself	you	we	they	everyone	each
24.	our	her	something	everybody	several	all	he	hers	nothing	your
25.	his	its	itself	himself	which	who	it	whom	whose	mine

10 Putting Pronouns to Work

In the space provided, write the pronoun that can correctly be substituted for the word or words shown in parentheses. Do not change the meaning of the sentence. Note the example.

0. Mr. Harris would like to see (*the person spoken to*).

0. <u>you</u>

1. (*Nearly all*) of the water has evaporated.

1. _____

2. (*The man spoken about*) may be able to do the work.

2. _____

3. June wishes that (*June*) had applied for the job.

3. _____

4. Mr. Davega said that (*Mr. Davega's*) loan application had been approved.

4. _____

5. (*The speaker*) plan to be in Tacoma next weekend.

5. _____

6. (*Not many*) of the customers complained about the increase in the price.

6. _____

7. (*An unknown person*) left the package in the lobby.

7. _____

8. Anne made (*Anne's*) reservations yesterday morning.

8. _____

9. (*The woman spoken about*) is a graduate of Columbia.

9. _____

10. Yes, I am certain that the general manager is (*Dave*).

10. _____

11. Please call (*the speaker*) collect at 555-4604.

11. _____

12. (*The speakers*) are eager to resume work on the project as quickly as possible.

12. _____

13. Is this (*something belonging to the person spoken to*)?

13. _____

14. When was the last time you spoke with (*Ms. Gorbea*)?

14. _____

15. (*Not a single person*) seems to know what the outcome will be.

15. _____

16. The speaker was unable to persuade (*any person in the audience*).

16. _____

17. Mr. Morton asked (*Mr. Phillips*) to attend.

17. _____

18. The auditors submitted (*the auditors'*) report.

18. _____

19. The cabinet has a dent in (*the cabinet*).

19. _____

20. (*The majority*) of the employees like the new plan.

20. _____

21. Mr. Roberts has no one to blame but (*Mr. Roberts*).

21. _____

22. The owners told (*the speakers*) about the damage.

22. _____

23. (*What person*) authorized the change?

23. _____

24. To (*what person*) is the letter addressed?

24. _____

25. (*Alice and I*) prepared the first draft.

25. _____

26. Six of the cartons are (*the speakers' cartons*).

26. _____

27. Dick and Ed said (*Dick and Ed*) worked overtime.

27. _____

28. (*Nearly all*) of the crops have been harvested.

28. _____

29. You can be very proud of (*the persons spoken to*).

29. _____

30. Jill fell and hurt (*Jill*) at work this morning.

30. _____

31. Is (*the speaker's*) account overdrawn?

31. _____

32. Lee's work is ready, but (*the speaker's work*) is not.

32. _____

33. Miss Davis has approved (*Pat and the speaker's*) plan.

33. _____

34. (*The person spoken to*) deserve greater recognition.

34. _____

35. Be sure to take good care of (*the person spoken to*).

35. _____

36. (*A large number*) disapprove of the mayor's actions.

36. _____

37. (*A large amount*) of the grain will be exported.

37. _____

38. (*Belonging to the person spoken to*) payment is due.

38. _____

39. Steve bought (*Steve*) a new delivery truck.

39. _____

40. The door could not have unlocked (*the door*).

40. _____

41. The voters have only (*the voters*) to blame.

41. _____

42. (*Not any*) of the receipts have been found.

42. _____

43. (*Not a thing*) has been done yet.

43. _____

44. (*Not any*) of the paint was properly mixed.

44. _____

45. (*Every person*) needs assistance occasionally.

45. _____

46. (*The time*) is exactly 8:30 p.m.

46. _____

47. The tree has lost most of (*the tree's*) leaves.

47. _____

48. Do you know (*belonging to someone*) coat this is?

48. _____

49. Maybe the handbooks are (*Carl and Arlene's*).

49. _____

50. Sheila and I served (*Sheila and I*) more coffee.

50. _____

11 Identifying Verbs and Verb Phrases

Underline the verb or verb phrase used as the simple predicate of the italicized noun or pronoun subjects in the following sentences. Note the examples.

0. *Dr. Mayes* <u>said</u> that *she* <u>would be</u> happy to serve as a consultant.

00. <u>Would</u> *you* <u>advise</u> us to invest in new equipment at this time, Ms. Quinlan?

1. When *we* arrived at the airport, *we* discovered that the *flight* had been canceled at the last minute.

2. Are *you* certain that the *documents* were in the file cabinet yesterday?

3. The *article* appeared in one of the professional journals last spring.

4. Several *members* of the staff attended the meeting, but *Al* and *I* did not.

5. *Mr. Willis* indicated that *he* had confirmed the specifications.

6. Your *representative* assured us that the *shipment* would arrive on time.

7. The *cost* of children's clothing often exceeds that of adults' clothing.

8. *Mrs. Gage* is a dedicated and competent employee, and *she* deserves the promotion.

9. Our *investment* in word processing equipment is paying big dividends.

10. *Who* was driving the delivery truck at the time of the accident?

11. Your *inquiry* has been referred to the manager of our Charleston office.

12. *Swimming* may be good exercise, but *jogging* is preferred by many of us.

13. This *color* appeals to me a great deal more than *either* of those does.

14. *Sales* in June of this year were much higher than *they* were in June of last year, according to the report prepared by Miss Hodgkins.

15. These new *regulations* will make it more difficult for any company to monopolize the market.

16. A corrected *statement of account* will be sent to you within a few days.

17. The recommended *procedure* is explained fully on pages 10-14 of the enclosed brochure, Mr. Stephenson.

18. What do *you* consider to be the most significant development in communications technology during the past decade?

19. The *supervisors* with whom *we* spoke seem to feel that stricter *enforcement* of those government regulations is essential.

20. *Advertising* plays a highly important role in today's society.

12 Classifying Verbs and Verb Phrases

Indicate whether the italicized verb or verb phrase in each sentence is transitive or intransitive by circling *T* (for *transitive*), *I* (for *intransitive*), or *I-L* (for *intransitive-linking*).

1. Mr. Torrance *preferred* to invest in real estate, not stocks and bonds.   **1.** T I I-L

2. This merchandise *should be returned* immediately.   **2.** T I I-L

3. Ms. Ellingson probably *will receive* their endorsement for reelection.   **3.** T I I-L

4. Free parking *is* available for your shopping convenience.   **4.** T I I-L

5. Your contribution *will help* someone who is less fortunate.   **5.** T I I-L

6. One of the witnesses *was cited* for contempt of court by Judge Pinkerton.   **6.** T I I-L

7. I thought that our new line of computers *was selling* well.   **7.** T I I-L

8. *Did* your company *bid* on that construction project?   **8.** T I I-L

9. Miss Holloway *will represent* us in Maine and New Hampshire.   **9.** T I I-L

10. Mrs. Lopez *seems* happy in her new job, doesn't she?   **10.** T I I-L

Draw one line under the simple or compound subject and two lines under the simple or compound predicate in each sentence. Then circle *A* if the voice of the verb or verb phrase is *active* or *P* if it is *passive*.

11. Lorraine needs and has requested several copies of their most recent catalog.   **11.** A P

12. Smoking is prohibited in many retail stores and public buildings.   **12.** A P

13. I sent a check for the balance of my account on October 16.   **13.** A P

14. Neither copy of the contract has been returned by Mrs. Fong.   **14.** A P

15. You may choose from a wide variety of styles and prices.   **15.** A P

16. You and I should have taken the time to study the proposal carefully.   **16.** A P

17. The cost of essential goods and services has risen sharply.   **17.** A P

18. This insurance plan provides an annuity of approximately $300 a month.   **18.** A P

19. Several improvements have been made during the past decade.   **19.** A P

20. Circumstances prevent our purchasing a new home at this time.   **20.** A P

13 Recognizing Tenses of Verbs

In the space provided, indicate the tense of the verb or verb phrase shown in italics by writing *present, past, future, present perfect, past perfect,* or *future perfect.*

1. The current interest rate *is* 9 percent.

1. _____

2. Several customers *submitted* claims.

2. _____

3. Mr. Jorgenson *will call* you next week.

3. _____

4. Both applicants *have* excellent qualifications.

4. _____

5. Cleo *had notified* us of the changes before we received Ms. Klein's memo.

5. _____

6. I *shall be* happy to assist you at any time.

6. _____

7. Your suggestions *were* extremely helpful.

7. _____

8. Miss Tremain *has been* manager of this department for approximately two years.

8. _____

9. Mr. Baker *will have retired* before July 1.

9. _____

10. Two employees of the bank *have been charged* with conspiracy to commit fraud.

10. _____

11. The author *described* many fascinating incidents.

11. _____

12. I *am* fully aware of Sally's contributions.

12. _____

13. You *were* correct in making those assumptions.

13. _____

14. The delay *will cause* some inconvenience.

14. _____

15. We *incurred* some unnecessary expense.

15. _____

16. Dr. Edwards *went* to Norfolk last Tuesday.

16. _____

17. By Friday we *will have completed* this job.

17. _____

18. Both suppliers *have assured* us of prompt service at reasonable prices.

18. _____

19. Our account *has been transferred* to the branch on Wilshire Boulevard.

19. _____

20. The conference *was* most worthwhile from every view-point, I believe.

20. _____

14 Putting Verbs to Work

Which of the verbs or verb phrases shown in parentheses is correct? Write your answer in the space provided.

1. You (*are, is*) to be congratulated on your promotion.

2. Bill usually (*do, does*) excellent work.

3. We (*reccommend, recommend*) no immediate changes.

4. Please (*procede, proceed*) with caution.

5. Mr. Burns (*has gone, has went*) to Philadelphia.

6. Those plans (*was, were*) unacceptable.

7. Who (*commited, committed*) that mistake?

8. By next Wednesday the offer (*will expire, will have expired*).

9. I (*am living, have been living*) in Milwaukee for almost two years.

10. I thought you (*was, were*) right.

11. Everyone (*recognize, recognizes*) a bargain.

12. This policy (*provide, provides*) full protection for you and the members of your immediate family.

13. Larry (*did, done*) the work himself.

14. Your secretary (*shall be, will be*) happy with the gift you bought her.

15. Before I realized it, my license (*had expired, has expired*).

16. Irene (*supervise, supervises*) a staff of 25 clerk-typists in our Burlington office.

17. Mike (*omited, omitted*) some details.

18. The laboratory (*has give, has given*) us a complete chemical analysis of the substance.

19. We frequently (*corespond, correspond*) with them.

20. The analysis (*was, were*) unacceptable to the head of our research department.

1. _____

2. _____

3. _____

4. _____

5. _____

6. _____

7. _____

8. _____

9. _____

10. _____

11. _____

12. _____

13. _____

14. _____

15. _____

16. _____

17. _____

18. _____

19. _____

20. _____

148

15 Identifying Words Used as Adjectives

Underline all words that are used as adjectives in the following sentences.

1. Please accept our sincere best wishes for outstanding success in your new assignment.

2. This weekly report indicates that we have a number of out-of-stock items.

3. Neither of these plastic containers seems suitable for our purposes.

4. Mrs. Lombard gave a complete description of the new procedures that we are to follow.

5. The entire surface was covered with an oily substance.

6. Both of those secretaries are recent community college graduates.

7. A number of politicians issue periodic newsletters to their constituents.

8. The current balance of your account is exactly $85.60.

9. Would it be possible to catch the New York-San Francisco flight if we were to leave now?

10. Both of the prospective buyers seem capable of making a substantial investment.

11. A professional decorator recommended the installation of dark green carpeting.

12. The firm's profits rose approximately 8 percent last year.

13. We noticed an immediate increase in sales soon after the new series of ads began appearing.

14. For some reason, neither of the adjacent warehouses was damaged during the recent storm.

15. Their company employs approximately 1,500 permanent workers and 100 part-time workers.

16. What would be an acceptable solution to this particular problem?

17. Your supervisor made a number of very complimentary remarks about your work.

18. Everyone made an extraordinary effort to ensure the success of the new business venture.

19. Do you honestly feel that it would be advisable for us to accept that proposal?

20. As a practical matter, it seems unlikely that anything else could have been done.

21. Each of the applicants has excellent personal and professional qualifications.

22. Knowledgeable insiders expect that a firm stand against the proposal will be taken by the board of directors at the March 10 meeting.

23. The preliminary report indicates that capital expenditures will be reduced slightly.

24. You will find that this organization provides numerous opportunities for advancement.

25. A large number of foreign investors expressed a strong interest in the project.

16 Indicating Degree of Adjectives

Write the comparative and the superlative degree forms of each adjective.

POSITIVE DEGREE	COMPARATIVE DEGREE	SUPERLATIVE DEGREE
1. low		
2. clear		
3. expensive		
4. good		
5. happy		
6. unusual		
7. new		
8. attractive		
9. friendly		
10. casual		
11. busy		
12. critical		
13. much		
14. far (*degree*)		
15. far (*distance*)		
16. familiar		
17. successful		
18. many		
19. little		
20. high		
21. quiet		
22. smooth		
23. costly		
24. deep		
25. cheap		

150

17 Putting Adjectives to Work

In the space provided, write the correct form of the adjective shown in parentheses.

0. Which of the two cartons is (*light*)?

1. Lyle works (*few*) hours than Kurt does.

2. Buying stocks may be (*risky*) than buying land.

3. They were (*careful*) than we were.

4. Miss Findley did the (*good*) work she could.

5. The article is in the (*recent*) issue of *Time*.

6. He seems (*happy*) today than he did yesterday.

7. This office is (*good*) than that one, I think.

8. Which contestant made the (*bad*) impression?

9. What is the (*tall*) building in the world?

10. Your information is (*current*) than mine.

11. Who is the (*cooperative*) person you know?

12. She is the (*shy*) person I have ever met.

13. Is this model (*expensive*) than that one?

14. The repairs will be (*costly*) than we thought.

15. We must give the matter (*far*) attention.

16. Albany is (*far*) from here than Detroit is.

17. We bought the (*sturdy*) furniture we saw.

18. Which of the three lawyers is (*shrewd*)?

19. Who has the (*old*) typewriter in the office?

20. Which of the twins is (*strong*)?

21. Your report is (*thorough*) than mine.

22. This container looks (*square*) than that one.

23. It is (*quiet*) in your office than in mine.

24. We must be (*thoughtful*) the next time.

25. You write (*many*) memos than I do.

0. lighter

1. _____

2. _____

3. _____

4. _____

5. _____

6. _____

7. _____

8. _____

9. _____

10. _____

11. _____

12. _____

13. _____

14. _____

15. _____

16. _____

17. _____

18. _____

19. _____

20. _____

21. _____

22. _____

23. _____

24. _____

25. _____

18 Using *a* and *an* Correctly

Write *a* or *an,* whichever is correct, before each word or group of words.

1. _____ bright future

2. _____ effective speaker

3. _____ good return

4. _____ formal complaint

5. _____ ideal arrangement

6. _____ high yield

7. _____ merit increase

8. _____ quiet place

9. _____ novelty

10. _____ reference manual

11. _____ telephone call

12. _____ uniformed guard

13. _____ X-ray machine

14. _____ youthful outlook

15. _____ justifiable complaint

16. _____ zealous worker

17. _____ opportunity

18. _____ appliance store

19. _____ stationery shop

20. _____ element of risk

21. _____ hour each day

22. _____ up-to-date store

23. _____ intricate problem

24. _____ acknowledgment

25. _____ surprise

26. _____ itemized statement

27. _____ honorarium

28. _____ enthusiastic response

29. _____ hotel manager

30. _____ idea

31. _____ large order

32. _____ keen interest

33. _____ objective evaluation

34. _____ descriptive brochure

35. _____ small package

36. _____ enclosure

37. _____ workable plan

38. _____ valid contract

39. _____ superfluous statement

40. _____ primary objective

41. _____ applicant

42. _____ license

43. _____ heir

44. _____ disappointment

45. _____ competitive price

46. _____ naive manner

47. _____ analysis

48. _____ defendant

49. _____ equal opportunity

50. _____ government agency

19 Distinguishing Adverbs and Adjectives

Indicate whether the italicized word is an adverb or an adjective by circling *Adj* (for *adjective*) or *Adv* (for *adverb*). In addition, study the spelling of each word carefully.

1. *sincerely* regret	1. Adj Adv	26. *friendly* person	26. Adj Adv
2. *business* associate	2. Adj Adv	27. *available* resources	27. Adj Adv
3. *completely* exhausted	3. Adj Adv	28. *cordially* invite	28. Adj Adv
4. *necessary* expenses	4. Adj Adv	29. *current* interest rate	29. Adj Adv
5. *approximately* a week	5. Adj Adv	30. *conveniently* located	30. Adj Adv
6. reply *immediately*	6. Adj Adv	31. *medical* examination	31. Adj Adv
7. *industrial* wastes	7. Adj Adv	32. *personal* attention	32. Adj Adv
8. left *yesterday*	8. Adj Adv	33. *personnel* records	33. Adj Adv
9. *too* elaborate	9. Adj Adv	34. *annual* report	34. Adj Adv
10. *financial* statement	10. Adj Adv	35. counted *individually*	35. Adj Adv
11. *original* copy	11. Adj Adv	36. tries *occasionally*	36. Adj Adv
12. *particularly* important	12. Adj Adv	37. *successful* meeting	37. Adj Adv
13. *quite* aggravating	13. Adj Adv	38. felt *ill* today	38. Adj Adv
14. the *second* notice	14. Adj Adv	39. a *moody* person	39. Adj Adv
15. *illegible* signature	15. Adj Adv	40. were *never* checked	40. Adj Adv
16. will *not* cooperate	16. Adj Adv	41. *quiet* neighborhood	41. Adj Adv
17. is *always* prompt	17. Adj Adv	42. a *choice* location	42. Adj Adv
18. may taste *bitter*	18. Adj Adv	43. *probably* will go	43. Adj Adv
19. a *similar* situation	19. Adj Adv	44. *outstanding* debts	44. Adj Adv
20. are *almost* ready	20. Adj Adv	45. *applicable* rule	45. Adj Adv
21. *sufficiently* covered	21. Adj Adv	46. *valuable* asset	46. Adj Adv
22. *eligible* bachelor	22. Adj Adv	47. *especially* attractive	47. Adj Adv
23. *very* unfortunately	23. Adj Adv	48. *permanent* residents	48. Adj Adv
24. for *most* people	24. Adj Adv	49. *most* complete ones	49. Adj Adv
25. for *late* arrival	25. Adj Adv	50. arrived *late*	50. Adj Adv

20 Using Adverbs

Indicate which form of the word in parentheses correctly completes each sentence.

0. I am late (*frequent*) than Mildred is.

0. <u>more or less frequently</u>

1. When is the report (*usual*) issued?

1. _____

2. Our supply is (*practical*) exhausted.

2. _____

3. John's statement is (*substantial*) correct.

3. _____

4. Negotiations have been (*official*) suspended.

4. _____

5. We (*real*) are interested in your ideas.

5. _____

6. The road has been closed (*temporary*).

6. _____

7. Your suggestion will be studied (*far*).

7. _____

8. Who submits the (*consistent*) accurate reports?

8. _____

9. Of all of them, who travels (*far*)?

9. _____

10. You (*definite*) should plan to attend.

10. _____

11. The author (*grateful*) acknowledged their help.

11. _____

12. These are (*unique*) suited to our needs than those.

12. _____

13. I (*accidental*) dropped the package.

13. _____

14. Which firm offers the (*competitive*) priced goods?

14. _____

15. Louis (*undoubted*) will be named general manager.

15. _____

16. This machine operates (*efficient*) than that one.

16. _____

17. We (*respectful*) disagreed with Ms. Saunders.

17. _____

18. Mr. Richardson resigned (*voluntary*).

18. _____

19. (*Unfortunate*), the folder was mislaid.

19. _____

20. Richard presented his ideas (*interesting*).

20. _____

21. We do not know how many were involved (*initial*).

21. _____

22. You most (*assured*) will succeed.

22. _____

23. The letter was (*incorrect*) addressed.

23. _____

24. Of the three, which is (*close*) watched?

24. _____

25. We were (*casual*) dressed than they were.

25. _____

154

21 Spelling and Defining Modifiers

Underline each incorrectly spelled adjective or adverb in each of the following sentences. Then write the correct spelling. Each sentence contains one error. Use your dictionary!

1. We sincerly regret this unavoidable delay.   1. _____

2. Currant interest rates are extremely high.   2. _____

3. She imediately reported a serious error.   3. _____

4. Finansial records are important documents.   4. _____

5. We probly have a sufficient quantity on hand.   5. _____

6. You are elgible for a minimum raise of $600.   6. _____

7. Free physical exams are given annualy.   7. _____

8. The truck suddenly rolled foreward.   8. _____

9. Tom operates several stores sucessfully.   9. _____

10. This model is noticably larger than that one.   10. _____

11. Please wrap each fragile item seperately.   11. _____

12. Their resent ads are attractively designed.   12. _____

13. The report you requested is allmost ready.   13. _____

14. Our new offices are unusualy spacious.   14. _____

15. We thoroughly enjoyed your informitive article.   15. _____

16. The responsable official reacted angrily.   16. _____

17. We truely appreciate your prompt response.   17. _____

18. Conveneint payment terms are easily arranged.   18. _____

19. We defanitely think it is worthwhile.   19. _____

20. The reccommended procedure is easy to follow.   20. _____

21. A more economicle model is urgently needed.   21. _____

22. They were sitting quitely in the fourth row.   22. _____

23. The difference was not particlarly noticeable.   23. _____

24. I personly think it was unfortunate.   24. _____

25. Incidently, we have tentative plans to attend.   25. _____

In the space provided, write the letter that identifies the best definition of each adjective or adverb listed below.

A. pertaining to an individual; private

B. nearby; side by side

C. qualified; entitled

D. liable; trustworthy

E. separately; one by one

F. in a very careful manner

G. aware; thankful

H. profitable; advantageous

I. at the present time

J. willing and able

K. required; unavoidable

L. useful

M. quickly; immediately

N. additional

O. at the beginning; first

P. in a foreboding manner; fatefully

Q. in a meaningful manner; importantly

R. thoughtful; observant

S. misleading

T. completely; entirely

U. financial

V. unintentionally; accidentally

W. taking place twice a year

X. entitled to acceptance

Y. insignificant; ordinary

26. authoritative _____

27. trivial _____

28. currently _____

29. necessary _____

30. supplementary _____

31. significantly _____

32. eligible _____

33. promptly _____

34. biannually _____

35. personal _____

36. individually _____

37. responsible _____

38. beneficial _____

39. appreciative _____

40. ominously _____

41. cooperative _____

42. particularly _____

43. initially _____

44. fiscal _____

45. practical _____

46. deceptive _____

47. incidentally _____

48. attentive _____

49. quite _____

50. adjacent _____

156

22 Identifying Prepositional Phrases

Underline each prepositional phrase. Then, in the space provided, write the object or objects of the preposition. Note the examples.

0. We took the truck <u>to the garage</u> <u>for a tune-up</u>.

0. garage; tune-up

00. Have you heard anything <u>from her or him</u>?

00. her, him

1. Mr. Orr met with them on the eighth or ninth.

1. _____

2. Please turn off the lights before leaving.

2. _____

3. We did not arrive at work until 12:30 p.m.

3. _____

4. By noon we will be about finished.

4. _____

5. This message is of interest to taxpayers.

5. _____

6. You will receive your order within a week.

6. _____

7. Going too fast, we went past the exit we wanted.

7. _____

8. We plan to move our offices within a year.

8. _____

9. Upon hearing the alarm, we walked down the stairs.

9. _____

10. The books fell off the shelves in her office.

10. _____

11. They ran down the street and into the store.

11. _____

12. It was below zero throughout the night.

12. _____

13. We were standing between them, not beside them.

13. _____

14. The building across the street is for sale.

14. _____

15. The stockholders are against the takeover.

15. _____

16. Do you like working after 6 o'clock?

16. _____

17. We drove through the tunnel that was built under the river several years ago.

17. _____

18. Around the first, you undoubtedly will be hearing more about it.

18. _____

19. We enjoyed working with you and her, and we hope to see both of you again soon.

19. _____

20. Please look up the information for Ms. Stephenson and him over the weekend.

20. _____

23 Recognizing Conjunctions and Interjections

Draw one line under each *subordinate conjunction;* draw two lines under each *coordinate conjunction, correlative conjunction,* or *conjunctive adverb.* Circle each *interjection.*

1. A receptionist is usually expected to answer the telephone in a pleasant, businesslike manner at all times.

2. The company plans to move its headquarters either to Reno or to Fresno.

3. Be sure to contact both Mr. Maxwell and Mrs. White before you cancel the order.

4. The hotel could not accommodate us because it had previously booked two large convention groups from the New England area.

5. We tried to settle the dispute between them, but we were not too successful.

6. She was there not only at the beginning of the meeting but also at the end.

7. We are happy to report that your sales representative is a person whom we always look forward to seeing.

8. Ms. Janson said that she did not order either the furniture or the dishes.

9. Neither the apartment nor the store below it was damaged too extensively; however, the cost of repairs is likely to be quite high.

10. Wow! That's a beautiful car, Joyce!

11. Well, no one around here seems to have taken that suggestion very seriously.

12. However costly the new equipment may be, we definitely need it immediately.

13. Please let Miss Pierce know where you will be staying before you leave.

14. Either Mark or I will make the necessary arrangements for the banquet.

15. Joan left early in the morning, but she did not arrive until late in the afternoon.

16. The premium must be paid on time; otherwise, our insurance coverage will lapse.

17. Did you notify either Henry or Mary of the decision that you made?

18. While you are in Buffalo, you may want to visit their new laboratories.

19. An athlete must be not only strong but also skillful.

20. If I remember correctly, this model is less expensive than that one.

158

24 Spelling *ei* and *ie* Words

Put *i* before *e* except after *c* or when sounded like *a*, as in *neighbor* and *weigh*. It isn't a bad rule—but there are many exceptions to it. Insert *ei* or *ie* in each of the following words.

1. consc--ntious _____
2. var--ty _____
3. rec--ve _____
4. gr--vance _____
5. anx--ty _____
6. effic--ncy _____
7. conven--nce _____
8. suffic--nt _____
9. cash--r _____
10. n--ther _____
11. qu--t _____
12. consc--nce _____
13. propr--tor _____
14. l--n _____
15. dec--ve _____
16. s--ze _____
17. acqu--sce _____
18. sover--gn _____
19. twent--th _____
20. counterf--t _____
21. or--ntation _____
22. propr--ty _____
23. c--ling _____
24. ch--f _____
25. l--utenant _____

26. ach--vement _____
27. h--ght _____
28. defic--ncy _____
29. l--sure _____
30. n--ghborhood _____
31. cl--nt _____
32. bel--ve _____
33. for--gn _____
34. --ther _____
35. exper--nce _____
36. fr--ght _____
37. misch--vous _____
38. conc--vable _____
39. y--ld _____
40. forf--t _____
41. br--fly _____
42. fr--ndship _____
43. h--r _____
44. fort--th _____
45. sc--ntific _____
46. front--r _____
47. recip--nt _____
48. retr--val _____
49. v--wpoint _____
50. w--ght _____

25 Defining and Using Business Terms

Select the correct definition for each italicized word. In the answer column, write the letter that identifies the definition. Use your dictionary if necessary.

1. *Biennial*   (a) twice a year; (b) once a year; (c) every two years; (d) continuously

       1. _____

2. *Semiannual*   (a) almost yearly; (b) every six months; (c) every two years; (d) every twelve months

       2. _____

3. *Quarterly*   (a) every six months; (b) every four months; (c) every three months; (d) at the rate of 25 cents

       3. _____

4. *Equity*   (a) partiality; (b) ownership right in property; (c) guilt; (d) unfair claim against property

       4. _____

5. *Depreciation*   (a) lack of interest; (b) an increase in value; (c) a decrease in value; (d) additional interest

       5. _____

6. *Biannual*   (a) twice a year; (b) once a year; (c) every two years; (d) continuously

       6. _____

7. *Beneficiary*   (a) one who gives; (b) one who receives; (c) one who takes by force; (d) one who takes without force

       7. _____

8. *Prudent*   (a) shrewish; (b) foolish; (c) shrewd; (d) prudish

       8. _____

9. *Prorate*   (a) to rate professionally; (b) to distribute proportionately; (c) to assess; (d) to divide

       9. _____

10. *Amortize*   (a) to mortgage; (b) to pay immediately; (c) to distribute payment or cost over a long period of time; (d) to cancel without prior notice

       10. _____

On a separate sheet of paper, write a brief definition of each of these business terms. Then write 15 sentences (one for each word) in which you use the words correctly. Use your dictionary if necessary.

11. debtor   16. conglomerate   21. merger

12. creditor   17. subsidize   22. corporation

13. proprietor   18. parity   23. inventory

14. monopoly   19. appraise   24. maintenance

15. partnership   20. retroactive   25. acquisition

26 Recognizing Kinds of Phrases

Write *V* after each *verb phrase*, *I* after each *infinitive phrase*, *G* after each *gerund phrase*, and *P* after each *prepositional phrase*.

1. to operate efficiently   1. _____   26. to the garage   26. _____

2. will be admitted   2. _____   27. asking them now   27. _____

3. in the conference room   3. _____   28. have been using   28. _____

4. to succeed in business   4. _____   29. until this afternoon   29. _____

5. for your approval   5. _____   30. to answer the telephone   30. _____

6. am considering   6. _____   31. should be corrected   31. _____

7. under the circumstances   7. _____   32. answering mail promptly   32. _____

8. between you and me   8. _____   33. by shouting loudly   33. _____

9. before evening   9. _____   34. are leaving   34. _____

10. to be eliminated   10. _____   35. had known   35. _____

11. explaining the policy   11. _____   36. your sending us a copy   36. _____

12. with him and her   12. _____   37. to lead the way   37. _____

13. to interfere often   13. _____   38. would have gone   38. _____

14. through his efforts   14. _____   39. in their opinion   39. _____

15. were planning   15. _____   40. advertising regularly   40. _____

16. over our budget   16. _____   41. around April 15   41. _____

17. did arrive   17. _____   42. was canceled   42. _____

18. of every supervisor   18. _____   43. directing traffic   43. _____

19. to obtain assistance   19. _____   44. off the list price   44. _____

20. have written   20. _____   45. to oversee the work   45. _____

21. at her insistence   21. _____   46. is leaving soon   46. _____

22. making them angry   22. _____   47. inside the building   47. _____

23. on the agenda   23. _____   48. entertaining visitors   48. _____

24. has been trying   24. _____   49. from the outset   49. _____

25. beside the cabinet   25. _____   50. taking inventory   50. _____

27 Identifying Dependent Clauses

Draw one line under each dependent clause that is used as an adjective. Then draw two lines under the word it modifies. Note the example sentence.

0. This is the list of <u>things</u> <u>that she wants me to do for her.</u>

1. We should try to call on those who have shown the most interest in these products.

2. Do you remember the name of the person whom Ms. Johnson recommended as a consultant?

3. I have forgotten what the deadline for filing the report is.

4. This is the place where Messrs. Horton and Feldman built their first retail store.

5. These buildings, which used to be private residences, have been taken over by the city.

6. Were you at the workshop that Mrs. Burton conducted last Friday afternoon?

Draw one line under each dependent clause that is used as an adverb. Then draw two lines under the word or words it modifies.

7. I wish that you had called me when you were in San Francisco last weekend.

8. Does either of them know where Mrs. Stern will be staying in Richmond?

9. I spoke to them after I had talked to you about the new procedures to be followed.

10. Please post the notice where everyone will be sure to see it.

11. We are unable to fill these orders because some of the items have been discontinued.

12. You should make your reservations now if you would like to attend this seminar.

13. Where did you go while you were on vacation last summer?

14. She should have discussed the matter with you before she submitted her resignation.

Underline each dependent clause that is used as a noun in the following sentences.

15. Ms. Everest wants to know who authorized the purchase of this equipment.

16. That is one of the things that seem to irritate most people.

17. Do you know of anyone who needs another copy of this manual?

18. Miss McLean, who is our Minnesota representative, will call you early next week.

19. Neither of us knows what the outcome of the current negotiations will be.

20. Please send this brochure to whoever requests additional information.

28 Correcting Spelling Errors

If one of the words in the line is misspelled, underline the word and write the correct spelling. If all words in the line are spelled correctly, write *OK*. Use your dictionary if necessary.

1. accelerate	accomodate	aggravate	correlate	1. _____
2. column	volumn	condemn	hymn	2. _____
3. stationery	stationary	voluntery	inflationary	3. _____
4. analyze	paralyze	visualyze	realize	4. _____
5. milage	acreage	mortgage	storage	5. _____
6. truely	purely	surely	safely	6. _____
7. receit	conceit	deceit	conceive	7. _____
8. abrupt	disrupt	corupt	bankrupt	8. _____
9. campaign	champagne	deign	arraign	9. _____
10. sucess	recession	process	concession	10. _____
11. occasion	assassin	session	accession	11. _____
12. accessible	acceptable	admissible	corruptable	12. _____
13. ecstasy	fantasy	embasy	grassy	13. _____
14. mistake	mispell	mismatch	misplace	14. _____
15. couragious	religious	courteous	insidious	15. _____
16. parasite	insight	excite	incite	16. _____
17. picnic	picnicking	picnickers	picnicks	17. _____
18. simalarly	advisory	usually	wholly	18. _____
19. swept	kept	warpt	adept	19. _____
20. pneumonia	numerous	pneurotic	pneumatic	20. _____
21. relavent	reverent	resonant	resultant	21. _____
22. assistance	residence	assistants	residents	22. _____
23. supervise	criticize	summarise	apologize	23. _____
24. weird	forfeit	neice	seize	24. _____
25. shipper	baggage	gasseous	stopping	25. _____

29 Adding Prefixes and Suffixes

Add the prefix (word beginning) or suffix (word ending) to the word indicated, and write the resulting word in the space provided.

1. un + necessary _____

2. pre + pay _____

3. employ + er _____

4. permit + ed _____

5. dis + respect _____

6. usual + ly _____

7. avail + able _____

8. pro + rated _____

9. reply + ing _____

10. im + material _____

11. enjoy + ing _____

12. mal + practice _____

13. re + possess _____

14. bi + lateral _____

15. omit + ing _____

16. un + leaded _____

17. inspire + ation _____

18. intra + office _____

19. counsel + or _____

20. digest + ible _____

21. excel + ent _____

22. sick + ness _____

23. apply + ance _____

24. recess + ion _____

25. whole + ly _____

26. arrange + ment _____

27. accept + able _____

28. help + ful _____

29. re + entry _____

30. mis + spell _____

31. il + logical _____

32. acquit + ed _____

33. in + flexible _____

34. un + broken _____

35. bi + lingual _____

36. cancel + ed _____

37. anti + social _____

38. sub + freezing _____

39. judge + ment _____

40. slip + ery _____

41. il + legal _____

42. inter + state _____

43. possess + ive _____

44. pre + mature _____

45. congest + ion _____

46. dis + possess _____

47. over + rated _____

48. local + ity _____

49. equip + ing _____

50. dis + appoint _____

30 Forming Plurals of Nouns

Write the plural of each noun in the space provided. If the noun has both an English plural and a foreign plural, give the foreign plural. If the noun has but one form (*series,* for example), place a check mark in the space provided. If necessary, use your dictionary.

1. envelope _____
2. alumnus _____
3. business _____
4. curriculum _____
5. privilege _____
6. bureau _____
7. ranch _____
8. bookshelf _____
9. crash _____
10. hero _____
11. staff _____
12. 10 _____
13. Mallory _____
14. spoonful _____
15. equipment _____
16. woman _____
17. tooth _____
18. criterion _____
19. stimulus _____
20. attorney _____
21. Mrs. _____
22. sheep _____
23. employee _____
24. high school _____

25. territory _____
26. son-in-law _____
27. portfolio _____
28. accessory _____
29. survey _____
30. analysis _____
31. income tax _____
32. governor _____
33. speech _____
34. quartz _____
35. half _____
36. A _____
37. Harris _____
38. Ms. _____
39. corps _____
40. Coleman _____
41. booth _____
42. child _____
43. material _____
44. thief _____
45. runner-up _____
46. Foley _____
47. committee _____
48. vehicle _____

49. principal _____

50. warehouse _____

51. agency _____

52. license _____

53. emphasis _____

54. energy _____

55. belief _____

56. activity _____

57. profession _____

58. piano _____

59. shelf _____

60. wrench _____

61. write-in _____

62. source _____

63. folio _____

64. notebook _____

65. volunteer _____

66. thousand _____

67. employer _____

68. enterprise _____

69. neighborhood _____

70. hazard _____

71. vacuum _____

72. luxury _____

73. Mr. _____

74. wish _____

75. letterhead _____

76. architect _____

77. regulation _____

78. disappointment _____

79. occupation _____

80. principle _____

81. amateur _____

82. vacancy _____

83. convenience _____

84. cliff _____

85. basis _____

86. handout _____

87. potato _____

88. column _____

89. handkerchief _____

90. magazine _____

91. reference _____

92. railroad _____

93. installment _____

94. stockholder _____

95. kilometer _____

96. wealth _____

97. B _____

98. Miss _____

99. stationery _____

100. price list _____

31 Using Singular and Plural Nouns

Which form of the noun shown in parentheses correctly completes the sentence? Write your answer in the space provided.

1. Each of the (*man, men*) hired an attorney.

2. Peggy has four (*sister-in-laws, sisters-in-law*).

3. We've had several (*crisis, crisises, crises*).

4. Both (*plaintiffs, plaintives*) were present.

5. How many (*ses, s's, ss*) appear in *Mississippi*?

6. Some (*tomatos, tomatoes*) were spoiled.

7. The (*analysis, analysises, analyses*) differ.

8. Many (*womans, women, womens*) are executives.

9. Have you visited the (*Wolfs, Wolves*) lately?

10. This spray kills (*mosquitos, mosquitoes*).

11. I typed two (*agenda, agendas, agendums*).

12. These (*formula, formulae, formulas*) are correct.

13. Who compiled the (*statistic, statistics*)?

14. Two (*companys, companies*) submitted bids.

15. That bank is run by (*womans, womens, women*).

16. Those (*knifes, knives*) are very sharp.

17. Be sure to save every (*receipt, receipts*).

18. Their (*employs, employees*) are paid well.

19. Do you write many (*memo, memoes, memos*)?

20. How many (*kilogram, kilograms*) does it weigh?

21. The (*columes, columnes, columns*) are uneven.

22. These (*securitys, securities*) are worthless.

23. Both (*benchs, benches*) are broken.

24. Those (*pianoes, pianos*) are on sale now.

25. Their (*wifes, wives*) were present.

1. _____
2. _____
3. _____
4. _____
5. _____
6. _____
7. _____
8. _____
9. _____
10. _____
11. _____
12. _____
13. _____
14. _____
15. _____
16. _____
17. _____
18. _____
19. _____
20. _____
21. _____
22. _____
23. _____
24. _____
25. _____

26. We asked the bureau (*chiefs, chieves*).

27. What is the current price of (*potatos, potatoes*)?

28. Should these (*shelfs, shelves*) be painted?

29. We ought to invite the (*Kellies, Kellys*).

30. How many (*20's, 20s*) do you have?

31. The temperature is in the (*40s, 40's*) today.

32. We have several (*hundred, hundreds*) copies.

33. It operates on (*batterys, batteries*), I think.

34. How many (*fish, fishes*) did you catch?

35. We have no more (*cataloges, catalogs*).

36. All (*taxes, taxs*) have been paid.

37. We saw several (*deer, deers*) along the road.

38. Both (*agendas, agendums*) have been prepared.

39. Ross and Peg are (*alumnae, alumni*) of Cornell.

40. What advertising (*media, medias, mediums*) does your company use?

41. (*Indexes, Indices*) of books usually are arranged alphabetically, aren't they?

42. Are these valid (*criteria, criterias, criterions*)?

43. What is the (*bases, basis*) of your statement?

44. May I borrow your (*scissor, scissors*)?

45. Who inspected the (*premise, premises*)?

46. Does he have the proper (*credential, credentials*)?

47. We should distribute the (*proceed, proceeds*).

48. The picnic is for the (*children, childs*) of the company's employees.

49. How many (*cupfuls, cupsful*) are required?

50. The group of tourists included several (*Germans, Germen*).

26. _____

27. _____

28. _____

29. _____

30. _____

31. _____

32. _____

33. _____

34. _____

35. _____

36. _____

37. _____

38. _____

39. _____

40. _____

41. _____

42. _____

43. _____

44. _____

45. _____

46. _____

47. _____

48. _____

49. _____

50. _____

32 Forming Possessives of Nouns

In the space provided, write the correct possessive form of the noun shown in parentheses. If an *of* phrase should be used, write it instead of a possessive noun.

1. (*Ms. Shultz*) office is on the third floor.

2. You deserve a (*month*) vacation.

3. We have each (*company*) address on file.

4. The (*carton*) lid fits improperly.

5. These (*lady*) coats are quite expensive.

6. (*Clark & Ross*) new store opens tomorrow.

7. I put it on (*Ed, our supervisor,*) desk.

8. Please give her a (*visitor*) pass.

9. Have you met (*Wes and Don*) wives?

10. Did you hear the (*President*) address?

11. My check was short two (*day*) pay.

12. We bought several (*dollar*) worth of gas.

13. Many (*child*) toys are very expensive.

14. (*Mark Harper Jr.*) business is real estate.

15. These (*client*) statements are ready.

16. What is their (*son-in-law*) first name?

17. Who drafted the (*meeting*) agenda?

18. (*Mary and Barbara*) father is a trustee.

19. (*Mr. Lodge*) resigning was a surprise.

20. The (*analysis*) correctness is doubtful.

21. The (*Perez*) home is on Tenth Street.

22. Each (*customer*) request is important.

23. What is this (*agency*) budget?

24. We need the (*committee*) endorsement.

25. This (*city*) streets need repairs.

1. _____

2. _____

3. _____

4. _____

5. _____

6. _____

7. _____

8. _____

9. _____

10. _____

11. _____

12. _____

13. _____

14. _____

15. _____

16. _____

17. _____

18. _____

19. _____

20. _____

21. _____

22. _____

23. _____

24. _____

25. _____

33 Using Possessive Nouns

Underline each noun that should be written in possessive form. Then write the correct possessive in the space provided. If no correction is necessary, write *OK*.

1. They sell doctors and nurses uniforms.

2. We appreciate Beverly helping us.

3. Is that St. Johns Cathedral?

4. The federal governments policy is unclear.

5. The Dennises last names are Hill and Lee.

6. Both accountants records were checked.

7. We took three weeks vacation.

8. Jack attended both sales meetings.

9. Who did the clerk-typists work for them?

10. My boss telephone extension is 2040.

11. Every employers cooperation is needed.

12. Mrs. Dodges friends were there.

13. Have you read *Gentlemens Monthly?*

14. The "Totals" columns are too narrow.

15. Each sales managers report is due today.

16. Are these James glasses?

17. Mrs. Bliss secretary wrote the letter.

18. It is an important tourist attraction.

19. We knew nothing of Sue being ill.

20. Tillie took a two-week trip to Tahiti.

21. Mrs. Strauss speaks before many civic groups.

22. This copy is Dr. Norris.

23. We bought less than a dollars worth of those.

24. Are you voting in this years election?

25. You should have seen the interviewers expression.

1. _____

2. _____

3. _____

4. _____

5. _____

6. _____

7. _____

8. _____

9. _____

10. _____

11. _____

12. _____

13. _____

14. _____

15. _____

16. _____

17. _____

18. _____

19. _____

20. _____

21. _____

22. _____

23. _____

24. _____

25. _____

34 Correcting Errors in Noun Usage

The following sentences contain errors in the spelling of nouns, the capitalization of nouns, and the formation and use of plural and possessive nouns. Underline each error, and write the necessary correction in the space provided. If a sentence is correct, write *OK*.

1. The company's products are made of alumium.
2. You'll have opportunitys to serve on committees.
3. Every organizations' policies will be affected.
4. Please return this notice with your remitance.
5. Each applicant will need a physicians statement.
6. It will be a pleasure and a priviledge, Ms. Dyer.
7. Is the corporation's managment in agreement?
8. Regular attendance is a requirment, isn't it?
9. A delay in distribution will cause inconvenience.
10. Please check these employers addresses.
11. This certificate fully explains the coverage.
12. What are the heighth and width of this room?
13. We should reduce our inventory to a minium.
14. It makes little diference to the superintendent.
15. Did she give a description of the hazzard?
16. What is the telephone extention of the laboratory?
17. Who notified the federal bureau of investigation?
18. This advertisment provides a complete description.
19. Have you met their new sales' manager?
20. Who is the director of the confrence?
21. Todays appointments have been canceled.
22. We run out of merchandise on occassion.
23. Every vehicle requires a valid lisence.
24. What is your local representatives name?

1. _____
2. _____
3. _____
4. _____
5. _____
6. _____
7. _____
8. _____
9. _____
10. _____
11. _____
12. _____
13. _____
14. _____
15. _____
16. _____
17. _____
18. _____
19. _____
20. _____
21. _____
22. _____
23. _____
24. _____

25. The settlement's terms are unknown.

25. _____

26. Don't place too much emphases on that inquiry.

26. _____

27. The language of the amenment is ambiguous.

27. _____

28. Please bring the matter to bills attention.

28. _____

29. Did he have the article in his posession?

29. _____

30. What is the companys' commitment to you?

30. _____

31. Confirmation of the specifications is required.

31. _____

32. Is it your intention to get a College degree?

32. _____

33. Have you studied advanced mathematic?

33. _____

34. This announcment contains too many statistics.

34. _____

35. The cancellation came as a suprise.

35. _____

36. Did you make an adjustment in the mileage?

36. _____

37. We sent a full contingent to new orleans.

37. _____

38. Have arrangements been made for a replacement?

38. _____

39. The current was turned off during the emergensy.

39. _____

40. I made a note of each expence on my calendar.

40. _____

41. Are you aware of marks latest achievement?

41. _____

42. She is one of our professional associates.

42. _____

43. Who are the beneficiarys of those changes?

43. _____

44. Your assistance increases our indebtedness to you.

44. _____

45. We must make a desision concerning the next edition within the next few weeks.

45. _____

46. We depend upon every employe's cooperation.

46. _____

47. What quanity of envelopes should we order?

47. _____

48. Were those statments made during the campaign?

48. _____

49. Please bring it to a managers attention.

49. _____

50. Were you aware of the dissappearance of a number of the documents?

50. _____

35 Using Personal Pronouns

Which of the pronouns shown in parentheses is correct? Write your answer in the space provided.

1. Mr. Lomax and (*her, she*) are our principal advisers.

2. Which of these catalogs are (*our, our's, ours*)?

3. Pauline is more efficient than (*I, me*).

4. Ms. Burke asked (*he, him*) to draft the report.

5. Mrs. Gregory told Jack and (*I, me*) about the change.

6. (*Their, Their's, Theirs, There's*) won first prize.

7. Was anyone aware of (*him, his*) planning to leave?

8. Louis mistook Sonia to be (*her, she*), my secretary.

9. Were (*them, they*) the ones who were responsible?

10. Mark and (*I, me*) are preparing the agenda.

11. (*Her, She*) and Robert usually do excellent work.

12. Did anyone comment about (*me, my*) not going?

13. I thought (*he, him*) to be the general manager.

14. The company has moved (*it's, its*) headquarters.

15. The responsibility is no longer (*mine, my*).

16. Which of the offices is (*your, your's, yours*)?

17. Miss Donen brought (*her, her's, hers*) own copies.

18. (*It, It's, Its*) unusually warm this spring.

19. (*Us, We*) secretaries deserve more recognition.

20. The managers met (*their, there, they're*) goals.

21. Was that story written by (*her, she*)?

22. (*Them, They*) are highly competent accountants.

23. Everyone but (*her, she*) was at work yesterday.

24. Maria seems to have a better idea than (*he, him*).

25. You and (*I, me*) should volunteer to help.

1. _____

2. _____

3. _____

4. _____

5. _____

6. _____

7. _____

8. _____

9. _____

10. _____

11. _____

12. _____

13. _____

14. _____

15. _____

16. _____

17. _____

18. _____

19. _____

20. _____

21. _____

22. _____

23. _____

24. _____

25. _____

26. Do you think (them, *those*) prices are reasonable?

27. Marvin said that (*he*, him) was being considered.

28. Would you want (he, *him*) for a supervisor?

29. Doris and Esther, (*you*, yous) are the winners!

30. The voters made (*their*, theirs) views clearly known.

31. The new vice president is (her, *she*).

32. Do you consider (he, *him*) to be successful?

33. How long have you worked for (*them*, they)?

34. Between you and (I, *me*), there is no alternative.

35. That store has closed (it's, *its*) doors for good.

36. The change will not affect you and (I, *me*).

37. Lester has as much experience as Roy or (her, *she*).

38. I doubt (them, *they*) or Tom will be attending.

39. A number of people objected to (*our*, us) smoking.

40. You can give a talk as well as (I, *me*).

41. Are you sure these are (their's, *theirs*)?

42. (Their's, Theirs, *There's*) nothing else to do.

43. (Their, There, *They're*) planning a reception.

44. All of (*us*, we) were pleased with the results.

45. Please notify Dr. Parker and (I, *me*) in advance.

46. The truck was lying on (it's, *its*) side.

47. The entire staff enjoyed (you, *your*) singing.

48. (Our's, *Ours*) cost less than those.

49. I believe this package is (your's, *yours*).

50. Jean said it was no concern of (her, her's, *hers*).

26. _____

27. _____

28. _____

29. _____

30. _____

31. _____

32. _____

33. _____

34. _____

35. _____

36. _____

37. _____

38. _____

39. _____

40. _____

41. _____

42. _____

43. _____

44. _____

45. _____

46. _____

47. _____

48. _____

49. _____

50. _____

36 Correcting Errors in Pronoun Usage

Underline each incorrectly used personal pronoun. Then write your correction in the space provided. If no correction is necessary, write *OK*.

1. She thought it was I who was to speak.

1. _____

2. We will appreciate you shipping the order promptly.

2. _____

3. They should have consulted you or I first.

3. _____

4. It's being considered by both of them, isn't it?

4. _____

5. I think them are the ones we should buy, don't you?

5. _____

6. They probably are as eager to move as us.

6. _____

7. Both of we sales representatives plan to attend.

7. _____

8. It was her who developed that advertising campaign.

8. _____

9. Ruth and him seemed pleased with our progress.

9. _____

10. Please keep mine separate from their's.

10. _____

11. Who notified you and she of the discrepancy?

11. _____

12. I think you and her deserve everyone's thanks.

12. _____

13. This is him speaking.

13. _____

14. No one has made a greater contribution than her.

14. _____

15. I am sure they mistook us to be them.

15. _____

16. The two of we should have answered the ad.

16. _____

17. Would you like to be him or her?

17. _____

18. Were them the ones that you requested?

18. _____

19. You and him ought to prepare your budgets this week.

19. _____

20. We have no objection to him going to Syracuse.

20. _____

21. Why didn't she phone or write you or I?

21. _____

22. You and us certainly have plenty of work to do.

22. _____

23. Would you like Joe and she to assist you next week?

23. _____

24. The bank has closed it's branch in Spring Valley.

24. _____

25. Each of yous should offer recommendations.

25. _____

26. Its all right to call before 8 o'clock.

27. You and her ought to visit their new offices.

28. Phyllis said the signature was not her's.

29. What was her reaction to you changing the furniture?

30. None of we received instructions to the contrary.

31. I am sure that her and Rose are stockholders.

32. Did either of you notice him talking to Shirley?

33. It came as no surprise to he or me.

34. Mr. Rodriguez and them agreed to review our request.

35. Do you consider him to be a good employee?

36. It was she who wrote the lead article in this issue.

37. Your opinion is as good as our's.

38. Everyone but he is in favor of the reorganization.

39. I think that its a matter of principle, don't you?

40. Those orders are her's, not mine, aren't they?

41. Them are not as good as the ones we bought last year.

42. Her and Rodney served on the panel last year.

43. Unfortunately, you had left before them and I arrived.

44. No one is more efficient than him or Kay.

45. Nothing is more important to we union members.

46. I am confident that you and she will be pleased.

47. Do you know when their's will be ready to ship?

48. She brought extra copies for you and I.

49. Us taxpayers should support that proposal.

50. Their looking for a modest increase this quarter.

26. _____

27. _____

28. _____

29. _____

30. _____

31. _____

32. _____

33. _____

34. _____

35. _____

36. _____

37. _____

38. _____

39. _____

40. _____

41. _____

42. _____

43. _____

44. _____

45. _____

46. _____

47. _____

48. _____

49. _____

50. _____

37 Using Indefinite Pronouns

Underline each error in the use of indefinite pronouns. Then write the necessary correction in the space provided. If the sentence is correct, write *OK*.

1. Janet hoped that somebody would help her.
2. An other of those machines is out of order.
3. We could not find no one willing to go.
4. Someone of them may be hired this week.
5. One should know what's best for oneself.
6. Some one ordered a bouquet of roses.
7. You should get some one else's opinion.
8. I think everyone of them is qualified.
9. No thing has been left undone, has it?
10. Those two are good about helping one another.
11. This is noone's problem but ours.
12. Everyones' suggestions will be considered.
13. Would you appear before anybody of legislators?
14. Did you receive any thing from anyone?
15. Someone must have told her some thing about it.
16. The three of them were assisting each other.
17. Is everyone of the totals correct?
18. Martin found nothing unusual about it.
19. We did not see no one in the warehouse.
20. Would anyone of these pens be satisfactory?
21. Any one's guess is as good as ours.
22. That certainly is some body of water.
23. Is there any thing we can do to assist you?
24. We are confident everyone will cooperate.
25. Everyone's business is no ones business.

1. _____
2. _____
3. _____
4. _____
5. _____
6. _____
7. _____
8. _____
9. _____
10. _____
11. _____
12. _____
13. _____
14. _____
15. _____
16. _____
17. _____
18. _____
19. _____
20. _____
21. _____
22. _____
23. _____
24. _____
25. _____

26. Maybe we should ask somebody else.

27. Every body was upset about the change.

28. Everything went wrong at the same time.

29. These type of shoes is very comfortable.

30. I seem to have someone else's notes.

31. The two of them write each other frequently.

32. Most of the rumors conflicted with one another.

33. Noone could recall the name of the witness.

34. Companies often know each other's plans.

35. Mr. Fein will be unable to see anyone today.

36. Anything of value should be protected carefully.

37. I think this kind is better than that one.

38. We promised nothing to no one.

39. There is something for every one, isn't there?

40. We welcome everybodys' constructive criticism.

41. Dr. Myers doesn't know neither of them.

42. These class of merchandise is too expensive.

43. Was any one with Jerry at the time?

44. Please mail every one of those statements.

45. One should try to improve one's self.

46. You, she, and he know each other's jobs.

47. You know them as well as anyone else does.

48. We appreciate everyone pitching in to help.

49. No one else's ideas have been considered.

50. Anyone would buy those kind of merchandise.

26. _____

27. _____

28. _____

29. _____

30. _____

31. _____

32. _____

33. _____

34. _____

35. _____

36. _____

37. _____

38. _____

39. _____

40. _____

41. _____

42. _____

43. _____

44. _____

45. _____

46. _____

47. _____

48. _____

49. _____

50. _____

38 Using *Who*, *Whom*, and Other Pronouns

In the space provided, write the pronoun or the contraction that correctly completes the sentence: *who, who's, whom, whose, whoever, whomever, which,* **or** *that.*

1. _____ was asked to participate besides Cleo and Carol?

2. To _____ did you address your inquiry about discount terms?

3. Give the prize to _____ submits the first correct entry.

4. Do you know _____ serving as executor of the estate?

5. Please feel free to invite _____ you wish, Ms. Kish.

6. I have no idea _____ responsibilities those are.

7. This is the house for _____ we paid $30,000 a few years ago.

8. We have decided to take the tour _____ you recommended.

9. There is no doubt as to _____ deserves the salary increase.

10. I left the message with the person _____ I thought was the cashier.

11. Neither of us knew _____ had been contacted about the report.

12. In _____ office did you see someone acting suspiciously?

13. _____ told you _____ we were interested in their proposal was misinformed.

14. The board of directors, all of _____ were present at the meeting, endorsed the proposed merger.

15. Everyone _____ has the qualifications _____ the job requires will be considered whenever a replacement for Miss Packard is needed.

16. Mr. Young, _____ we have been investigating, seems to be innocent of any wrongdoing.

17. She is someone for _____ all of us have the highest regard.

18. We were too confused to know _____ to ask for directions.

19. Please find out _____ is calling.

20. We certainly would like to meet _____ came up with _____ idea, wouldn't you?

39 Correcting Errors in Pronoun Usage

Underline each incorrectly used pronoun; then write the correct pronoun in the space provided. If the sentence is correct, write _OK_.

1. We don't have nobody else on the payroll.

2. Who did you ask to approve the draft?

3. Did you hear those news on the radio?

4. You and her should offer some suggestions.

5. Mrs. Hills prefers these kind of shoes.

6. Ralph did the work hisself.

7. Fred, as well as myself, may resign.

8. Part of the credit should go to you and I.

9. Rita and myself spoke to him.

10. Davis Brothers is the firm for whom I work.

11. Send a copy to whomever requests one.

12. They did most of the work theirselves.

13. How much do that styles of furniture cost?

14. Ann, who we regard highly, will retire Friday.

15. Whom is to be appointed manager?

16. Each of you should work by yourselves.

17. Whose going with you to the convention?

18. You should discourage them gossiping.

19. She endorsed the check herself.

20. Is he someone who accepts responsibility?

21. As for myself, I would prefer to stay.

22. We don't know who's briefcase this is.

23. We aren't certain ourselfs.

24. Which of them colors do you prefer?

25. What is the price of those type of scissors?

1. _____

2. _____

3. _____

4. _____

5. _____

6. _____

7. _____

8. _____

9. _____

10. _____

11. _____

12. _____

13. _____

14. _____

15. _____

16. _____

17. _____

18. _____

19. _____

20. _____

21. _____

22. _____

23. _____

24. _____

25. _____

40 Correcting Errors in Agreement

If a pronoun does not agree with its antecedent, underline the pronoun and write the correct pronoun in the space provided. If no correction is necessary, write _OK_.

1. The company has moved into their new offices.

2. Each of us must do their share of this work.

3. Any doctor will give you his opinion, I'm sure.

4. Neither of those trees will shed their leaves.

5. Several have given me their advice.

6. A typist must check everything he or she does.

7. A meal of fish and chips lost their appeal to me.

8. Every owner and every manager gave their approval.

9. Some of us need to do their work more carefully.

10. Everyone must contribute whatever he can.

11. The members of the staff held its meeting today.

12. The scissors had a scratch on it.

13. Some of the medicine has lost their potency.

14. Neither of the dogs stopped their barking.

15. We inspected the premises and found it safe.

16. Phil and myself audited those accounts.

17. Did the owners give you their permission?

18. Everything should be in their proper place.

19. Every man and woman gave their full support.

20. The jury argued among itself.

21. Each of the walls had cracks in them.

22. Ms. Barbera moved into her new apartment.

23. The letter is addressed to you and myself.

24. A manager must budget his time carefully.

25. Which of the two women left their purse here?

1. _____
2. _____
3. _____
4. _____
5. _____
6. _____
7. _____
8. _____
9. _____
10. _____
11. _____
12. _____
13. _____
14. _____
15. _____
16. _____
17. _____
18. _____
19. _____
20. _____
21. _____
22. _____
23. _____
24. _____
25. _____

41 Matching Words and Definitions

In the space provided, write the letter that identifies the definition of each word.

A. in the United States, the principal dish of a meal

B. an analysis of the cause of something

C. to shift from one position to another with uncertainty

D. having a bad reputation

E. an amount received when custom forbids a fee

F. implied rather than stated

G. forecast based on the usual course of events

H. capable of being understood in more than one way

I. a thought or an idea

J. to show a relationship of some kind

K. lifeless; unenthusiastic

L. superior; supreme; dominant

M. person designated to receive income from an insurance policy

N. a company owned by another company

O. fully developed; clear

P. depending on supposition; conditional

Q. inclined to be silent; restrained

R. to make firm; to limit

S. to convert or change into cash

T. fair; credible; reasonable

U. to support or to make more certain

V. one-sided

W. person who attempts to reconcile a dispute

X. estimate based on a trend

Y. declaration in advance of occurrence based on experience; a foretelling of something

1. ambiguous _____

2. beneficiary _____

3. corroborate _____

4. implicit _____

5. diagnosis _____

6. entrée _____

7. explicit _____

8. fluctuate _____

9. honorarium _____

10. hypothetical _____

11. infamous _____

12. correlate _____

13. concept _____

14. mediator _____

15. liquidate _____

16. lackadaisical _____

17. paramount _____

18. plausible _____

19. prognosis _____

20. prediction _____

21. reticent _____

22. stabilize _____

23. subsidiary _____

24. projection _____

25. unilateral _____

42 Identifying Subjects

Draw one line under the complete subject of each sentence. Then draw another line under the simple or compound subject of the sentence. Note the example.

0. <u>Mr. Hawkins</u> and <u>Ms. Coleman</u> are co-owners of the consulting firm that we use.

1. This type of machine probably cannot handle the volume of work that you have.

2. Miss Appleby, would you be willing to serve as chairperson of this committee?

3. The owner and manager of a local employment agency advised us to hire temporary workers during peak periods.

4. An award for Dr. Abrams, an outstanding economist, was presented at the banquet.

5. Of the many suggestions given to the council, yours was the best, in my opinion.

6. To ignore market needs would be the worst thing we possibly could do.

7. Our new secretary-treasurer is Mr. Harold Harriman.

8. Of the two proposed building sites, the one nearer the city is preferred by most of us.

9. There is only one item on this order that we will be unable to ship immediately.

10. Reference to Mrs. Ferrara's outstanding contribution to the success of the fund-raising campaign was made in the final report.

11. For your records, we are enclosing a photocopy of the September 20, 1979, contract.

12. This weight of paper is inappropriate for use as letterhead stationery.

13. Pedro M. Blanco, M.D., is the editor in chief of that particular professional journal.

14. Writing frequently takes up a large part of an executive's day in the office.

15. Would you please verify the accuracy of these figures before you issue the report?

Draw one line under the complete subject of each dependent clause in the following sentences. Then draw another line under the simple or compound subject of the dependent clause.

16. We do not know who is in charge of their customer relations department.

17. It seems that you and she are the leading candidates for that managerial position.

18. When I saw Miss Connors this morning, she did not mention her plans to resign.

19. Some of the tourists were complaining because the exchange rate had dropped somewhat.

20. Since you will be out of the office next week, I would like to meet with you tomorrow.

43 Changing Word Order

If a sentence is shown in normal word order, change it to inverted word order. If a sentence is shown in inverted word order, change it to normal word order.

1. In an effort to improve employee morale, the company has made several changes.

2. You should make your reservations now if you would like to attend.

3. Will these price and wage guidelines go into effect before the end of this year?

4. Does Maria believe that the reorganization will improve productivity?

5. To achieve the desired results, we will need to work even harder.

6. Dr. Davis has been an active member of the association for several years.

7. To each of our customers, prompt and courteous service is of prime importance.

8. Are both of them graduates of a community or junior college?

9. Somewhere in your report, please include a statement of market trends.

10. Has their attorney contacted you during the past week?

44 Choosing Correct Verbs

Draw one line under the simple or compound subject. Then choose the correct verb (shown in parentheses), and draw two lines under it.

1. You (*are, is*) our first choice to serve as chairperson of the committee.

2. I (*know, knows*) that my subscription will expire within another week or two.

3. We sincerely (*hope, hopes*) that you will be pleased with this substitute.

4. Each of you (*has, have*) an equal amount of work to do.

5. Among the unusual items on display (*are, is*) a building made of walnut shells.

6. Gene and Terry (*has, have*) told us that they often (*work, works*) overtime.

7. Neither of the reports (*was, were*) delivered to Mr. Delgado on time.

8. Every man and woman in the office (*are, is*) entitled to at least two weeks' vacation.

9. There (*are, is*) five application letters on your desk.

10. Every dog and cat in this city (*need, needs*) a license before January 1.

11. Why (*doesn't, don't*) either of them assume part of the responsibility?

12. The proceeds of the sale (*amount, amounts*) to less than a hundred dollars.

13. Every man and woman (*has, have*) responsibilities that must be met promptly.

14. (*Are, Is*) there anything else that you would like me to do?

15. Either of the apartments (*seem, seems*) large enough for us.

16. That new set of tools (*are, is*) for sale at a greatly reduced price, Ms. Pullman.

17. We heard that you (*was, were*) planning to move to Alaska sometime next year.

18. There (*are, is*) two expiration notices in this batch of mail, Mr. Walker.

19. A number of voters (*has, have*) complained about rising taxes and inflation.

20. Florida and California (*produce, produces*) a variety of fruits and vegetables.

21. The typewriter, as well as those two calculators, (*need, needs*) to be repaired.

22. (*Was, Were*) the jury arguing among themselves?

23. Watching his tactics (*was, were*) most amusing to many of us.

24. Mr. Hillman, you (*know, knows*) that both of us (*has, have*) to be paid for that work.

25. Either my brother or my parents (*pay, pays*) the rent on the first of the month.

26. The jury (*was*, *were*) out for almost seven hours.

27. Either Mr. Hawley or Miss Perrins (*are*, *is*) to conduct the afternoon session.

28. Neither the Owenses nor the Joneses (*tries*, *try*) to outdo their neighbors.

29. A number of our customers (*place*, *places*) their orders early every year.

30. His typing skill (*make*, *makes*) it possible for him to earn extra money.

31. Our vice president and general manager (*participate*, *participates*) in many seminars.

32. Washington and Oregon (*has*, *have*) many natural resources.

33. A long list of prospective advertisers (*are*, *is*) enclosed.

34. That television set, as well as these radios, (*need*, *needs*) to be repaired.

35. The number of people receiving these benefits (*continue*, *continues*) to increase.

36. Neither she nor they (*know*, *knows*) about the change in our top management.

37. It (*seem*, *seems*) that no one (*bother*, *bothers*) to keep in touch with them.

38. Salt and pepper (*are*, *is*) probably the most common of all seasonings.

39. The director of marketing and an accountant usually (*work*, *works*) together in developing a tentative sales budget.

40. My associates and I (*appreciate*, *appreciates*) your extraordinary cooperation.

41. Neither the owner nor the tenants (*want*, *wants*) to install closed-circuit television in the building.

42. The board of directors (*was*, *were*) unanimously in favor of the proposal.

43. Approximately $800 (*remain*, *remains*) in the account.

44. *The New York Times* (*are*, *is*) available in the library.

45. Sixty days (*has*, *have*) gone by since we received a payment from them.

46. Some of the firm's advertising claims (*was*, *were*) considered to be misleading.

47. About half of the offices (*has*, *have*) been rented so far.

48. Part of the blame (*lie*, *lies*) with us.

49. I thought that some of the merchandise (*was*, *were*) overpriced.

50. (*Are*, *Is*) there anything that we (*are*, *is*) overlooking?

45 Using Verbs in Relative Clauses

Which of the verbs shown in parentheses is correct? Write your answer in the space provided.

1. Juan is only one of those who (*has, have*) shown an interest.

    1. _____

2. This is one of the machines that (*need, needs*) repairing.

    2. _____

3. What is the brand of coffee that (*cost, costs*) least?

    3. _____

4. Is that the answer that you (*was, were*) expecting?

    4. _____

5. The plan, which (*seem, seems*) sound to me, is theirs.

    5. _____

6. Kay is the only one who (*are, is*) applying for the job.

    6. _____

7. I'd like one of those—whichever (*are, is*) least expensive.

    7. _____

8. Is that the report that (*contain, contains*) sales data?

    8. _____

9. Research is one of the things that (*are, is*) essential.

    9. _____

10. She is among those who (*go, goes*) to Montreal frequently.

    10. _____

11. Is that the column that (*appear, appears*) in *Newsweek*?

    11. _____

12. Ours is one of the meetings that (*was, were*) canceled.

    12. _____

13. We have many employees who (*show, shows*) initiative.

    13. _____

14. I usually am the one who (*arrive, arrives*) late.

    14. _____

15. Who is the person whom you (*admire, admires*) most?

    15. _____

16. Do you have a copy of the contracts that (*was, were*) issued?

    16. _____

17. There is only one office that (*require, requires*) carpeting.

    17. _____

18. How many cities are there that (*has, have*) that problem?

    18. _____

19. I have only one of the sets that (*are, is*) incomplete.

    19. _____

20. They are the only ones who (*attend, attends*) regularly.

    20. _____

21. You are the one who (*deserve, deserves*) the credit.

    21. _____

22. Laura is one worker who (*take, takes*) things seriously.

    22. _____

23. It is something that (*serve, serves*) no useful purpose.

    23. _____

24. I am one of the clerks who (*file, files*) every day.

    24. _____

25. Please tell whoever (*want, wants*) to know about it.

    25. _____

46 Correcting Spelling Errors

Underline each misspelled word. In the space provided, write the correct spelling. If all the words in the line are spelled correctly, write *OK*.

1. maintainance	summarize	obsolete	similar	1. _____
2. basicly	substantial	calendar	interpret	2. _____
3. unforeseen	equallize	volunteer	discipline	3. _____
4. souvenir	deferred	conferred	differed	4. _____
5. garantee	vertical	technician	mediocre	5. _____
6. embarrassment	insureable	manageable	advisable	6. _____
7. parallell	agreeable	aggravate	dissatisfied	7. _____
8. synthetic	rigerous	acclaim	rescind	8. _____
9. fascinate	durable	imaginery	serviceable	9. _____
10. recipe	receipt	twelvth	negative	10. _____
11. inferrence	liaison	omission	pastime	11. _____
12. ninth	forty	fourth	ninty	12. _____
13. formally	formerly	Febuary	Wednesday	13. _____
14. heighth	weight	whether	wherever	14. _____
15. usage	auxilliary	vigorous	remodeling	15. _____
16. proceed	succeed	successful	proceedure	16. _____
17. remittance	milage	vaguely	surely	17. _____
18. untill	movable	affiliate	adjourn	18. _____
19. reccommendation	occurrence	optimistic	repetitious	19. _____
20. consultent	consensus	susceptible	temperament	20. _____
21. outragous	inflammable	hoping	salable	21. _____
22. tremenduous	legitimate	management	permanent	22. _____
23. unforgettable	trasable	shining	lapsed	23. _____
24. owing	resembelance	interesting	unanimous	24. _____
25. perogative	inquiry	pamphlet	transferable	25. _____

188

47 Forming Tenses of Verbs

In the answer column, write the verb shown in parentheses in the tense indicated.

1. Joan (*go—past*) to the reception for Mr. Esposito.

2. You (*be—present*) an excellent writer.

3. Pat (*represent—future*) us clerical workers.

4. They (*be—past*) responsible for the delay.

5. Who (*take—past*) your order, Ms. Bullard?

6. Carl (*shirk—past perfect progressive*) his duties.

7. On July 1, I (*work—future perfect progressive*) for you a year.

8. Irene (*do—present*) her work on time and well.

9. He (*go—past perfect*) before we arrived.

10. The statements (*mail—past perfect*) by Ms. Helms.

11. Jeff (*be—present progressive*) very cautious.

12. Who (*attend—future progressive*) the conference?

13. They (*sit—past progressive*) in the last row.

14. We (*follow—present perfect*) your instructions.

15. I (*work—past perfect progressive*) on it.

16. He (*review—present perfect progressive*) them.

17. By then, the house (*sell—future perfect*).

18. How (*do—present*) this machine work?

19. I (*meet—present perfect*) both of them.

20. They (*know—past*) our marketing plans.

21. I (*plan—present progressive*) to leave at noon.

22. They (*discuss—past progressive*) budgets.

23. What (*be—present*) your immediate plans?

24. Ann (*forget—past*) to tell Mrs. Thurmond.

25. Marilyn (*write—present perfect*) two articles.

1. _____

2. _____

3. _____

4. _____

5. _____

6. _____

7. _____

8. _____

9. _____

10. _____

11. _____

12. _____

13. _____

14. _____

15. _____

16. _____

17. _____

18. _____

19. _____

20. _____

21. _____

22. _____

23. _____

24. _____

25. _____

48 Expressing Tenses Correctly

If the verb expresses the wrong tense or if the tense is formed incorrectly, underline the error and write the necessary correction in the space provided. If no correction is necessary, write *OK*.

1. We have did all that you asked us to do.

2. Your supervisor knowed you had been ill.

3. They already had chose someone else.

4. The sun will sit at 7:50 p.m. this evening.

5. Our customers knows where to get bargains!

6. I don't think she has wore that suit before.

7. How many of the dishes were broke?

8. You may chose the one that you like best.

9. Ellen teached him to run the calculator.

10. The driver winded in and out of traffic.

11. One of the sweaters had shrank badly.

12. Have you ever eat mangoes or papayas?

13. A thief stoled some of her jewelry.

14. The papers were tore in half.

15. Some of the vegetables were froze.

16. We had ate before they arrived.

17. He wishes he had did a better job.

18. I wish I had knew you would be there.

19. These plants have growed rapidly.

20. The problem had came up before, I think.

21. They done all they could to help us.

22. He had spoke of that possibility.

23. Has he went to Wichita yet?

24. Maria hasn't began her new job yet.

25. Have you wrote to Mr. Swanson lately?

1. _____

2. _____

3. _____

4. _____

5. _____

6. _____

7. _____

8. _____

9. _____

10. _____

11. _____

12. _____

13. _____

14. _____

15. _____

16. _____

17. _____

18. _____

19. _____

20. _____

21. _____

22. _____

23. _____

24. _____

25. _____

190

49 Expressing the Correct Mood

Which of the italicized verbs shown in parentheses is correct? Write your answer in the space provided.

1. I wish I (*was, were*) able to make better progress.

2. We request that orders (*are, be, is*) handled promptly.

3. If the meeting (*are, is*) successful, we'll be pleased.

4. Miss Welch acts as though she (*was, were*) President.

5. If Thomas Edison (*was, were*) alive, he would be shocked.

6. Dale suggested that the dues (*are, be*) increased.

7. What would you do if you (*was, were*) she?

8. I move that the meeting (*are, be, is*) adjourned.

9. We would buy now if the price (*was, were*) a little lower.

10. If I had been asked, I would (*go, have gone*).

11. (*Was, Were*) Bill happy, he would not complain.

12. The bank insists the balance (*are, be, is*) paid today.

13. Don't you wish she (*was, were*) here to help us now?

14. If Roy (*was, were*) there, I did not see him.

15. We feel that the increase (*are, be, is*) inadequate.

16. It is important that they (*are, be, is*) consulted first.

17. Lynn requested that the speaker (*arrive, arrives*) early.

18. We recommend that he (*take, takes*) the exam again.

19. It is imperative that some action (*are, be, is*) taken.

20. It looks as though it (*are, be, is*) raining hard.

21. Do you think that (*was, were*) truly significant?

22. If I (*am, are, be*) chosen, I will be surprised.

23. The IRS requires that all taxes (*are, be, is*) paid.

24. If the figures (*are, be, is*) accurate, we'll use them.

25. If Gary (*had been, was*) there, I would have seen him.

1. _____

2. _____

3. _____

4. _____

5. _____

6. _____

7. _____

8. _____

9. _____

10. _____

11. _____

12. _____

13. _____

14. _____

15. _____

16. _____

17. _____

18. _____

19. _____

20. _____

21. _____

22. _____

23. _____

24. _____

25. _____

50 Using Active and Passive Voice

If the sentence contains a verb in active voice, rewrite the sentence and use a verb in passive voice. If the sentence contains a verb in passive voice, rewrite it and use a verb in active voice. Then, before the number of the sentence, write *A* if you think the active-voice sentence is better or *P* if you think the passive-voice version is better.

1. This policy provides you and your family full protection. _____

2. We are returning the damaged merchandise. _____

3. The directive was issued by the governor. _____

4. Some consultants charge exorbitant fees. _____

5. A copy of your article was sent to me by the publisher of *Tomorrow's Manager*. _____

6. The mayor will lay the cornerstone during the ceremonies next week. _____

7. Someone must have left the door unlocked. _____

8. Did Miss Ryman give you my address? _____

9. You should make your request in writing. _____

10. One of them must have canceled the order. _____

11. The check should have been deposited by you yesterday. _____

12. Every company values the goodwill of its customers. _____

51 Correcting Errors in Verb Usage

The verbs *lay, lie, set, sit, raise,* and *rise* are used in the following sentences. Underline each incorrectly used verb, and write the correct verb. If no correction is necessary, write *OK.*

1. Whose papers are those lying over there?

2. I love to lay in the shade in the summertime.

3. The doctor asked the patient to lay down for a while.

4. One of the cars was laying in the ditch.

5. We lay more bricks than they did.

6. Please lie the package over there on the counter.

7. Those papers have laid there more than a week.

8. We have laid more carpeting than they have.

9. I set in the receptionist's office an hour.

10. This case may sit a precedent.

11. You should set close to the exit.

12. Who sits the prices of those products?

13. Is she firmly set in her ways?

14. How many eggs was that chicken setting on?

15. Please remember to sit the clock ahead an hour.

16. We wish that we had set with them.

17. Who sat the carton on my desk?

18. The cost of everything has risen lately.

19. Have we risen enough for a down payment?

20. They are raising their prices 10 percent.

21. What time will the sun raise tomorrow?

22. Wasn't someone raising the roof yesterday?

23. Has the cost of living raised more?

24. The temperature raised quickly this morning.

25. Salvage experts have risen the sunken ship.

1. _____
2. _____
3. _____
4. _____
5. _____
6. _____
7. _____
8. _____
9. _____
10. _____
11. _____
12. _____
13. _____
14. _____
15. _____
16. _____
17. _____
18. _____
19. _____
20. _____
21. _____
22. _____
23. _____
24. _____
25. _____

52 Correcting Spelling Errors

Underline each misspelled word, and write it correctly in the answer column. If no correction is necessary, write *OK*.

1. Is there a shortage of gasolene?

2. Your neighborhood druggist will fill the perscription.

3. The hotel has spacious banquet facilitys.

4. Are these details worrysome to you too?

5. The taxes are witheld by all employers.

6. You will need to exorcise your best judgment.

7. How can we accomodate so many travelers?

8. How much are blueberries and rasberries?

9. Is your office in Acron or in Cleveland?

10. His wish is to termanate the agreement amicably.

11. Be sure to analyze the data carfully.

12. He is in charge of the maintainance department.

13. That is an employee's perogative.

14. Should some corporations be subsidized?

15. Was the witness subpenaed to testify?

16. We considered his behaviour incongruous.

17. Are those pans made of alumium or copper?

18. Such testimony is inadmissable.

19. Does he have the rank of corpral or sergeant?

20. That discussion is irrelevant.

21. He was asked not to exaggerrate or prevaricate.

22. The surface was oilly in places.

23. A vitamin deficeincy can be serious.

24. Children should be immunized against measels.

25. The mechanic bought a pair of plyers.

1. _____

2. _____

3. _____

4. _____

5. _____

6. _____

7. _____

8. _____

9. _____

10. _____

11. _____

12. _____

13. _____

14. _____

15. _____

16. _____

17. _____

18. _____

19. _____

20. _____

21. _____

22. _____

23. _____

24. _____

25. _____

53 Using Infinitives and Other Verbals

If an incorrect noun, pronoun, or other word is used with an infinitive, a gerund, or a participle, underline the error and write the correction. If no correction is necessary, write *OK*.

1. We thought Mr. Bliss resigning was strange.

2. You should try and get a replacement quickly.

3. Who dropped the cartons' lying over there?

4. Anyone's committing forgery will be prosecuted.

5. I remember them being annoyed at the delay.

6. The one's showing improvement are he and she.

7. We applaud you taking such a strong stand.

8. It came as a surprise to we living in this area.

9. We certainly didn't appreciate them misleading us.

10. Which of the movies is to be showed next?

11. Have you ever overdrawn your checking account?

12. All of us ought to congratulate her.

13. Did you see Dr. Ross waiting outside?

14. No one else knew of him rejecting the offer.

15. Who pruned the shrubs growing by the fence?

16. Who reported someone's loitering in the lobby?

17. The animal escaping from the zoo was an accident.

18. We want them too be cooperative.

19. The visitors' waiting outside are Ed and Anna.

20. I doubt that you would want to be him.

21. Please ask she to call me tomorrow morning.

22. We appreciate you telling us.

23. We noticed your helping them again.

24. Do you consider she to be qualified?

25. The items thrown out were useless.

1. _____

2. _____

3. _____

4. _____

5. _____

6. _____

7. _____

8. _____

9. _____

10. _____

11. _____

12. _____

13. _____

14. _____

15. _____

16. _____

17. _____

18. _____

19. _____

20. _____

21. _____

22. _____

23. _____

24. _____

25. _____

54 Eliminating Dangling Modifiers

If the sentence contains a misplaced participle or participial phrase, rewrite the sentence and position the modifier where it will not "dangle." Change the wording of the original sentence as little as possible—but as much as necessary to ensure that the sentence conveys a logical thought. Write *OK* if the sentence does not contain a dangling modifier.

1. We went to a place having a beautiful view to eat. _____

2. Could you see the movie sitting that far away? _____

3. Warped and full of knotholes, the carpenter threw the board to the ground. _____

4. Did you see the car going up the street being pulled by a tow truck? _____

5. Transcribed by an efficient secretary, incorrect punctuation will not appear in a letter.

6. Being a competent accountant, the reports were prepared accurately by Miss Helms.

7. Place the potatoes in the oven wrapped in aluminum foil. _____

8. Anything written by Professor Harding attracts a great deal of attention. _____

9. Wearing a light blue suit, Ms. Kean said the man looked out of place on the beach. _____

10. Bearing the endorsement of Mr. Edwards, the cashier accepted the check for deposit.

55 Choosing Correct Modifiers

Which of the modifiers shown in parentheses is correct? Draw a line under your answer.

1. (*Almost, Most*) all of the applicants answered the questions (*correct, correctly*).

2. Would you please file (*these, this*) stack of papers (*immediate, immediately*)?

3. Unless she made (*an awful, a very*) bad mistake, she shouldn't feel (*bad, badly*).

4. (*Them, Those*) letters were supposed to be sent to a (*real estate, real-estate*) office in Erie.

5. The house with a (*red tile, red-tile*) roof was damaged (*extensive, extensively*).

6. (*These, This*) kind of paper doesn't look as (*good, well*) as it should.

7. One of the drivers stopped (*real, very*) (*sudden, suddenly*).

8. We couldn't see (*clear, clearly*) through the (*mud streaked, mud-streaked*) windshield.

9. The (*acrid smelling, acrid-smelling*) fumes made several of us feel (*sick, sickly*).

10. I could tell that she didn't feel (*good, well*) because she spoke so (*slow, slowly*).

11. Please ship the order (*direct, directly*) to our (*Rock Island, Rock-Island*) warehouse.

12. The customers looked (*angry, angrily*) when they heard the items were (*out of stock, out-of-stock*).

13. They rented a (*four room, four-room*) apartment in a (*high priced, high-priced*) neighborhood.

14. We (*seldom, seldomly*) buy (*ice cream, ice-cream*) bars for our picnics.

15. Is he a (*high school, high-school*) or a (*junior college, junior-college*) graduate?

16. Are you (*quiet, quite*) certain the storm damaged the crops (*bad, badly*)?

17. She sings (*beautiful, beautifully*)—even when she doesn't feel (*good, well*).

18. She seemed (*disgusted, disgustedly*) when she heard the gems were not (*real, really*) diamonds.

19. Please put all of (*them, those*) papers in (*neatly arranged, neatly-arranged*) stacks.

20. It was (*real, really*) thoughtful of you to entertain us (*out of town, out-of-town*) visitors.

21. (*Almost, Most*) people think that the situation looks (*different, differently*) today.

22. It snowed (*hard, hardly*) for a few minutes and then stopped (*sudden, suddenly*).

23. (*These, This*) kind of cloth looks (*more, most*) expensive than that one.

24. (*Stock market, Stock-market, Stockmarket*) prices fell (*sharp, sharply*) in today's trading.

25. As (*usual, usually*), your ideas were presented (*good, well*).

26. It seems that (*almost, most*) everyone had ideas that were (*different, differently*) from ours.

27. The company treats everyone (*fair, fairly*) and pays its employees (*good, well*).

28. What is the price of (*that, those*) kind of coal in (*3 and 5 ton, 3- and 5-ton*) lots?

29. The official acted (*confident, confidently*) and spoke (*brief, briefly*) at the meeting.

30. Do you think either of them dresses (*to, too, two*) (*casual, casually*)?

31. You may be (*sure, surely*) that we'll pack the others (*secure, securely*).

32. It was an (*all together, all-together, altogether*) different story (*than, then*).

33. (*Almost, Most*) all of us think their merchandise is priced (*reasonable, reasonably*).

34. Every motorist (*sure, surely*) knows he or she should go (*slow, slowly*) in a school zone.

35. Look (*careful, carefully*) and then proceed (*cautious, cautiously*).

36. The (*writer's, writers'*) name was written (*legible, legibly*).

37. Everything considered, we didn't do (*to, too, two*) (*bad, badly*) last year.

38. Everyone applauded the (*first rate, first-rate*) performance (*enthusiastic, enthusiastically*).

39. She has a (*remarkable, remarkably*) (*good, well*) record as a marketing representative.

40. There was (*quiet, quite*) a disturbance in the (*fifth floor, fifth-floor*) showroom.

41. We did the work (*different, differently*), and it is (*almost, most*) ready to hand in.

42. Do you think (*almost, most*) anyone could handle such responsibilities (*easily, easy*)?

43. He did (*near, nearly*) as (*many, much*) work as both of us together.

44. Such (*ill-advised, illy advised*) actions should be avoided (*all ways, always*).

45. They handle themselves (*good, well*) in (*almost, most*) every situation.

46. As (*usual, usually*), we went (*direct, directly*) to the train station after work.

47. Some people talk so (*loud, loudly*) that no one else can be heard (*easily, easy*).

48. The new (*Evening Star, Evening-Star*) reporter worked for us (*previous, previously*).

49. These figures are (*up to date, up-to-date*), and they will be (*useful, usefully*) to us.

50. Are (*them, those*) briefcases (*real, really*) made of leather?

198

56 Correcting Errors in Preposition Usage

Draw a line *through* each unnecessary preposition. If an incorrect preposition is used, draw a line *under* it and write the correct preposition. If the sentence is correct as shown, write *OK*.

1. Why don't you open up the discussion with a question?

1. _____

2. Miss Selden was angry with the delay in the delivery.

2. _____

3. Your flight will arrive in Duluth at about 6 p.m.

3. _____

4. Does anyone know where Ms. Farrell is at today?

4. _____

5. This survey is different than the one they designed.

5. _____

6. Did you see the bus swerve off of the highway?

6. _____

7. You have a copy identical to the one I have.

7. _____

8. The contract will be retroactive from August 1.

8. _____

9. The work should be divided among Willie and Andy.

9. _____

10. She was going in her office when I saw her.

10. _____

11. Mike seems unwilling to stand up to anybody.

11. _____

12. Were you angry at your secretary this morning?

12. _____

13. One of the vases fell off of the table and broke.

13. _____

14. This model is different than the one we ordered.

14. _____

15. We seldom differ with them on critical issues.

15. _____

16. Everyone must comply to her directives.

16. _____

17. Lyle was angry at his boss yesterday.

17. _____

18. All of these conform with your specifications.

18. _____

19. Would you like to sit in on the meeting?

19. _____

20. Who opened up the new office next door?

20. _____

21. When will that job be done with?

21. _____

22. Do you like strawberries better then raspberries?

22. _____

23. Who was there besides you and Mr. Brady?

23. _____

24. Do you know what Faye was angry about?

24. _____

25. The desk sitting besides mine is in the way.

25. _____

57 Using Conjunctions

Underline the conjunction or conjunctions in each sentence. If necessary, rewrite the sentence to show each correction that should be made in the choice or placement of a conjunction or in the wording of the sentence elements joined by a conjunction. Add or delete words wherever appropriate.

1. We carry not only a full line of men's suits but of men's and children's shoes. _____

2. Mr. Lee has and will be running again for reelection. _____

3. Please answer the telephone promptly and with a pleasant, courteous manner. _____

4. Lisa likes to transcribe better then she does supervising others. _____

5. Ray either must retype the letter or I will have to do it myself. _____

6. These foods are not only nutritious but they are inexpensive. _____

7. We left at four and so we could arrive a few minutes early. _____

8. Mrs. Lombardi resigned and because she received a better job offer. _____

9. It makes little difference either to him nor to me. _____

10. Your office is as large, if not larger than, mine. _____

58 Choosing the Right Word

Which of the words shown in parentheses correctly completes the sentence? Write your answer in the space provided.

1. When did she (*emigrate, immigrate*) from Japan?

2. Larry has been (*anxious, eager*) about his health.

3. What is their (*principal, principle*) objection?

4. I asked him to (*lend, loan*) me $20.

5. A large (*amount, number*) of people were there.

6. Her job is to (*council, counsel*) employees.

7. We should drive no (*farther, further*) today.

8. She gave a (*credible, creditable*) excuse.

9. The building is (*all ready, already*) to occupy.

10. The yield is (*fewer, less*) than we expected.

11. Roy is (*liable, likely*) to resign soon.

12. How much (*capital, capitol*) will be needed?

13. They plan to (*adapt, adept, adopt*) a baby.

14. She was (*accepted, excepted*) from one duty.

15. Do you know what (*affect, effect*) it will have?

16. Is that TV available in a (*console, consul*) model?

17. When we arrived, they (*all ready, already*) had left.

18. Did you attend the (*council, counsel*) meeting at city hall last night?

19. What is the (*principal, principle*) ingredient?

20. All of us are (*anxious, eager*) to celebrate.

21. That pie smells (*awful, very*) good, doesn't it?

22. How much will the bank (*lend, loan*) them?

23. Are there (*few, less*) people in the audience?

24. (*Can, May*) I go with you tomorrow?

1. _____

2. _____

3. _____

4. _____

5. _____

6. _____

7. _____

8. _____

9. _____

10. _____

11. _____

12. _____

13. _____

14. _____

15. _____

16. _____

17. _____

18. _____

19. _____

20. _____

21. _____

22. _____

23. _____

24. _____

25. I think she's (*angry with, mad at*) herself today.

25. _____

26. How much does the job pay (*a, an, per*) week?

26. _____

27. I'll go, (*provided, providing*) you do too.

27. _____

28. She's on the telephone (*continually, continuously*).

28. _____

29. This one is (*as, so*) good (*as, so*) that one.

29. _____

30. What is the (*principal, principle*) of the loan?

30. _____

31. Please look into the matter (*farther, further*).

31. _____

32. Max (*affected, effected*) a German accent.

32. _____

33. Who planned this new (*ad, add*)?

33. _____

34. Are you (*adapt, adept, adopt*) at skiing?

34. _____

35. Did you talk with the (*principal, principle*)?

35. _____

36. We met on the steps of the (*capital, capitol*).

36. _____

37. The court held the owner (*liable, likely*).

37. _____

38. Please (*accept, except*) our apologies.

38. _____

39. The proposal needs (*farther, further*) study.

39. _____

40. We can (*adapt, adept, adopt*) them to our needs.

40. _____

41. The (*affect, effect*) may be higher prices.

41. _____

42. What (*advice, advise*) did they offer you?

42. _____

43. You may obtain a visa from the (*console, consul*).

43. _____

44. The Ryans (*emigrated, immigrated*) to Quebec.

44. _____

45. Farmers exported a large (*amount, number*) of corn and other kinds of grain.

45. _____

46. (*Provided, Providing*) the meeting is held in Memphis, Miss Soriano and I will attend.

46. _____

47. The reason (*because, that*) the office will be closed is Monday is a holiday.

47. _____

48. That nuclear power plant operates (*continually, continuously*) to provide electricity in this area.

48. _____

49. I doubt that you will be (*awfully, terribly, very*) surprised to hear that news.

49. _____

50. The company is (*liable, likely*) to relocate its headquarters within the next year or so.

50. _____

59 Correcting Grammatical Errors

Underline each grammatical error, and write the necessary correction in the space provided. If no correction is required, write *OK*.

1. Have either of them responded to your request?

1. _____

2. Do you know which of these is their's?

2. _____

3. I wish that both of you had went with us.

3. _____

4. The secretary and treasurer are Ms. DelRio.

4. _____

5. Has this training film been showed before?

5. _____

6. One of the restaurants lost their license.

6. _____

7. They should of been much more careful.

7. _____

8. Neither he or she seemed interested in the job.

8. _____

9. The reason we left is because we were through.

9. _____

10. If I was you, I'd ask for a raise now.

10. _____

11. Do you know who's papers these are?

11. _____

12. They asked Paul and myself to help them.

12. _____

13. Was any of the containers dented?

13. _____

14. Some officials often travel outside of the country.

14. _____

15. Would you please check them figures again?

15. _____

16. That news come as no surprise to us.

16. _____

17. Please try and get in touch with them immediately.

17. _____

18. We don't need no more of those spare parts.

18. _____

19. That certainly is somebody of water, isn't it?

19. _____

20. The bonus will be divided between the employees.

20. _____

21. Our new contract is retroactive from May 15.

21. _____

22. Did anyone comment on Tim typing it himself?

22. _____

23. They did most of the work theirselves, I think.

23. _____

24. Do you use these kind of business forms?

24. _____

25. Neither of the women lost their glasses.

25. _____

26. Whom do you think has the necessary qualifications?   26. _____

27. Diane and myself offered to edit the report.   27. _____

28. I think you and he ought to visit them tomorrow.   28. _____

29. Us secretaries may need to work overtime.   29. _____

30. The cost of living has raised about 1 percent.   30. _____

31. Do you know who's going beside Ray and Kay?   31. _____

32. Were you aware of the workers walking out?   32. _____

33. Everyone has his personal preferences.   33. _____

34. Is that Ms. Hodges office?   34. _____

35. Do you know their son-in-laws' names?   35. _____

36. We deserve three week's vacation, don't we?   36. _____

37. We would like for you and she to go with us.   37. _____

38. He is only one of them that has been asked.   38. _____

39. Anyone of them will be satisfactory.   39. _____

40. You have a better chance than me.   40. _____

41. The three witnesses contradicted each other.   41. _____

42. Give a copy to whomever asks for one.   42. _____

43. Has some of the prices gone up again?   43. _____

44. One of the cartons was laying outside the door.   44. _____

45. Every man and woman must meet their obligations.   45. _____

46. There was only two or three items missing.   46. _____

47. Does the accountants have that responsibility?   47. _____

48. The jury argued among itself for an hour.   48. _____

49. The proceeds amounts to more than $200.   49. _____

50. Lynn, as well as others, support the recommendations we have made to the general manager.   50. _____

204

60 Using End Punctuation Marks

Insert periods, question marks, and exclamation points wherever they are needed in the following sentences. If necessary, place a caret (∧) below the line and write the punctuation mark above the line. Note the example sentence. Capitalization is correct as shown.

0. Those prices are f.o.b. Houston, aren't they?

1. Please have them ship the order cod directly to our St Louis warehouse

2. This signature indicates that Fred Miller Jr does not use a comma in his name

3. What a shock that was

4. Ms. Collins would like to know whether she should plan to arrive early

5. The balance of their account is approximately $200, isn't it

6. Harris Bros offers the widest selection of home appliances, in my opinion

7. Please be sure to address the Mailgram to Miss Ruth J Mendosa

8. Apparently, Ms Horton was not consulted before the change was made   Why

9. How much did the desk cost the chair the carpeting

10. If you had to train these new employees, how would you proceed

11. Would you be willing to rehire Mr. Siever as a sales representative

12. Do we have an adequate supply of stationery on hand   Certainly

13. We paid $125 plus tax for each of these stenographer's notebooks

14. They were fortunate to obtain a home-improvement loan at 85 percent interest

15. If you wish, you may place those ads over the phone between 9 am and 6:30 pm

16. Jim Norton asked whether he should plan to attend the conference

17. Will you please send us your check for last month's rent

18. Ask him if all the letters and invoices have been filed for this month

19. What confusion there was in the office this morning

20. Have you checked to see whether anyone has found Mrs Rowe's package

21. There is $12 due, isn't there

22. Mr Helitzer asked me to call the Colony Inn and make a reservation for a group of six

23. We thought your flight was due to arrive at 8:30 pm

24. The amount of the loan that we requested was $1,500

25. Do we have all the latest fashions in women's clothing   Yes

26. Would it be possible to have the shipment sent cod

27. The letter should have been addressed to Mr James L Hopkins, Jr

28. How much do we owe John Cynthia Fred

29. Dr Vargas is the head of the medical department at Brill & Haines, Inc

30. What a surprise it was for Mel

31. If you were in charge of the office, how would you run it

32. When you arrive in Phoenix, give me a call and I'll pick you up at the airport

33. Miss Hamilton has asked whether her vacation could be extended two weeks

34. Why she didn't ask him to leave a message is a mystery to me

35. Not one of those orders was shipped on time   Why

36. Someone ought to help Jane with that collating, don't you think

37. Miss Bartlett, our receptionist, earned $150 a week when she first started working for us

38. Michael Teague, PhD, will be the principal speaker

39. These are fantastic bargains

40. Does the local YWCA have a swimming pool

41. Dolores received an MBA degree from Northwestern in 1979

42. Messrs Fernandez and Lawrence are on our company's board of directors

43. We aren't sure how much the repairs will cost

44. Both of them have the authority, don't they, to approve such requisitions

45. Will you please sign and return both copies of the enclosed contract

46. Now, on to the next question   How much will we be able to save

47. Do ask her, however, whether she mailed the invoice to Jeannette Wyman, MD

48. The investigation is being conducted by the local IRS office

49. You can obtain that data from the US Bureau of the Census.

50. Mr Jeffreys wants to know when a firm decision will be made

61 Correcting Spelling Errors

Underline each misspelled word, and write it correctly in the answer column. If the line contains no misspelled word, write *OK* in the space provided.

1. percentage	permanent	priviledge	receive	1. _____
2. patient	peculiar	prepayed	seized	2. _____
3. simalar	strictly	salary	diary	3. _____
4. nickel	pickle	cycle	bicycle	4. _____
5. recede	secede	suceed	proceed	5. _____
6. miscellaneous	parallell	recommend	occasion	6. _____
7. perspective	prospective	protective	perport	7. _____
8. symbolic	allergic	picnicked	frolicing	8. _____
9. responsible	collapsable	dispensable	probable	9. _____
10. separate	temperate	perpetrate	concentrate	10. _____
11. truly	duly	purely	wholely	11. _____
12. malign	benign	align	consign	12. _____
13. foundry	boundry	humor	assessor	13. _____
14. respectible	respectively	flexible	accessible	14. _____
15. stationery	stationary	pneumonia	pneurology	15. _____
16. subtle	vacumn	triumph	enough	16. _____
17. thirty	eighty	fourty	seventy	17. _____
18. derisive	incisive	decisive	devisive	18. _____
19. contentious	superstitious	religious	prodigious	19. _____
20. stimulate	accummulate	regulate	congratulate	20. _____
21. mechanism	organism	pledge	knowledge	21. _____
22. playwright	copywright	incite	excite	22. _____
23. withold	patients	patience	underrate	23. _____
24. engross	digress	regression	succesion	24. _____
25. errosion	corrosion	explosion	contusion	25. _____

62 Gaining Word Power

Choose the verb that correctly completes each sentence. Use your dictionary if necessary.

abscond	complement	exhilarate	ostracize	stimulate
accede	compliment	exonerate	perpetuate	sublimate
adhere	emulate	incite	rationalize	terminate
alleviate	evoke	invoke	scintillate	vegetate

1. The stars seem to —?— on a clear winter's night.

2. Jim tried to —?— his behavior during the robbery.

3. Parents often —?— their own desires for the sake of their children.

4. Mary was allowing herself to —?— on the farm.

5. There is nothing like a cold shower to —?— you in the morning.

6. The new plan should —?— traffic congestion.

7. His wish is to —?— the agreement.

8. One speaker tried to —?— his audience to commit acts of violence.

9. The defendant probably will —?— the Fifth Amendment instead of answering the questions.

10. I shall —?— to your wishes.

11. Its purpose is to —?— an earlier measure.

12. How can we —?— his memory?

13. You should —?— to company policy.

14. Did he —?— with the payroll?

15. His statement didn't —?— a favorable response.

16. Youngsters often —?— their parents.

17. John's ironclad alibi will —?— him, I'm sure.

18. Some club members may attempt to —?— her.

19. These ads should —?— sales.

20. If Sharon does well, remember to —?— her.

1. _____

2. _____

3. _____

4. _____

5. _____

6. _____

7. _____

8. _____

9. _____

10. _____

11. _____

12. _____

13. _____

14. _____

15. _____

16. _____

17. _____

18. _____

19. _____

20. _____

208

63 Using Commas

Insert commas where necessary in the sentences below and on the following page.

1. We are proud to present James J. Parker Ph.D. as our next district representative.

2. Their newest book *Management by Directives* is published by Paul & Lewis of Akron Ohio.

3. Please address this letter to Maureen H. Haley whose home address is 1104 Eighth Avenue Indianapolis Indiana 46291.

4. Furthermore we are uncertain as to whether we shall move or not at least within the near future.

5. Reaching maturity it has been said is not simply a matter of reaching old age.

6. To arrive at a reasonable estimate we must obtain their help.

7. In the absence of any proof of personal injury the judge dismissed the case.

8. However you must evaluate the risk involved before you invest in stocks.

9. Following the steps listed at the top of the next page please retype the report.

10. We believe that very few if any changes need to be made in the outline.

11. Two of the group John and Bill submitted their resignations on Friday May 2.

12. Yes we completely agree with you Phyllis.

13. Please write directly to Mr. J. P. Lang 140 West End Avenue Tulsa Oklahoma 74115.

14. Of the 10500 questionnaires we mailed 4850 have been returned so far.

15. There are 500 employees give or take a few in their Detroit plant.

16. The manager of Duke's Department Store Mr. J. F. Albright Jr. attended the meeting that was held in Norman Oklahoma last Monday.

17. It is requested that you schedule your vacation during June July or August.

18. A recent report which has not yet been published indicates that companies are giving their employees longer vacations.

19. The amount you save not the amount you earn is what counts.

20. Please use a large manila envelope when you mail these materials.

21. A small neatly wrapped package was sitting outside the receptionist's office.

22. The president of the organization namely Miss Eileen Barton personally invited Harold T. Simpson Ph.D. to speak at the August conference.

23. Mark is a capable conscientious worker.

24. The new blue carpet gave the office a cool elegant appearance.

25. My youngest brother Herman and his wife Mary moved to Dallas about eight years ago.

26. Please be sure to include pencils notebooks etc. on the next order Mr. Saunders.

27. However important the convention may be our budget will not permit us to attend this year.

28. Exhausted after the lengthy hearing the judge adjourned the case until next Wednesday.

29. In June 1979 the distance given on the sign was changed to 8 520 kilometers.

30. One of the attorneys commented "I wouldn't take this case for anything would you?"

31. In my opinion many many thousands of dollars could be saved if we were to try harder.

32. Lorraine's office is on the fifth floor; John's the fourth floor.

33. A new sidewalk which was laid at the request of the property owners extends from Marcus Avenue to Willow Road.

34. Thank you Mrs. Weeks for all that you did to make the campaign a success.

35. Mr. Alan Hall Jr.'s office is on the twelfth floor I believe.

36. Of the $25 $2.50 is your commission.

37. Miss Hale president of the local chapter of the National Secretaries Association has written several articles for our magazine.

38. To show the work flow chart the information in graph form.

39. We are enclosing a copy of *Dream Homes* which has been acclaimed by architects interior decorators and countless others.

40. When you have finished the inventory Mr. Orval make a typewritten record.

41. Miss Akers formerly secretary to the general manager is now an administrative assistant.

42. The company's losses this year as given in the report exceed those of last year.

43. This spring I intend to drive to Cleveland where I have many relatives.

44. I have not answered Mr. Young's letter but I shall do so before Monday.

45. Anyone who wants to succeed in business cannot be satisfied with mediocre work.

46. The colors are not strictly speaking complementary.

47. Facts not personal opinions should decide your course of action.

48. Please sign the card mail it to our Chicago office and pay when the package arrives.

49. We won't be able to give our answer however until we talk with our lawyer Mr. Grier.

50. The article first appeared in the February 5 1979 issue of *Time* magazine and I think it is just as relevant today as it was then don't you?

64 Using Semicolons and Commas

Insert commas and semicolons where necessary in the sentences below and on the next page.

1. We are enclosing your credit card Mr. Hansen note that it is nontransferable.

2. He will be in Ames Iowa Omaha Nebraska and Duluth Minnesota this week.

3. Please cancel my reservation at the Taft then make one for me at the Hilton.

4. Ms. Lane vice president for marketing will return Tuesday March 10.

5. Your message was delivered at three and we left the office at four.

6. Work has fallen behind schedule consequently we cannot move until June.

7. If you will be making a trip this summer why not let us help you plan it?

8. The order was shipped on June 10 it should reach you by June 20.

9. Mr. Ward will be in Baltimore Tuesday therefore you may expect a call from him then.

10. However annoyed you may be don't lose your temper.

11. Imported silks tropical worsteds and lightweight shetlands have been fashioned into sport clothes of commanding appearance all are available at our store.

12. Our electric mowers always the favorite in any store will be demonstrated at Martin's.

13. Ms. Key is our general manager Mr. Burton is her secretary and Mr. Hall whom you have met is our director of marketing.

14. She attended the University of Illinois he attended Michigan State University.

15. Mr. Baker chairman of the finance committee Miss Lane and Mrs. Stone will be unable to attend the meeting scheduled for November 20.

16. Thank you for accepting our invitation John we look forward to seeing you again.

17. When you write a letter don't be vague instead be as specific as you can.

18. As the hours went by the auditor became more weary and frustrated.

19. Mr. Kane started work as a salesclerk then he became a field supervisor now he is our general sales manager.

20. The merchandise was shipped on May 4 by Air Express therefore you should have received it the next day.

21. Mrs. Phipps was born in Iowa Mr. Phipps in Nebraska.

22. We have meetings scheduled for Monday May 4 Tuesday May 19 and Friday May 29.

23. We import thousands and thousands of TV sets and radios and other items every year.

24. If the small blue bag weighs 22 pounds 11 ounces what would its weight be in kilograms?

25. The cost of raw materials has risen thus we can expect a rise in the price of finished goods.

26. Most of the airports were closed but all the bus and train stations were open yesterday.

27. The meeting ended at six therefore you should have had no difficulty getting home.

28. Before you decide to move consider the advantages of staying where you are.

29. Nevertheless it may be necessary to interview two or three more candidates before you find the person you believe has all the qualifications to do this type of work.

30. It is very difficult to decide what to do next.

31. The Whartons who live next to us are not the Whartons you described.

32. Carmen was wearing a hat decorated with bananas oranges lemons and other fruits.

33. This beautiful four-color brochure contains a reproduction of a snapshot showing Miranda sitting on the veranda of Cedar Farms a famous resort.

34. We should order the new model however long we must wait for it to be delivered Mrs. Dalton.

35. Is the top of that table wood plastic or something else?

36. All the figures were arranged in a long narrow column.

37. The population of this city is 53486 according to the most recent census.

38. The harbor of Palma de Mallorca is indeed magnificent.

39. Everything will turn out just fine in my opinion.

40. They are going to Canada we to Mexico.

41. You will of course be fully reimbursed for your travel expenses.

42. The next time you are in the neighborhood please call me.

43. Do you plan to spend the holidays at home or do you plan to visit friends in the country?

44. The farmers all of them hard workers reported that they were having problems.

45. Ed has the authority doesn't he to approve my request?

46. Their address is 166 Fifth Avenue Rockford Illinois 61108.

47. Please call 967-4004 and ask for Operator 12.

48. The lot is 96 feet 8 inches by 45 feet 10 inches.

49. We need enough to cover approximately 1 800 square meters.

50. Ilene would you be willing to answer the letter that Mr. Claussen wrote to me?

65 Using Colons, Dashes, and Parentheses

Insert colons, dashes, and parentheses where needed. If there is not enough space to insert the punctuation within the line, place a caret (/\) below the line and write the punctuation above it.

1. The theme of this year's meeting will be as follows Big Opportunities for Small Businesses.

2. These are the incoming officers Cynthia Hines, president; Victor Noriega, secretary.

3. Sales during the past four years see Table 2 on page 10 have been most impressive.

4. You must make up your mind soon either accept the proposal or reject it.

5. Paul Ferris Jr. no, not Paul Ferris Sr. founded the company in August 1976.

6. You will find this statement on page 3 "Productivity is the key to business survival."

7. He will arrive at 330 p.m. on Wednesday, March 14.

8. A truthful statement is this People cannot live by bread alone.

9. These are the months of our carpet sales March, August, and December.

10. Kathleen no, I mean Kathryn would you take a letter to Mr. Kingston, please?

11. Here are our officers for the coming year Walter Lang, president; Isabel Grey, vice president.

12. Suits, coats, and dresses all are on sale at greatly reduced prices.

13. How much would it cost to run ads of these lengths 4 lines? 6 lines? 10 lines?

14. Portland, Springfield, Albany any one of them would be an excellent site.

15. We awarded the contract to the lowest bidder Alioto & Associates Construction Company.

16. Cary or maybe it was Gary told us of the progress being made in eliminating pollution.

17. The meetings are scheduled for these dates February 16, March 24, and April 6.

18. Peggy yes, Peggy said that she will be resigning at the end of this month.

19. Large quantities of grain for example, corn, wheat, and oats are stored in huge silos.

20. Several items for example, pens, pencils, and notebooks will be needed in the auditorium.

21. IBM, Xerox, Wang these and others will be considered when we buy new equipment.

22. Jean's sole objective is this to move to the top of the management ladder.

23. The papers we submitted are these Form 1040, Schedule A, and Schedule D.

24. The report Edwin Moore prepared it has been widely acclaimed by industry leaders.

25. The general session will begin at 830 a.m. and end at 10 a.m., I believe.

66 Matching Words and Definitions

Select the most appropriate definition for each word. In the space provided, write the letter that identifies the definition. Use your dictionary if necessary.

A. a sculptured likeness of a person or a thing

B. to charge with an offense of some kind

C. interest beyond the maximum legal rate

D. a claim against property for the amount of a debt

E. violation of a sworn oath or vow to tell the truth

F. place of legal residence

G. a minor offense or crime

H. restraint by threat

I. an unchanging factor

J. to read or study with close attention

K. a person named in a divorce suit in some instances

L. to call before a court to answer an indictment

M. to put in order

N. to harass or annoy

O. one who writes letters or other messages

P. a boundary; the outer limits

Q. one who associates with another in wrongdoing

R. anguish; trouble; misfortune

S. to yield; to die

T. one who conveys property to another conditionally

U. one to whom property or a right is transferred

V. a law enacted by a legislative body

W. to postpone or delay intentionally and habitually

X. to begin and carry on a legal suit

Y. to court; to chase

1. statue _____

2. peruse _____

3. domicile _____

4. arraign _____

5. parameter _____

6. accomplice _____

7. correspondent _____

8. indict _____

9. prosecute _____

10. statute _____

11. perjury _____

12. duress _____

13. lien _____

14. pursue _____

15. corespondent _____

16. perimeter _____

17. misdemeanor _____

18. persecute _____

19. usury _____

20. arrange _____

21. assignee _____

22. mortgagor _____

23. procrastinate _____

24. succumb _____

25. distress _____

67 Correcting Grammatical Errors

Underline each grammatical error. Write the necessary correction in the answer column. If no correction is needed, write *OK.*

1. Everyone must do their own work.

2. Was there any other damaged ones?

3. I would like to go too Los Angeles this year.

4. She does much better work than him.

5. Tony and myself have finished the report.

6. As for myself, I would prefer to stay here.

7. We slept until almost 8 o'clock.

8. They done what they could to help us.

9. Have you wrote to either of them?

10. This one is more small than that one.

11. One member of the committee is him, Fred Lyons.

12. Which one of these is our's?

13. Us secretaries do most of the hard work.

14. Who would you like to see?

15. Whoever finishes before five may leave early.

16. Everyone of them must do outstanding work.

17. Both of them has been confirmed.

18. The proceeds amounts to $54.50.

19. Neither he or Larry works for Arnold's.

20. The question is, How do it work?

21. The majority of the members is here.

22. A number of records was destroyed.

23. Either you or him ought to be there.

24. None of the construction were done.

25. Is any of them eligible for promotion?

1. _____

2. _____

3. _____

4. _____

5. _____

6. _____

7. _____

8. _____

9. _____

10. _____

11. _____

12. _____

13. _____

14. _____

15. _____

16. _____

17. _____

18. _____

19. _____

20. _____

21. _____

22. _____

23. _____

24. _____

25. _____

Underline each incorrectly used verb and write the correct verb in the answer column. If no correction is necessary, write *OK* in the answer column.

26. I thought you was planning to go on vacation.

26. _____

27. Do you know who done all the work?

27. _____

28. Only a few of them is correct.

28. _____

29. There is several questions to be answered.

29. _____

30. How was we supposed to know their plans?

30. _____

31. He done all that we asked him to do.

31. _____

32. Have either of you ate at Clara's Cafe?

32. _____

33. Neither were received on time.

33. _____

34. Young & Young are the agency we use.

34. _____

35. Some of the papers has been misfiled.

35. _____

36. Sears carry all our products.

36. _____

37. Where was the orders being sent?

37. _____

38. I think we have ran out of envelopes.

38. _____

39. Was they the ones that submitted the low bid?

39. _____

40. Either of these routes is satisfactory.

40. _____

41. She said you was in your office.

41. _____

42. Some of them undoubtedly is incorrect.

42. _____

43. When was these instructions given?

43. _____

44. That is where he is going today.

44. _____

45. Neither of them has taken the examination.

45. _____

46. The letter came while you was gone.

46. _____

47. Most of them is ready now.

47. _____

48. We seen them leaving the building.

48. _____

49. The thief run down the street.

49. _____

50. One of the machines work well.

50. _____

68 Supplying Punctuation

Insert quotation marks, underscores, and other punctuation marks where needed in the following sentences. If necessary, write the punctuation mark above the line with a caret (∧) below it.

1. She asked whether I read The Wall Street Journal regularly.

2. The real problem the manager said is that our productivity has slipped somewhat.

3. His reply was We have no record of that particular order Mr. Graham.

4. One speaker shouted Americans cherish the democratic form of government.

5. All the spokesperson would say is No comment at this time ladies and gentlemen.

6. Are you sure you understand the provisions of the contract asked the banker.

7. Dr. Steinberg replied How many times must I explain those instructions to them

8. This he said is an outrage That rumor has no factual basis whatsoever

9. Miss Kent asked whether all the merchandise for the men's department had been delivered.

10. Our bookstore the manager said has sold more than a hundred copies of Antarctica Today.

11. Tom said that he was not sure when he would be able to call on those customers.

12. It has been said that all that glitters is not gold

13. Please check the dictionary to see what the term widow means to a printer.

14. In lieu of actual expenses, each participant will receive a per diem allowance of $65.

15. The Mailgram said Please send 100 copies of the article Computers for Home Use

16. Everyone was plumb done in at the end of that meeting!

17. Did anyone say Let's postpone action on that proposal until the next meeting

18. He exclaimed I'll quit first

19. Who said The stockholders will be pleasantly surprised at the end of this year

20. Tony said that he has been running from dawn until dusk for the past month.

21. Wasn't it Ben Franklin who said that a penny saved is a penny earned

22. Does the Spanish term casita mean little house

23. According to an article in Business Week, the shortage is temporary the speaker said.

24. This she said is a hopeless state of affairs. I don't see how it can be resolved.

25. How many times is the letter l used in the word parallel?

69 Choosing Synonyms

Which of the three words is closest in meaning to the word shown in italics? Write your answer in the space provided. Use your dictionary if necessary.

1. *indispensable*	unnecessary	optional	essential	1. _____	
2. *eminent*	famous	impending	early	2. _____	
3. *illicit*	unlawful	legal	permissive	3. _____	
4. *suave*	unpolished	urbane	sullen	4. _____	
5. *stupendous*	dull	fickle	huge	5. _____	
6. *subsist*	sustain	starve	die	6. _____	
7. *conspicuous*	tasteless	unseen	noticeable	7. _____	
8. *contaminate*	pollute	dilute	purify	8. _____	
9. *complement*	praise	favor	counterpart	9. _____	
10. *complaisant*	amiable	lazy	shiftless	10. _____	
11. *flexible*	rigid	fixed	pliable	11. _____	
12. *avert*	avoid	cause	eliminate	12. _____	
13. *bizarre*	fair	just	odd	13. _____	
14. *translucent*	opaque	luminous	effusive	14. _____	
15. *vulgar*	course	common	acceptable	15. _____	
16. *escalate*	climb	increase	ascend	16. _____	
17. *benign*	gracious	evil	malignant	17. _____	
18. *nominal*	monetary	trifling	appointed	18. _____	
19. *notorious*	infamous	famous	unknown	19. _____	
20. *sagacious*	spicy	shrewd	shrewish	20. _____	
21. *transient*	permanent	fleeting	sticky	21. _____	
22. *purport*	profess	confess	brag	22. _____	
23. *espouse*	support	divorce	separate	23. _____	
24. *enmity*	hostility	love	friendship	24. _____	
25. *implicate*	pacify	involve	absolve	25. _____	

218

70 Indicating Correct Capitalization

Draw three lines below each letter, word, or phrase that should be capitalized.

1. during the next fiscal year, capital expenditures are expected to decrease slightly.

2. Our attorney, ms. judith m. pierce, will meet us at the fiesta inn on biscayne boulevard.

3. The clerk said, "perhaps you would like to order a copy of *games people play.*"

4. Please be sure to bring the following:
   1. at least 2 dozen notebooks
   2. ballpoint pens or pencils

5. Note: we'll meet you at jfk international airport at 3:30 p.m.

6. The president held the news conference in the east room of the white house monday evening.

7. Do we have india ink and manila folders on hand?

8. One of the proposed sites is about a mile south of rock island.

9. The president of our company had this to say: "we are not interested in their proposal."

10. Before joining our organization, she was a lieutenant in the marine corps.

11. I seldom use "very truly yours" as a complimentary closing.

12. I believe there is an authorized ford agency at 1400 north tenth street.

13. Is the new warehouse in kansas city, kansas, or in kansas city, missouri?

14. Didn't former president nixon live in the city of new york at one time?

15. Ms. Inez Torres, vice president and general manager, is an avid reader of *the new york times.*

16. I would very much appreciate it, professor, if you would serve as our speaker this year.

17. Everyone will have a long weekend for the fourth of july and washington's birthday.

18. The late vice president nelson a. rockefeller served as governor of the state of new york.

19. We would appreciate it, sir, if you would send us a map of new england.

20. Was the senior senator from new york state born in the north or in the south?

21. How many people use the salutation "my dear sir or madam" when writing to a sales manager?

22. Chicago, the windy city, is the home of the merchandise mart.

23. Does trans world airlines have daily service to those european cities?

24. Were roman numerals used for the date on the base of the statue of liberty?

25. Southerners and northerners during the civil war were fictionalized in *gone with the wind.*

71 Choosing Antonyms

From the choices, write the word that is *opposite* in meaning to the italicized word.

1. *ambiguous*	clear	large	fuzzy	1. _____
2. *appropriate*	fit	ideal	unsuitable	2. _____
3. *acquit*	convict	deny	pardon	3. _____
4. *flexible*	malleable	rigid	elastic	4. _____
5. *foretell*	recall	predict	prophesy	5. _____
6. *polite*	discourteous	civil	refined	6. _____
7. *multiple*	manifold	double	single	7. _____
8. *contract*	expand	shrivel	condense	8. _____
9. *complex*	simple	difficult	hard	9. _____
10. *denial*	disavowal	rejection	admission	10. _____
11. *deprive*	withhold	remove	provide	11. _____
12. *derogatory*	degrading	detracting	complimentary	12. _____
13. *adolescent*	young	mature	youthful	13. _____
14. *mundane*	earthly	unusual	ordinary	14. _____
15. *negative*	disagreeable	positive	opposite	15. _____
16. *provincial*	cosmopolitan	narrow	simple	16. _____
17. *radical*	traditional	extreme	unusual	17. _____
18. *stationary*	fixed	immobile	movable	18. _____
19. *round*	circular	square	oval	19. _____
20. *somber*	grave	happy	melancholy	20. _____
21. *sincere*	hypocritical	genuine	honest	21. _____
22. *minute*	small	huge	infinitesimal	22. _____
23. *meager*	sparse	scant	plentiful	23. _____
24. *emulate*	copy	ignore	imitate	24. _____
25. *encumber*	free	hinder	burden	25. _____

220

72 Using Abbreviations

If an abbreviation is incorrect for any reason, underline it and write it correctly—or if the expression should not be abbreviated, the complete expression. If the sentence is correct, write *OK*.

1. In Ft. Collins it was 10°C at 11:30 a.m.

2. The meeting is scheduled for Tues. afternoon.

3. Do you prefer the title *Ms.* or *Miss.*, Roberta?

4. Have you ever visited New Orleans, La.?

5. Wasn't Dr. Karl in St. Paul last Aug.?

6. Ed Hill, Doctor of Philosophy, spoke last.

7. Sister Mary Ruth, O.P., was here this p.m.

8. Have you seen Mr. Paul Roberts, Senior?

9. Are these statistics from a govt. publication?

10. This is a good co. to ask for a contribution.

11. The meeting will be held in Sept., I think.

12. They are taking swimming lessons at the YMCA.

13. Is that station an affiliate of NBC or CBS?

14. The date on the cornerstone is A.D. MCMLVII.

15. Did Chas. Ash read the government regulations?

16. Is the speed limit still 55 km/h?

17. Did one of the ships transmit an S.O.S.?

18. She works for either IBM or AT&T.

19. Please order 20 kg of lawn fertilizer.

20. Our attorney is Wm. J. Sloane.

21. He is a graduate of the Univ. of Miss.

22. These figures were provided by the U.S. Dept. of Labor.

23. Is Ms Frye a C.P.A.?

24. Industry leaders met with Gov. Higgins.

25. It is now 3 a.m. o'clock in the morning.

1. _____

2. _____

3. _____

4. _____

5. _____

6. _____

7. _____

8. _____

9. _____

10. _____

11. _____

12. _____

13. _____

14. _____

15. _____

16. _____

17. _____

18. _____

19. _____

20. _____

21. _____

22. _____

23. _____

24. _____

25. _____

73 Gaining Word Power

Read the statement, and then choose the word that answers the question. Use your dictionary if necessary. In the answer column, write the word you have chosen.

1. Her remark to the new employee was meant to hurt. Was her remark **(a)** cursory, **(b)** vicarious, or **(c)** caustic?

1. _____

2. The applicant failed the test because he barely glanced at the study materials. Did he study in **(a)** an acrid, **(b)** a perfunctory, or **(c)** a punctilious manner?

2. _____

3. Lonely children often turn to reading for companionship, becoming lovers of books. Do they become **(a)** jingoists, **(b)** bibliophiles, or **(c)** stoics?

3. _____

4. Wise people disapprove the idea of violence. Do they **(a)** deprecate, **(b)** emulate, or **(c)** procrastinate violence?

4. _____

5. Agricultural agencies are endeavoring to rejuvenate worn-out soil. Would such land be **(a)** maudlin, **(b)** expiated, or **(c)** exhausted?

5. _____

6. The new clerk frequently and openly disregarded the rules in the office. Was the behavior **(a)** didactic, **(b)** flagrant, or **(c)** circumspect disobedience?

6. _____

7. Much time is wasted each day in senseless, idle chatter. Would you describe such talk as **(a)** surreptitious, **(b)** inane, or **(c)** acrimonious?

7. _____

8. Cancer can be cured if it is discovered in the beginning stages. Would that be in the **(a)** incipient, **(b)** incisory, or **(c)** sibilant stages?

8. _____

9. His tendency to laugh made it difficult for him to take part in dramatics. Is this trait **(a)** lethargy, **(b)** risibility, or **(c)** antipathy?

9. _____

10. Roy has the capacity to share another person's ideas and feelings. Does Roy show **(a)** empathy, **(b)** sympathy, or **(c)** pity?

10. _____

74 Expressing Numbers Correctly

Underline each incorrectly expressed number; then write the number correctly in the answer column. If the numbers in a sentence are written correctly, write *OK*.

1. We sold several 100 tickets.

2. $85 was not a reasonable price.

3. Please buy 8 1-liter bottles of soda.

4. He built twelve homes in 3 years.

5. She paid two dollars for it.

6. We charge seven cents each for them.

7. Was 10010 used as a ZIP Code in the 50's?

8. We canceled our June 5th order.

9. Two of the 24 bottles were broken.

10. Could you leave at three p.m.?

11. We sold four hundred tickets before 2 p.m.

12. The loan was for ninety days only.

13. The baby is one year 15 days old.

14. 3½ tons of coal were used this month.

15. We received a fifteen percent discount.

16. 38% of the accidents were minor ones.

17. I need 12 large, 6 small, and 18 medium.

18. There are twenty-three schools in the city.

19. He gave his date of birth as 2/1/63.

20. Please ship 6 of model 420.

21. She was 10 years old on the 12th of July.

22. Their address is 1 Park Avenue.

23. I found 6 15-cent stamps.

24. One-half of the group went; the other half did not.

25. Our address is 3,347 East 10th Street.

1. _____

2. _____

3. _____

4. _____

5. _____

6. _____

7. _____

8. _____

9. _____

10. _____

11. _____

12. _____

13. _____

14. _____

15. _____

16. _____

17. _____

18. _____

19. _____

20. _____

21. _____

22. _____

23. _____

24. _____

25. _____

75 Using Hyphens

Insert hyphens wherever they are needed in these sentences.

1. She is a write in candidate.

2. The building is 20 stories high.

3. Mel keeps the files up to date.

4. The platform was flag draped.

5. This station gives up to the minute news.

6. Hit and miss methods are inefficient.

7. A two thirds majority is necessary.

8. We need more income tax forms.

9. She is self supporting.

10. This 24 page booklet is free.

11. Did you stand up for yourself?

12. The ex President was on television.

13. A made to order suit will cost more.

14. She has a three room apartment.

15. Who operates the local drive in?

16. These are nicely arranged plants.

17. We passed the three mile limit.

18. She is very old fashioned.

19. Japan is very pro Western.

20. It has a water repellent finish.

21. She had a coat made to order.

22. We sat through a three hour movie.

23. Do you have a data processing department?

24. Six and one half percent is the rate now.

25. We need to represent our side of that in house dispute.

26. Who is secretary treasurer?

27. Do you have self control?

28. James is well known and quiet spoken.

29. They have a real estate agency.

30. This company is privately owned.

31. Both long and short term securities are available.

32. He has an out of state license.

33. It was an awe inspiring view.

34. Twenty two members were present.

35. We have the technical know how.

36. The election was a cliff hanger.

37. He is the leader of the AFL CIO.

38. The right hand margin is too wide.

39. Please double check these figures.

40. She is a Wall Street broker.

41. He owns a real estate business.

42. Jim has one half; I, the other half.

43. It is a well written document.

44. She is a clerk typist.

45. We use a numeric filing system.

46. It was a nerve racking experience.

47. He has a wait and see attitude.

48. Chile is a South American country.

49. This is our fourth annual report.

50. It is only one twenty second of an inch thick.

76 Using Apostrophes

Insert an apostrophe (or 's) where needed to form possessives and contractions.

1. We shouldve bought several dollars worth of diesel fuel.

2. Were you aware of Anthony leaving at 12 oclock yesterday.

3. Were looking for a days pay for a days work, arent we?

4. Theyre having a sale of mens and boys shoes next week.

5. Youll want to know that well be unable repair those trucks of yours.

6. The business executives luncheon will be held after Tuesdays election; wed like to attend.

7. Larry has three of Bobs IOUs., each of which dates from the late 70s.

8. Please plan to arrive a little before two oclock if its at all possible.

9. When others tell you how good you are, its a compliment; when you tell others how good you are, its considered bragging.

10. You may solicit contributions from the people in Mr. Jones department.

11. "Come to work at 10 oclock," said Miss Harris secretary.

12. I think Max report has fewer errors in it than anyone else.

13. Its been in the low 50s for several days in a row.

14. He always forgets to cross his ts and dot his is.

15. Do you know whos planning to make the arrangements for the sales staffs dinner?

16. I dont think Laura spreading gossip will gain her the respect of the secretaries.

17. No ones prices are more reasonable than theirs.

18. The medical departments located on the second floor.

19. I dont think its more than an hours drive from here to Moline.

20. The cashier put a stack of 10s on top of the counter.

21. Its almost certain to be several weeks work, isnt it?

22. Steve and Gregg sister is planning to attend Rock Valley Junior College.

23. The Longs, our next-door neighbors, own and operate the towns only bakery.

24. Mr. and Mrs. Kenneth Sheahan Jr. house will be finished soon, wont it?

25. The sales meeting will be held at a motel near OHare Field in Chicago.

77 Using Punctuation and Capitalization

Insert all necessary punctuation marks. If a letter should be capitalized, draw three short lines below it. If a letter should not be capitalized, draw a light diagonal line (/) through it.

1. Ms Beth Messina executive vice president reported a breakdown in the labor management negotiations.

2. One of the nations top notch economists spoke at our sales conference.

3. If necessary well send each of them a Mailgram before 4 oclock today.

4. By June 1 we expect to have a new text editing machine.

5. He has owed us $125 for three months now he asks for a 90 day extension.

6. You were not here consequently we gave our order to someone else.

7. Yes Miss Ahrens I shall introduce Mr. Howard Mrs. Jones and Mr. Frye.

8. The associations books were audited yesterday and I believe they were approved.

9. A growing business has to answer this question if we surpass optimum size how do we safeguard efficient operation

10. He visited Fond du Lac Wisconsin Marquette Michigan and Terre Haute Indiana.

11. Your qualifications particularly your educational background are outstanding.

12. Political leaders who are responsive to the needs of their constituents are actively supporting the legislation proposed by senator Harrison.

13. This top quality roofing retains its color provides insulation and enhances the beauty of your home.

14. When your account is inactive its subject to no interest or other charges.

15. The Government inquiry deals with operations of multinational corporations.

16. The policy we have followed for some time is to answer letters within 24 hours.

17. Send it to his home address 290 Madison Avenue Burlington Vermont 05401.

18. For the past two years I have been a Stenographer for the Barnes Company.

19. Your application which was submitted to our Personnel Department in october, has been carefully reviewed by Mrs James c Carson our personnel director.

20. Before you invest heavily in that companys stock you should take a very very close look at its prospects for continued growth.

78 Correcting Grammatical Errors

Underline each grammatical error, and write the necessary correction in the space provided. If a sentence is correct as shown, write *OK*.

1. Has everyone received their office manual?   1. _____

2. Is there two or three out-of-stock items?   2. _____

3. Who is on vacation beside him and her?   3. _____

4. You should of applied for that job, don't you think?   4. _____

5. We've already distributed copies to most everyone.   5. _____

6. I'm convinced I should have chose the other one.   6. _____

7. Please check all of them addresses very carefully.   7. _____

8. The committee usually meets once a month, don't it?   8. _____

9. Bob is only one of those who was absent today.   9. _____

10. Whom do you think will be appointed regional manager?   10. _____

11. The number of orders have been most gratifying.   11. _____

12. Has anyone else wrote to Ms. Caruso lately?   12. _____

13. Do you think your new supervisor is to aggressive?   13. _____

14. May be you should have consulted her first.   14. _____

15. The reason we didn't go is because we had to work.   15. _____

16. Are they quiet sure the orders have been mislaid?   16. _____

17. There is nothing left for you and myself to do.   17. _____

18. This pair of scissors seem to be very dull.   18. _____

19. Did anyone see their entering the building?   19. _____

20. There ready to ship right now, aren't they?   20. _____

21. Neither of the women left their notes here.   21. _____

22. You are one of those who always does good work.   22. _____

23. They will have to do the checking theirselves.   23. _____

24. The staff submitted its expense reports on time.   24. _____

25. If I wasn't too tired, I'd go with you and her.   25. _____

26. Do you know where Mr. Coswell is at?

27. She is one of those who has worked hard.

28. This machine is efficienter than that one.

29. I'm not sure whether this is mine or your's.

30. Had you heard of Jane taking flying lessons?

31. A number of them were on vacation.

32. If you was Rosemary, what would you do?

33. Do you recommend that the plans are canceled?

34. I doubt that any one else noticed it.

35. Where will you be setting?

36. A number of tours is available to groups only.

37. Do either of them need our assistance?

38. Pencils, notebooks, and etc. are on each desk.

39. Do you like this types of clothing?

40. I wish we had knowed their plans earlier.

41. The situation didn't look too well to us.

42. This is the most perfect rose in the exhibit.

43. Doesn't this lemonade taste very bitterly?

44. Be sure to look careful before you proceed.

45. Don't you have none of them on hand?

46. Please feel free to stop into see us anytime.

47. These are already to be shipped, aren't they?

48. This carton looks squarer than either of those.

49. Did you read the article wrote by Dr. Helms?

50. Are these the ones you was checking yesterday?

26. _____

27. _____

28. _____

29. _____

30. _____

31. _____

32. _____

33. _____

34. _____

35. _____

36. _____

37. _____

38. _____

39. _____

40. _____

41. _____

42. _____

43. _____

44. _____

45. _____

46. _____

47. _____

48. _____

49. _____

50. _____

79 Correcting Errors in Word Choice

Underline each error in word choice, and write the necessary correction in the space provided. If no correction is necessary, write *OK*.

1. The firefighters were on the seen immediately.

2. It was indeed a beautiful scene.

3. Which of them did you chews for yourself?

4. The doctor overcharged several patience.

5. Please be sure the currant is turned off.

6. Are you quiet sure you will attend?

7. The attendants may decrease even more.

8. He doesn't know weather to resign or not.

9. You have every write to return it.

10. Was this in today's correspondents?

11. Which addition of the book do you have?

12. That signature is totally eligible.

13. Is the equipment stationery?

14. Several of these accounts are overdo.

15. The affect has been insignificant so far.

16. Where would you like to spend your vacation?

17. Do you have excess to a typewriter at home?

18. We complement you on your outstanding success.

19. No one should accede the speed limit.

20. Those requirements may be waved in some cases.

21. What is the shortest root we can take to Winnipeg?

22. Every employ has an equal opportunity.

23. What was their principle objection?

24. The Bureau of the Senses issued these figures.

25. That is truly a handy devise, don't you think?

1. _____

2. _____

3. _____

4. _____

5. _____

6. _____

7. _____

8. _____

9. _____

10. _____

11. _____

12. _____

13. _____

14. _____

15. _____

16. _____

17. _____

18. _____

19. _____

20. _____

21. _____

22. _____

23. _____

24. _____

25. _____

26. We appreciate your corporation in this matter.

26. _____

27. Ms. Helmsley has been of grate assistance.

27. _____

28. It must be time for a coffee brake, isn't it?

28. _____

29. They were standing on the bough of the ship.

29. _____

30. Be sure to bring along some extra close.

30. _____

31. Would you sue anyone for liable?

31. _____

32. Both patients are too week to walk.

32. _____

33. We took a crews up the Hudson River last fall.

33. _____

34. The groom wore a tuxedo, and she wore a bridle gown.

34. _____

35. Are they members of the bored of directors?

35. _____

36. Smoking is not aloud in some retail stores.

36. _____

37. How much does this bail of hay weigh?

37. _____

38. When it rains, it pores—or so it seems.

38. _____

39. One couple has adapted two children.

39. _____

40. This receipt calls for two cups of flower.

40. _____

41. The hole shipment was defective.

41. _____

42. The board was nailed to the sealing.

42. _____

43. This is the forth error we have discovered.

43. _____

44. Were they formally introduced?

44. _____

45. What is the cost of that peace of steak?

45. _____

46. Have you ever sewn seeds by hand?

46. _____

47. These shoes have souls of leather.

47. _____

48. An announcement will be made eminently.

48. _____

49. The moral of our employees is very high.

49. _____

50. Several abandoned buildings were raised.

50. _____

80 Supplying Punctuation

Insert whatever punctuation marks are needed in the following sentences. If there is not enough space to insert the punctuation mark within the line, put a caret (∧) below the line and write the punctuation mark above it. Capitalization is correct as shown.

1. Occasionally almost every company makes mistakes in filling customers orders.

2. The questionnaires have not been returned therefore we should send follow up cards.

3. These figures are up to date arent they

4. Is there anything else in your opinion that we ought to take into consideration

5. Ms. Ralston asked me when the next meeting would be held

6. Come in and bring your notebook and the minutes of the last meeting

7. Moreover Basset & Sons was the lowest bidder

8. Three large metal drums of oil were delivered this morning

9. However helpful the advice may be dont offer it unless its requested.

10. We have many many models from which you can choose Ms Guerra.

11. Your last letter however indicated that you wanted a July 1 shipment

12. Dont you agree that he was careless actually too careless

13. If your letter attempts but fails to make a sale you need to analyze why it didnt do the job you intended

14. His brother Bill served four years in the Navy

15. Many of our employees are brushing up on their office skills at your school and we certainly appreciate the personal attention that you give to each of them

16. After it is vacuumed the rug will look as good as new

17. Before beginning to file Judy finished all her other work.

18. Who is the better secretary Alice or Sue

19. Before starting to rake the gardener weeded the flower bed

20. As the hours went by the prospects of an immediate solution grew dimmer.

21. The two calculators that we ordered last month will arrive tomorrow wont they

22. You may be able to get a 30 day extension

23. Using a sprayer instead of a brush the painter finished the job quickly

24. However carefully we may check we may miss a few errors

25. Several airlines make the New York Madrid trip daily

26. We were fortunate to obtain a 60 day loan at 95 percent interest.

27. If you place your order today we will guarantee delivery within three days.

28. Mrs. Peretta is the head of the accounting group Ms Lamont of the advertising staff.

29. I think it was Jim not Kim who served on the committee last year.

30. We received your Order No 8668 on the 14th of September Miss Farrell.

31. This well established firm is well known in this area.

32. It is a well recognized fact that a round trip ticket will not necessarily save a customer money.

33. Each morning he took a three mile walk along the bitterly cold seashore.

34. Everyone believes Professor Lynch to be a well informed person.

35. The store attempted to collect punitive as well as actual damages.

36. In arranging for your ticket you will find that it is difficult to obtain reservations during July August and September.

37. He called the office asked for Mr. Peters and tendered his resignation.

38. We are planning to revise our price list next month and we will send you a copy as soon thereafter as possible.

39. After making a careful investigation of your references Mr. Howard we are convinced that you are the right man for the Salem Oregon store.

40. Mr. George Carey who was the office manager in our Dayton Ohio store will be our vice president.

41. Our major expenses are as follows shipping maintenance and advertising.

42. Please send us your payment immediately this as you know is our third request.

43. Be sure to gather all the data before not after you make the decision.

44. In my opinion Lambert Lambert & Lambert is the leading law firm.

45. The check lying on the table is yours.

46. To add to your typing speed is to add to the ease and sureness with which you work.

47. The genuine aluminum frame gives you a number of advantages Mr. Corey.

48. Work on the new edition which is to be published in April is almost completed.

49. On page 10 there are four typographical errors on page 14 there are two factually incorrect statements.

50. Sitting in the last row of the auditorium we were unable to hear the panel.

81 Matching Terms and Definitions

In the space provided, write the letter that identifies the correct definition of each of the following words or expressions.

A. for each person

B. reproduction

C. existing condition

D. summary

E. common spirit of group enthusiasm

F. honorary rank after retirement

G. concerning

H. to mention

I. by the day

J. by virtue of an office

K. full discretionary power

L. for example

M. possible event

N. a school that one has attended

O. a civil wrong

P. that is

Q. at first sight

R. let the buyer beware

S. manner of operation

T. policy of abstaining from interference

U. booklet

V. final proposal

W. for the time being

X. a formal charge

Y. member of a diplomatic staff

1. cite _____

2. per diem _____

3. per capita _____

4. prima facie _____

5. attaché _____

6. i.e. (*id est*) _____

7. alma mater _____

8. tort _____

9. contingency _____

10. facsimile _____

11. e.g. (*exempli gratia*) _____

12. modus operandi _____

13. ex officio _____

14. status quo _____

15. in re _____

16. caveat emptor _____

17. emeritus _____

18. ultimatum _____

19. indictment _____

20. brochure _____

21. résumé _____

22. carte blanche _____

23. laissez-faire _____

24. esprit de corps _____

25. pro tem (*pro tempore*) _____

For each word in the right-hand column, select the most appropriate definition from those given at the left. In the space provided, write the letter that identifies the definition. If necessary, use the dictionary.

A. emaciated; thin

B. ardent; zealous

C. polished; diplomatic

D. inanely foolish; silly

E. unplanned; haphazard

F. a hiding place

G. talkative

H. appendage

I. apathy; lethargy

J. self-satisfied

K. routine; mechanical

L. argumentative; belligerent

M. wasted away

N. not excusable

O. in existence

P. careful; meticulous

Q. vague

R. bitter; mocking

S. believing anything

T. impoverished; needy

U. learned

V. overconfident; brazen

W. tasteless; dull; flat

X. deserving of blame

Y. puzzling

26. complacent _____

27. gullible _____

28. erudite _____

29. gaunt _____

30. loquacious _____

31. suave _____

32. sardonic _____

33. enigmatic _____

34. desultory _____

35. presumptuous _____

36. indefensible _____

37. perfunctory _____

38. indigent _____

39. fatuous _____

40. insipid _____

41. punctilious _____

42. fervid _____

43. torpor _____

44. culpable _____

45. indeterminate _____

46. extant _____

47. contentious _____

48. cache _____

49. atrophied _____

50. appurtenance _____

82 Checking for Correctness

Underline each grammatical or factual error. Then write the necessary correction in the space provided. If the sentence contains no error, write *OK*.

1. Part of the series have been shown already.

1. _____

2. The Smithsonian Institution is in New York City.

2. _____

3. A number of the windows was broken by vandals.

3. _____

4. Harrison & Associates represent Barker Bros., Inc.

4. _____

5. General Motors is one of the largest employees.

5. _____

6. If he had been there, I would have saw him.

6. _____

7. I wish I had gave them the discount they requested.

7. _____

8. One of the statements were incorrect.

8. _____

9. The Personal Department maintains employee records.

9. _____

10. She is a much better speaker than him.

10. _____

11. None of the officers was at the meeting.

11. _____

12. The amount of orders surprised all of us.

12. _____

13. He gave Louis and myself a raise of $10 a week.

13. _____

14. It was awfully kind of you to help us.

14. _____

15. Labor Day is the first Tuesday in September.

15. _____

16. Ohio is known as the Buckeye State.

16. _____

17. Chicago is larger than any city in Illinois.

17. _____

18. Etymology is the study of insects.

18. _____

19. Pittsburgh is the capital of Pennsylvania.

19. _____

20. You gave an awfully good report this morning.

20. _____

21. The entire matter requires farther study.

21. _____

22. They'll do the proofreading theirselves.

22. _____

23. A kilometer is about five-eighths of a mile.

23. _____

24. *C.O.D.* means "cash on delivery."

24. _____

25. The plural of *basis* are *bases*.

25. _____

83 Rewriting for Courtesy

Rewrite each sentence in order to express its meaning more courteously.

1. You won't get your order because you didn't give us the information we need. _____

2. Send me a copy of your new catalog just as soon as you can. _____

3. You should know by now that our standard terms are 2/10, n/30. _____

4. You don't have the authority to sign this contract, do you? _____

5. Thank you in advance for all the help you will give me. _____

6. The merchandise was damaged because of your negligence or someone else's. _____

7. Just as you do, we make mistakes once in a while. _____

8. We have so many applicants that I doubt you will be hired. _____

9. You know very well that no one undersells us. _____

10. To handle this kind of a job, you need a lot more experience. _____

84 Rewriting for Conciseness

Rewrite each sentence, using fewer words to express the same thought.

1. It is on the last day of June that the meeting will be held. _____

2. We are returning all the merchandise that is defective. _____

3. This is a location that is very convenient. _____

4. In the event that Model 404 is not available, please substitute Model 606. _____

5. The sale will begin on Wednesday, and it will end on Saturday. _____

6. Ms. Jenner, who is the head of the Word Processing Department, will retire next year. _____

7. Enclosed, please find our check in the amount of $124.50. _____

8. There was one route that was closed for more than four hours. _____

9. We cannot accept it for the reason that it is incomplete. _____

10. We have storage facilities that are modern and that are spacious. _____

85 Avoiding Objectionable Expressions

Underline the objectionable expressions in the following sentences. Then, in the space provided, rewrite the sentences, using acceptable expressions.

1. May I take this opportunity to thank you for your assistance? _____

2. We need to meet at an early date. _____

3. Attached hereto is a copy of Invoice 4357. _____

4. I thought it would be possible to get a copy free of charge. _____

5. Please call in advance of delivering this order. _____

6. Please return the enclosed card to the writer within two weeks. _____

7. In compliance with your request, we have reserved Booth 6 for you. _____

8. I am writing in re your Order 2446. _____

9. The error has been duly noted; it will be corrected in your next statement. _____

10. Our credit policies are along the same lines as theirs. _____

86 Correcting Errors in Verb Usage

Underline each incorrect verb or verb phrase, and write the necessary correction in the space provided.

1. Gene, as well as his administrative assistant, were at the trade show in Portland.

2. The mayor will lie the cornerstone of the new office building next Tuesday afternoon.

3. This is one of those things that has no value to us.

4. None of these orders has been processed.

5. The fabric shrunk more than we had expected it to.

6. Neither he nor his assistants has the data.

7. Have some of the wheat been harvested already?

8. I thought the driver run into a fire hydrant.

9. The owner and the general manager decides what the retail sales price will be.

10. I done my very best to convince both of them.

11. Aren't measles a childhood disease?

12. If she was there, I would have seen her, I'm sure.

13. Was there any other sites available?

14. The number of claims for refunds were quite small.

15. Much of the land were uncultivated.

16. Are either of the new series very popular?

17. The river was completely froze over last winter.

18. The owner and publisher of the *Cherry Valley News* is to be at the Cherryvale fashion show.

19. Aren't Palm Springs located in the desert?

20. She don't get too excited about such rumors.

21. Is these trousers on sale today?

22. Those vases were broke when I got home with them.

1. _____

2. _____

3. _____

4. _____

5. _____

6. _____

7. _____

8. _____

9. _____

10. _____

11. _____

12. _____

13. _____

14. _____

15. _____

16. _____

17. _____

18. _____

19. _____

20. _____

21. _____

22. _____

23. I think that a number of customers is interested in trying out this new machine.

23. _____

24. The jury done reached a verdict already.

24. _____

25. Some of the items is out of stock.

25. _____

26. I think she would of been better off if she had decided to stay with that company.

26. _____

27. Some of the letters were wrote by Dr. Favata.

27. _____

28. If I was you, I would take advantage of the offer.

28. _____

29. The contract states, "The balance will be repaid in monthly installments of $154.75."

29. _____

30. Barbara suggested that the dues are raised to $20.

30. _____

31. If it wasn't raining so hard, we could leave now.

31. _____

32. This decision is likely to sit a precedent.

32. _____

33. If there is some good reasons for the delay, I have not heard them.

33. _____

34. The new movie was showed at a "sneak preview" attended by the cast and their guests.

34. _____

35. Why has the cost of living rose so high?

35. _____

36. Does anyone know what the sales for last month was?

36. _____

37. That is only one of the things that bothers us.

37. _____

38. The papers on that desk is mine.

38. _____

39. Who is the ones responsible for the delay?

39. _____

40. Several of the strikers was carrying picket signs.

40. _____

41. The ledgers kept by the founder still exists.

41. _____

42. It would be nice if they would makeup their minds.

42. _____

43. Thomas & Winters are the ad agency we use.

43. _____

44. Why don't you try and visit them this week?

44. _____

45. We haven't done hardly anything with it so far.

45. _____

46. We were wishing that you had went with us too.

46. _____

47. Several of our staff takes their vacation in July.

47. _____

48. I wish that we had chose the other one, don't you?

48. _____

49. We could do nothing but set and wait for them.

49. _____

50. Several ships was laying at anchor when we saw them.

50. _____

87 Correcting Errors in Pronoun Usage

Underline each incorrectly used pronoun, and write the necessary correction in the space provided. If no correction is necessary, write *OK*.

1. Don't you think that anyone of them would be suitable for our purposes?

1. _____

2. Lori knows more about the new procedures than him.

2. _____

3. A breakfast of bacon and eggs has lost their appeal to a number of people.

3. _____

4. Please invite whoever you would like to attend.

4. _____

5. Lois said that Jerry did most of the work hisself.

5. _____

6. Who did you ask to approve the requisition?

6. _____

7. Wasn't one of the cartons lying on their side?

7. _____

8. Which of those briefcases is your's?

8. _____

9. It would have been better if they had done the work theirselves, wouldn't it?

9. _____

10. As for myself, I would prefer to sit and wait.

10. _____

11. You and him ought to be promoted soon.

11. _____

12. Who do you work for, Ms. Langford?

12. _____

13. What is the name of the store from whom you bought your new typewriter?

13. _____

14. They left it up to Sharon and myself to decide what to do about it.

14. _____

15. Why should we have to do that ourselfs?

15. _____

16. Is Sylvia someone whom accepts responsibility?

16. _____

17. Pat works harder than any body else in the office.

17. _____

18. Whom is to be appointed to the board of directors?

18. _____

19. Everyone knows they must be at work on time.

19. _____

20. Each of you should work by yourselves.

20. _____

21. How much do them styles of furniture cost?

21. _____

22. Do you have any idea who's notes these are?

22. _____

23. When did you hear those news?   23. _____

24. Everyone which we saw seemed highly interested.   24. _____

25. What ever the outcome, we'll be satisfied.   25. _____

26. This is the order for what we waited a month.   26. _____

27. Did anyone complain about them leaving early?   27. _____

28. That certainly is somebody of legislators!   28. _____

29. May I see them on the top shelf, please?   29. _____

30. The president and chief executive officer, Phillip Lange, announced their resignation.   30. _____

31. We checked the accounts and found no thing wrong with them.   31. _____

32. Us secretaries have submitted our suggestions.   32. _____

33. One of you must have forgotten his copy.   33. _____

34. We need some one who has at least a year's experience.   34. _____

35. Neither of the orders had errors in them.   35. _____

36. Were the jury arguing among itself?   36. _____

37. Every home owner wants the best protection he can get without paying an exorbitant price for it.   37. _____

38. I don't think that no one else will be interested.   38. _____

39. Their leaving at 7 o'clock this evening, aren't they?   39. _____

40. I thought you and him would be the winners.   40. _____

41. Isn't she a member of there medical staff?   41. _____

42. Didn't anyone ask he to be a member of the panel?   42. _____

43. His objections, that seem reasonable to me, need to be studied further.   43. _____

44. Did you hear about them embezzling $25,000?   44. _____

45. The one's waiting outside are Burt and Betty.   45. _____

46. We are waiting for he and she to return our call.   46. _____

47. The majority of the class expressed its approval.   47. _____

48. Whom do you think gave the best speech?   48. _____

49. Aren't them the machines you told us lathe operators about a few weeks ago?   49. _____

50. If these are Dan's and Tony's, those must be our's.   50. _____

88 Correcting Errors in Modifier Usage

Underline each incorrectly used adjective or adverb, and write the necessary correction in the space provided. If no correction is necessary, write *OK*.

1. We felt badly about the loss of those accounts.

2. Why does some medicine taste so bitterly?

3. Which of the twins is shortest?

4. I think you gave the bestest answer of all.

5. Who keeps the most neat office in your building?

6. We should have ordered a more large size of paper.

7. What is the less expensive means of transportation?

8. There sure must be an error in this statement.

9. Are you quiet certain they will not attend?

10. Most everyone participated in the election.

11. The cost of petroleum products has risen rapid.

12. We must handle these vases as careful as we can.

13. When does your company's physical year begin?

14. This is the originalest of the three plans.

15. The remedy may be worser than the illness.

16. To me, the old procedure is gooder than the new one.

17. Have you read either of them reports?

18. Is either of these types of fasteners acceptable?

19. Alaska is larger than any state in the United States.

20. Do you know who's responsibility it is?

21. We should put ever piece of furniture we have on sale.

22. Both of them often speak in a very abrupt manner.

23. We don't feel any differently about it now than we did a year or so ago.

24. She has not felt too good for a week or so.

1. _____

2. _____

3. _____

4. _____

5. _____

6. _____

7. _____

8. _____

9. _____

10. _____

11. _____

12. _____

13. _____

14. _____

15. _____

16. _____

17. _____

18. _____

19. _____

20. _____

21. _____

22. _____

23. _____

24. _____

25. We must be real sure there is no conflict of interest before we proceed.

25. _____

26. Please ship the order direct to our Dayton branch.

26. _____

27. Do you have an office in the Fort-Worth area?

27. _____

28. Both of them are always real considerate.

28. _____

29. They seemed to be in very well spirits yesterday.

29. _____

30. Those gems are really diamonds, aren't they?

30. _____

31. I think you did very good on the employment test.

31. _____

32. There are to many statistics in his report.

32. _____

33. I think they had left all ready, hadn't they?

33. _____

34. Be sure to issue an up to date report to the members of the local press.

34. _____

35. Business was very slowly during the fourth quarter.

35. _____

36. Do you feel well about the decision?

36. _____

37. We received less complaints than we had expected.

37. _____

38. You have always treated us very fair.

38. _____

39. It is all most time for us to leave.

39. _____

40. The pollution seemed worser than ever.

40. _____

41. We should buy a latter edition of this handbook.

41. _____

42. This soil looks too poorly to grow such crops.

42. _____

43. Why did the driver in front stop so sudden?

43. _____

44. This machine seems to operate different than it did.

44. _____

45. She is one of the more cooperative people I have ever worked with.

45. _____

46. May be we should examine the claim more closely.

46. _____

47. This stationery is an unusually size.

47. _____

48. You probable are correct in your assumptions.

48. _____

49. She is the patientest person around here.

49. _____

50. Which of the three candidates is more likelier to win this fall's election?

50. _____

89 Correcting Errors in Preposition Usage

Underline each error in preposition usage, and write the necessary correction in the space provided. If a preposition should be omitted, draw a line through it and write *Omit*. If a preposition should be added, use a caret (∧) to show where it should be inserted; then write the preposition in the space provided. If no correction of any kind is required, write *OK*.

1. The truck ran in to a brick wall, or so it seems.

1. _____

2. This calculator is different than the one I had.

2. _____

3. Do you know where they are going to tomorrow?

3. _____

4. Please stop in at your earliest convenience.

4. _____

5. Were you sitting besides your supervisor?

5. _____

6. Stock prices fell off slightly yesterday.

6. _____

7. Why not divide the reward between the three of them?

7. _____

8. Would you be willing to stand in for Fay?

8. _____

9. Do you know where Ms. Collins was at yesterday?

9. _____

10. Why were you so angry at your secretary?

10. _____

11. We have differed from them on several occasions.

11. _____

12. These increases will be retroactive from June 1.

12. _____

13. It isn't easy to comply to some of their requests.

13. _____

14. We differed on the effects of the cutback.

14. _____

15. I think our costs are identical to theirs, don't you?

15. _____

16. It conforms with the specifications they gave us.

16. _____

17. We put the cartons onto the loading dock.

17. _____

18. He seems to have walked in to a difficult situation.

18. _____

19. The auditors seem to have caught onto the irregular accounting procedures that were being used.

19. _____

20. Some customers are rather difficult to wait on.

20. _____

21. It would be a relief too both of them.

21. _____

22. We will meet you up on your arrival.

22. _____

23. Who is going beside Karen and Patricia?

23. _____

24. Several cases of empty bottles fell off of the truck. 24. _____

25. Where did the thieves break in at? 25. _____

26. The meeting will begin at about 2:30 p.m. 26. _____

27. Please let us hear from you on or before March 10. 27. _____

28. I leaned the boards again the wall of the building. 28. _____

29. We will wait out side your office. 29. _____

30. The work should be distributed evenly among you, her, and him. 30. _____

31. The car went passed us at a high speed. 31. _____

32. Several patients went into the waiting room. 32. _____

33. We should leave with in an hour, shouldn't we? 33. _____

34. They were sitting acrost from us. 34. _____

35. These figures do not correspond with those. 35. _____

36. Who will have to account for the fees collected so far, Phyllis or Marilyn? 36. _____

37. What type furniture would you like to buy? 37. _____

38. Was this invoice inside of that envelope? 38. _____

39. Everyone accept Miss Ashworth was there. 39. _____

40. They were graduated City College in June. 40. _____

41. We could not help from being impressed. 41. _____

42. You should smell of any perfume before you buy it. 42. _____

43. Flight 420 will arrive about a half hour late. 43. _____

44. Are you planning to open up your own office? 44. _____

45. Who took down the drapes in her office? 45. _____

46. Do you listen to the news both in the morning and night? 46. _____

47. Have you ever driven the Pennsylvania Turnpike? 47. _____

48. It would of been better if we had waited a while longer for them. 48. _____

49. How often have you corresponded to that client? 49. _____

50. That would be better then nothing, wouldn't it? 50. _____

90 Supplying Punctuation and Capitalization

Insert the necessary periods, question marks, and other punctuation marks in the following sentences. Use a caret (∧) and write the mark above it wherever space is too limited to write within the line. Draw three short lines under each letter that should be capitalized.

1. The office manager posted this notice there is to be no smoking by employees in the main office Smoking is permitted only in the cafeteria and in the lounges.

2. Approximately 100 people attended the meeting actually we expected only 75.

3. On March 15 124 inquiries were received in response to the ad in Business week.

4. We Ms Ellis and I will interview the candidates in Mr Paulsons office.

5. The notices are to be sent to the following companies Jones & Cunningham Harper Smith & Frank and Peter Proctor & Sons.

6. This new procedure will save time as well as money.

7. How to write short stories novels magazine articles and editorials is taught in this popular home study course.

8. Mr Robert J. Burns Jr has been appointed editor in chief of our local paper *The Evening standard*.

9. Radio TV newspapers billboards these are among the media we plan to use.

10. Our bureau chief, Miss Mildred Perez asked who made those recommendations

11. The motorist asked Is the freeway constructed as far as Bakersfield

12. Would you please send Miss oBrien a copy of that memo from executive vice president hale

13. Please forward these payroll records to Nina James manager of the accounting department

14. David together with his parents lives in New Jersey

15. How far is it from here to Montreal to Winnipeg to Regina

16. This typewriter as you can easily see is not a recent model.

17. Parker & Sons sent the order cod but we had asked them to charge it to our account.

18. Mrs Carrie Cooper former owner of Carries curio corner moved to Maine.

19. All of those who have been on our preferred customer list for a year or more will be sent notices of special sales.

20. Miss Simmons not Ms Symonds is in charge of our womens ready to wear department.

21. Did Paul actually shout get out of my office this minute

22. If not well have to begin searching for another supplier right away.

23. The enrollment data see table 8 on page 24 was provided by the US office of education.

24. A number of people for example Enrique Entrialgo Sara Simpson and Wally Wolfe have the training and the experience required to do that job in a most outstanding manner.

25. His brother George has worked for a firm in marengo illinois for a number of years.

26. Do you know where I would be able to obtain a copy of the February 19 1979 issue

27. Mrs Campbell joined our executive training program in February 1980 and was placed in a middle management position a few months later.

28. Please quote prices in 5 10 and 15 ton lots.

29. The new warehouse is just a few miles south of new london connecticut.

30. Would you be able to meet with us on May 10 Miss Timmons

31. I believe the parent company has its headquarters in one of the new england states.

32. Every employee should study such subjects as business english mathematics and accounting.

33. We who live in this area must pay federal state and local income taxes.

34. Was the president speaking from the oval office of the white house?

35. Does that airline offer new york madrid service every day of the week?

36. I have no idea whether they are easterners or westerners do you

37. Opportunities for advancement in my opinion are numerous in most companies.

38. Senator elect Noble and ex mayor Marvin were the principal speakers.

39. Cora Kildare phds belief is that such tests are invalid.

40. The sites under consideration are as follows butte montana laramie wyoming and boise idaho.

41. Several motorists, all of whom were exceeding the 40 kmh speed limit, were given tickets.

42. Please send it to 1224 south 24 avenue belvidere illinois 61008.

43. Each of the write in candidates was required to file an up to date report of contributions.

44. The spokesperson for the governor issued a strongly worded statement to the press.

45. Well it seems incredible to me that none of her coworkers would accept part of the credit.

46. If sales continue at this pace every employee will receive an end of year bonus.

47. Model 8640 or Model 9696 whichever is less expensive is the one we should buy.

48. We received the brochure on friday may 15 however we have not distributed it yet.

49. Fortunately no one was injured in the accident at the corner of elm and ash streets today.

50. Living in new york city you must visit the statue of liberty the american stock exchange etc many many times every year dont you

91 Using Numbers and Abbreviations

For each number or abbreviation that is incorrectly expressed or incorrectly used, underline the error and write the necessary correction in the space provided. If a word, an abbreviation, or a symbol used with a number is incorrect, underline it and indicate the appropriate correction also. If the sentence requires no correction, write *OK*.

1. Ms. Dedman began working here on 2/16/80, I believe.

1. _____

2. Isn't their office at 9,660 Lakewood Boulevard?

2. _____

3. Several 100 copies have been distributed already.

3. _____

4. Please indicate which of them is your 1st choice.

4. _____

5. Mr. Reese is attending a conference in Saint Louis, MO.

5. _____

6. The construction began on Sept. 8th of last year.

6. _____

7. The information appears on Page 60 of this booklet.

7. _____

8. Sixteen of the 40 orders were delivered within 8 days of the date they were received.

8. _____

9. This carton contains 24 1-liter cans of tomato juice.

9. _____

10. What is the name of the hotel at #1 Fifth Avenue?

10. _____

11. 1,200 questionnaires have been returned so far.

11. _____

12. At least ⅔ of the members must approve it.

12. _____

13. During July and August, the store will close at five p.m. Monday through Friday.

13. _____

14. We have received a large no. of inquiries about it.

14. _____

15. Is your meeting with Miss. Fisher at 10 today?

15. _____

16. Isn't he a member of the class of 78?

16. _____

17. These cost only 8¢ each in most stores.

17. _____

18. Is your current home address 2424 16 Avenue?

18. _____

19. We paid the balance in 6 installments of $50.00 each.

19. _____

20. It costs $4.50 a meter, not 45 cents a meter.

20. _____

21. They gave us a ten-percent discount, didn't they?

21. _____

22. We lived at 60 North 15th Street for 2 years or so.

22. _____

23. This container holds 1 qt., 4 ozs.　　23. _____

24. Your appointment is for 10:30 a.m. this morning.　　24. _____

25. Be sure to invite Col. Wm. F. Fong, Junior.　　25. _____

26. Two of her Bros. work for the US Postal Service.　　26. _____

27. They should arrive sometime this p. m.　　27. _____

28. Gov. Judson will make a two-hour stopover in Erie.　　28. _____

29. Phyllis Johnson, C.P.A., audited the firm's books.　　29. _____

30. $100 is all that we were able to collect last week.　　30. _____

31. Their youngest child is only 8 months old.　　31. _____

32. One-half of the work is done; the other half won't be ready for another day or two.　　32. _____

33. The office is only four and one-half miles from here.　　33. _____

34. I was 18 years four months old when I enrolled.　　34. _____

35. How long has Dr. Steven Sheahan, M.D., been the head of your company's medical department?　　35. _____

36. Did they go to Kansas City, KS, or Kansas City, MO?　　36. _____

37. It is about 18°C. this a.m.　　37. _____

38. We should try to catch a two-o'clock flight.　　38. _____

39. She began working for Wilton & Williamson, Inc. July 8th, 1979.　　39. _____

40. That song was popular during the gay 90s.　　40. _____

41. Kay received her PHD degree from the Univ. of Texas.　　41. _____

42. Please give me 12 large envelopes, six small envelopes, and 18 letterheads.　　42. _____

43. We recently bought six of their model twenty home computers for trial use by our sales staff.　　43. _____

44. This one retails for about five dollars.　　44. _____

45. We paid six-tenths percent more than they did.　　45. _____

46. Who owns that new twenty-four-story office building?　　46. _____

47. We have a number of employees in their early 20's.　　47. _____

48. The cost will be $1224.88 fob their Mobile plant.　　48. _____

49. Wasn't Pres. Carter elected in '76?　　49. _____

50. Please order notebooks, pencils, and etc.　　50. _____

92 Correcting Misspelled Words

Underline each misspelled word; then write the word correctly spelled in the space provided. If no correction in spelling is necessary, write *OK*.

1. Did you attend the annual meeting of the assocciation in Ames, Iowa, last week?

1. _____

2. Please check all those refferences carefully.

2. _____

3. This is an excellent oportunity for you.

3. _____

4. We do not have adequate storeage facilities.

4. _____

5. The necessary materials are unavailable now.

5. _____

6. Please return the agreement at your conveneince.

6. _____

7. What does their repersentative recommend?

7. _____

8. You should exercise your perogative, Dr. Li.

8. _____

9. This notice is similiar to the one distributed by Fay.

9. _____

10. Medical records are stored seperately from other personnel records.

10. _____

11. It was a dissappointment to our management.

11. _____

12. We need to develope better inventory records.

12. _____

13. Data proccessing involves the use of computers.

13. _____

14. We requested a desision immediately.

14. _____

15. In your judgement, are the arrangements acceptable?

15. _____

16. Their acceptance of the allowance was surprising.

16. _____

17. Approximately fourty were in attendance.

17. _____

18. Will you need an explaination of the specifications?

18. _____

19. Proper maintainance is of vital importance.

19. _____

20. She submited several worthwhile suggestions.

20. _____

21. The adjacent property has a morgage on it.

21. _____

22. We are forewarding the original copy to you.

22. _____

23. To the best of our knowledge, they kept expenses to a minimum.

23. _____

24. Many corporations operate in foriegn countries. 24. _____

25. He has a temporary lisense to operate that vehicle. 25. _____

26. We sincerly believe they handled the criticism in a manner that did credit to them. 26. _____

27. Who is chairperson of the advisery committee? 27. _____

28. It was a fasinating laboratory experiment. 28. _____

29. His illness was diagnosed as neumonia, I believe. 29. _____

30. Most of the wearhouse personnel are cooperative. 30. _____

31. We proceded to grant them a 30-day extension. 31. _____

32. What is the most desirable heighth? 32. _____

33. We are most greatful for that independent analysis. 33. _____

34. It is a priviledge to offer you our appraisal. 34. _____

35. It was difficult to adhere to those goverment guidelines. 35. _____

36. Reference to any indededness was omitted. 36. _____

37. We must fullfill all those fundamental requirements. 37. _____

38. Who are the attornies for the indicted officials? 38. _____

39. Incidently, the payee's endorsement was missing. 39. _____

40. We must endever to establish greater credibility. 40. _____

41. An organization is dependant upon everyone's whole-hearted cooperation and assistance. 41. _____

42. There is no significant difference between them. 42. _____

43. In so far as the language of the article is concerned, we have no objections to that of the revised draft. 43. _____

44. He will be eligible for promotion next Wensday. 44. _____

45. As a practical matter, there is no signifcant hazard to anyone's health. 45. _____

46. What is the experation date of your supervisor's subscription to that magazine? 46. _____

47. That certainly is extremely valueable commercial property, and I'm surprised they don't recognize that fact. 47. _____

48. These frames are more dureable because they are made of aluminum. 48. _____

49. Several of the secretaries worked overtime. 49. _____

50. I'm not sure whether this is the ninth or nineteenth. 50. _____

252

93 Correcting Errors in Word Choice

Underline each error in word choice, and write the necessary correction in the space provided. If no correction is necessary, write *OK*.

1. Are you sure that is the write one to use?

1. _____

2. What did they serve for desert last night?

2. _____

3. We were not specially eager to attend the reception.

3. _____

4. Irregardless of its cost, we should buy it.

4. _____

5. The purpose of Memorial Day is to honor those who are diseased, isn't it?

5. _____

6. She is a person of high principals.

6. _____

7. They were all most ready to leave when we arrived.

7. _____

8. Do you know whether they're going with him?

8. _____

9. The moral of the staff is unusually high.

9. _____

10. Is that tent made of canvass?

10. _____

11. Like Cleopatra, we saled the Nile in a barge.

11. _____

12. We have no idea what affect it will have on them.

12. _____

13. It should have been sent in a large envelop.

13. _____

14. That is a valuable peace of property.

14. _____

15. Why is the company lowering it's prices now?

15. _____

16. Be sure to flower the rolling pin first.

16. _____

17. Is this the most currant information available?

17. _____

18. Maybe you should have a fiscal checkup.

18. _____

19. Shouldn't it be shipped in a led container?

19. _____

20. The judge wrapped the gavel on the bench in an effort to restore order in the courtroom.

20. _____

21. We had no choice but to toe the car to a garage.

21. _____

22. We are not holy in agreement with them.

22. _____

23. It is the result of ordinary ware and tare.

23. _____

24. Would some lie open these drains?

24. _____

25. She is uncertain weather she should go or not.

25. _____

26. This fabric is much too course, isn't it?

26. _____

27. When I spoke to him, he sounded very horse.

27. _____

28. Wouldn't it be nice to get a rise in pay?

28. _____

29. What is your receipt for success?

29. _____

30. That horror movie was enough to raise anyone's hare.

30. _____

31. One of the clerks made an error in edition.

31. _____

32. If they are under 21, they are miners.

32. _____

33. Both of them are airs to a fortune.

33. _____

34. I think he worked as a nurse's aid.

34. _____

35. She has a huge stack of correspondents on her desk.

35. _____

36. Smoking isn't aloud in this part of the building.

36. _____

37. We have far less secretaries than we need.

37. _____

38. They may be held libel for damages.

38. _____

39. Do you think he is liable to go to Los Angeles?

39. _____

40. What is the net wait of this package?

40. _____

41. What kind of breakfast serial do you like?

41. _____

42. We drove passed the entrance to the parking lot.

42. _____

43. We cannot be sure of his presents or his absence at that particular meeting.

43. _____

44. It is unwise to do anything to access.

44. _____

45. What is the shortest root from here to Montreal?

45. _____

46. We complement you on your recent promotion!

46. _____

47. Are both of these machines stationery?

47. _____

48. What is the amount of the lean against that house?

48. _____

49. Why would they ask you to wave your rights?

49. _____

50. Be careful not to overdue yourself.

50. _____

94 Choosing Synonyms and Antonyms

Rewrite each of the following sentences, providing an appropriate synonym for the word shown in italics.

1. Each of us has a variety of *mundane* tasks to perform. _____

    _____

2. It was an *ignominious* thing for them to do. _____

    _____

3. Why did they have to behave in such a *fatuous* manner? _____

    _____

4. Their victory gives them every right to *exult*. _____

    _____

5. Dr. Mallory wrote a very *prosaic* article for the March issue. _____

    _____

6. She certainly seemed very *irascible* this morning. _____

    _____

7. He approaches almost everything with *sanguinity*. _____

    _____

8. Why did they have to be so *surreptitious* about the proposed merger? _____

    _____

9. Some of the points that were raised did not seem *germane*. _____

    _____

10. Anything more that we might say would be *superfluous*. _____

    _____

Rewrite each of the following sentences, providing an appropriate antonym for the word shown in italics.

11. Their participation in the experiment gave them a great deal of *notoriety*. _____

    _____

12. One of my co-workers is a highly skilled *professional* photographer. _____

_____

13. Her attitude about such things is usually very *negative*. _____

_____

14. Did the accident victim suffer any *external* injuries? _____

_____

15. Why were they pushing the car *backward* down the street? _____

_____

16. How much did you *win* while you were in Las Vegas? _____

_____

17. Do you think they will *fail* in that endeavor? _____

_____

18. Do you *agree* with us? _____

_____

19. Must the *buyer* pay the commission? _____

_____

20. Why don't we try to catch an *earlier* flight? _____

_____

21. Isn't that conclusion *logical*? _____

_____

22. We should wait *inside* for them. _____

_____

23. The tank is nearly *full*. _____

_____

24. Its value is likely to *increase*. _____

_____

25. Would you prefer a *darker* shade of green? _____

_____

95 Editing Rough Drafts

Indicate all necessary corrections in grammar, spelling, punctuation, capitalization, number expression, and so on, in the letters shown below and on the next page. Then type the edited letters on plain standard-size stationery. Supply a return address, an inside address, a date line, and other parts necessary to make each letter complete.

Dear Doctor deWitt,

It was a priviledge to meet you and to have an opportunity to discuss with you the possibility of setting up a series of traning seminars for our secretarial staff. These type of on the job preparation for advancement to supervisery positions would be most beneficial, not only to the secrettarys who participate but also to the company itself.

Youll be pleased to know that I have all ready met with Ms Marcella OMalley, our General Mgr., and discussed the details of the proposal you outlined during your visit this a.m. Thus both her and me are quiet eager to receive from you a writen description of the content, lenth, and etc. of the program you feel better suits our needs. Of course wed like to know the cost too!

Within a weak or 10 days of the time we hear from you, we oughta be able to give you a defanite anser concerning our ability to go-ahead with this valueable training program.

Sincerly your's,

(Your Name), Manager
Personal Training Section

cc: Mr. Marcella O'malley

In addition to making all the necessary corrections in grammar, spelling, and so on, be sure to divide the letter into as many paragraphs as you think appropriate before typing it.

Ladys And Gentleman:

In Oct. 1979 I submited an article to you for publication in the Febuary 11th 1980 adition of your magazine. I know you received the article and was planning to publish it right away cause a Mr. Terry Lawrence wrote me and told me it had been accepted for publication on that date. When I didnt hear any thing farther, I assumed you would go ahead and print the article--and send me a check in payment of it, of course. Well as you can see Feb. '80 was quite a while ago, and I still haven't received payment. Moreover the article hasn't and apparently wont be published, as I've bought and read ever single issue since the Fall of 79. I've wrote to you at least once a month since February, 1980, and all you've done is tell me your sorry about the mixup. you'll agree, I'm sure that I have been more than patient and that the time has come for me to put the matter in the hands of an attorney. Which is what I will do next monday if I do not receive a satisfactory settlement offer from you before then. Very sincerly yours,

96 Editing Rough Drafts (Continued)

Make all the necessary corrections in punctuation, capitalization, grammar, and so on, in each of the following letters. Then, prepare a clean typewritten or handwritten copy of each of them. Use any arrangement and punctuation styles that you wish. NOTE: Supply all the missing parts of each letter.

Dear Mrs Bailey,

Many thanks for your recent invitation to attend the Lakewood Chamber of commerce Dinner on Dec. second and to speak on the subject "Business As Usual?". As much as I wish it was possible for me to except I find that I'll be unable to do so. The reason is because I will be in Ogden UT where I'll be conducting a Management Seminar for a group of business executives.

If you don't have nobody else in mind, may be you would like to consider Ms. Priscilla Osmond, as associate of me for sevral years. She is a highly-skilled speaker and I am sure that you and the members of your organization would be very very impressed by her knowlege of all aspects of business operation and mgmt. So far as I know, she shall be available on the date of your diner and happy to hear from you.

Should you wish to invite Ms Priscilla, please write to her at Belford Institute, 4140 North 12th Street, New York, NY 10,020. If you preffer, of course, you may telephone her at 555-1000.

Please accept my very best wishes for a most successful dinner meeting, Mrs. Osmond.

                              Very Truly yours,

Dr. Wm. R. Barbetta

Morristown Products Corp

6,644 Linden Blvd.

Warwick RI, 02887

Dear Doctor Barbetta;

It is a pleasure to respond to your **resent** request for infor about Miss Jacqueline Greene qualifications to serve as a financial analyst in your organization. I hope the following comments will be helpfull to you.

   Miss Green come to us direct from the Community College in Norfolk from which she graduated about six year's ago. Her 1st job with us was that of administrative assistant to our senior vice president, Harley J. Martin. Within a year however she become a member of our Accounting De- partment, with which she remained untill her and her husband moved to Rhode Island a few months ago. Had she been able to remain with us, we undoubtedly would of placed her in a position similar to the one for which she has applied with your company.

                              Sincerely Yours,

                              (Your Name)
                              Vice President, Personnel

260